YUKON RIVER STEAMBOATS
A PICTORIAL HISTORY

The **White Horse** passing through Five Finger Rapids in 1904. YA
Macbride Museum Collection

A Pictorial History

by Stan Cohen

PICTORIAL HISTORIES PUBLISHING COMPANY
MISSOULA, MONTANA

LIBRARY OF CONGRESS CATALOG
CARD NO. 82-81717

ISBN #0-933126-19-0

First Printing May 1982
Second Printing May 1983

Typography by Signal Diversified Services
Cover by Bruce Donnelly
Printed by D. W. Friesen & Sons
Altona, Manitoba, Canada

PRINTED IN CANADA

PICTORIAL HISTORIES PUBISHING COMPANY
713 SOUTH THIRD WEST
MISSOULA, MONTANA 59801

CONTENTS

INTRODUCTION vi

PHOTO CREDITS vii

CHAPTER ONE – 1897-1955 1

CHAPTER TWO – CONSTRUCTION 45

CHAPTER THREE – TOWNS ALONG THE RIVER 51

CHAPTER FOUR – WINTER 61

CHAPTER FIVE – WRECKS AND FIRES 71

CHAPTER SIX – WAR YEARS 77

CHAPTER SEVEN – REMAINS 83

CHAPTER EIGHT – KENO, KLONDIKE, NENANA, TUTSHI 89

APPENDIX 110

INTRODUCTION

Perhaps no other form of transportation in North America has invoked so much nostalgia or has given rise to such romanticism as the steamboat. These colorful old boats plied their way up and down most of the large rivers on the continent during the last 150 years, and many books, songs and movies about this era have perpetuated the romantic idea.

Nowhere else on the continent was there such a proliferation of steamboats and for so long a period of time as on the Yukon River. The river was home to boats of one kind or another for close to 90 years, and the era did not end until 1955, long after the other river systems had switched to more economical means of river transportation.

The Yukon River flows through some of the most remote territory on the continent, bisecting Alaska and cutting through much of the Yukon. The river created an avenue for travel and became very important to the settlements along its course.

Most of the gold strikes in the late 1800s and early 1900s occurred along the Yukon or one of its tributaries. This naturally spurred development of river transportation. If it had not been for those gold strikes, who can say what course the development of the North Country would have taken.

Today there are only a few steamboats that have survived their colorful past. Fortunately for present generations several of them have been restored and are on display in Alaska and the Yukon. From them we can learn about the past and experience some of the history that they helped to create.

One especially impressive restoration is that of the steamer **Klondike** at Whitehorse. Parks Canada has totally restored this boat, and in doing so has created an atmosphere on board that takes you back more than 40 years to a time that was not quite so hectic.

I wish to thank the personnel of the various archives in Alaska and the Yukon for assisting me in my search for photos. I would also like to thank Bill McBurney and Robert Simond of the National Historic Parks and Sites Branch of Parks Canada in Ottawa for the use of the excellent photos of the **Klondike**. Also Jacquelyn McGiffert for editing the manuscript, Bruce Donnelly for the art work and Marlene Waylett of Signal Diversified Services for typesetting.

So get on board, look at the scenery, enjoy the trip into the past and dream a little . . .

— Stan Cohen

PHOTO CREDITS

The photographs in this book, spanning the history of approximately 90 years of steam-boating on the Yukon River in Canada and Alaska, came from a variety of sources. There are many hundreds of photographs available in various archives in the two countries, and it is hoped that the collection presented in this book will give the reader an adequate interpretation of the colorful story of the boats on the river.

Most of the present-day photographs were taken by the author over a period of years on annual trips to Alaska and the Yukon. The historical photographs are acknowledged by their archival source and collection name whenever possible as follows:

AHFAM Anchorage Historical and Fine Arts Museum, Anchorage

AHL Alaska Historical Library, Juneau

DP Dedman's Photo Shop, Skagway, Alaska

PABC Public Archives of British Columbia, Victoria

PAC Public Archives of Canada, Ottawa

PC Parks Canada, Ottawa

SC Stan Cohen

UAA University of Alaska Archives, Fairbanks

USA United States Army Archives, Washington, D.C.

UW University of Washington, Special Collections, Seattle

YA Yukon Archives, Whitehorse

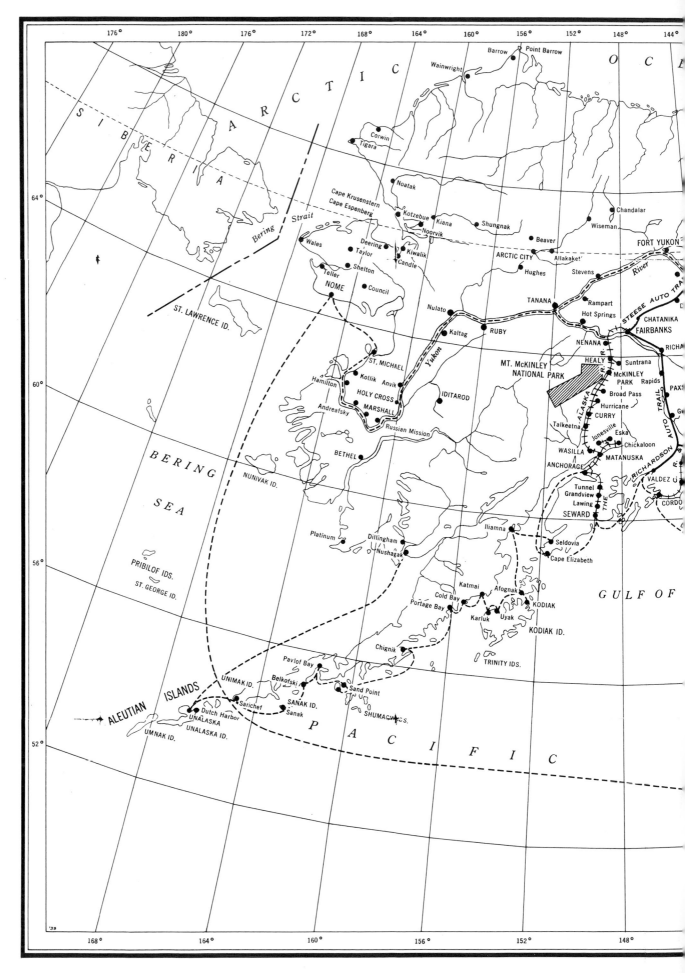

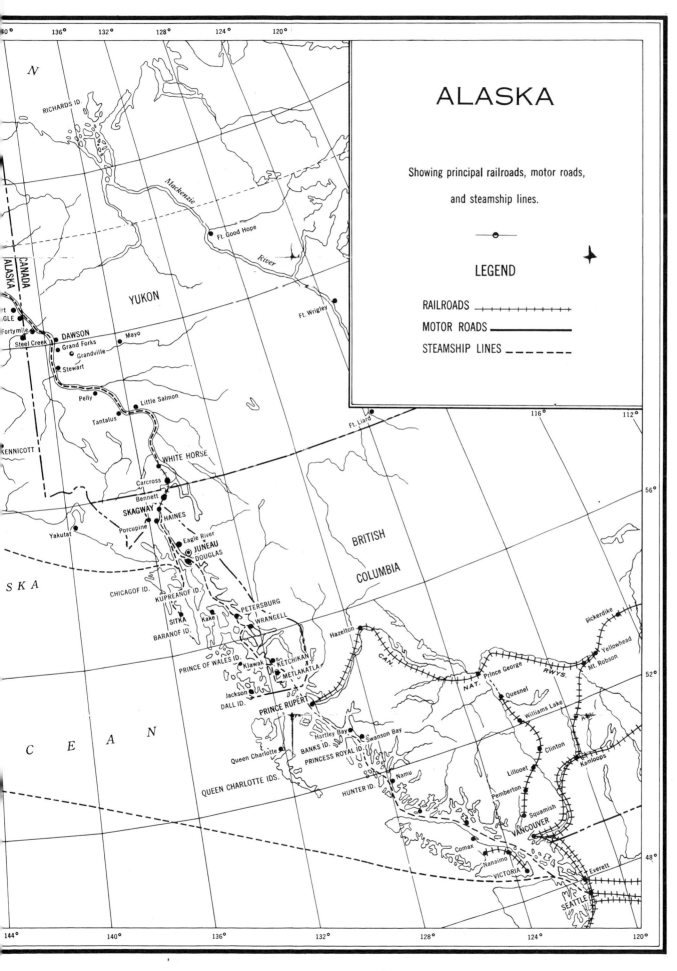

ALASKA

Showing principal railroads, motor roads,

and steamship lines.

LEGEND

RAILROADS ——+++++++++++++++—

MOTOR ROADS ————————

STEAMSHIP LINES — — — — — —

N

RICHARDS ID.

Mackenzie

Ft. Good Hope

River

YUKON

Ft. Wrigley

CANADA
ALASKA

EAGLE

Fortymile

DAWSON   Mayo

Steel Creek

Grand Forks

Grandville

Stewart

Pelly   Little Salmon

Tantalus

Ft. Liard

KENNICOTT

WHITE HORSE

Carcross

Bennett   56°

SKAGWAY   HAINES

Porcupine

Yakutat   BRITISH

Eagle River

JUNEAU   COLUMBIA

DOUGLAS

SKA

CHICAGOF ID.

KUPREANOF ID.

PETERSBURG   Bickerdike

SITKA   Kake   WRANGELL   Yellowhead

BARANOF ID.   Hazelton   CAN.   Mt. Robson   52°

PRINCE OF WALES ID.   KETCHIKAN   NAT. Prince George   RWYS.

Klawak   METLAKATLA   Quesnel

Jackson   Williams Lake

DALL ID.   PRINCE RUPERT   RK.

O   C   E   A   N   Hartley Bay   Clinton

Queen Charlotte   BANKS ID. Swanson Bay   Lillooet   Kamloops

PRINCESS ROYAL ID.   Pemberton

QUEEN CHARLOTTE IDS.   Namu   Squamish

HUNTER ID.   VANCOUVER

Comax

Nanaimo   Everett   48°

VICTORIA

SEATTLE

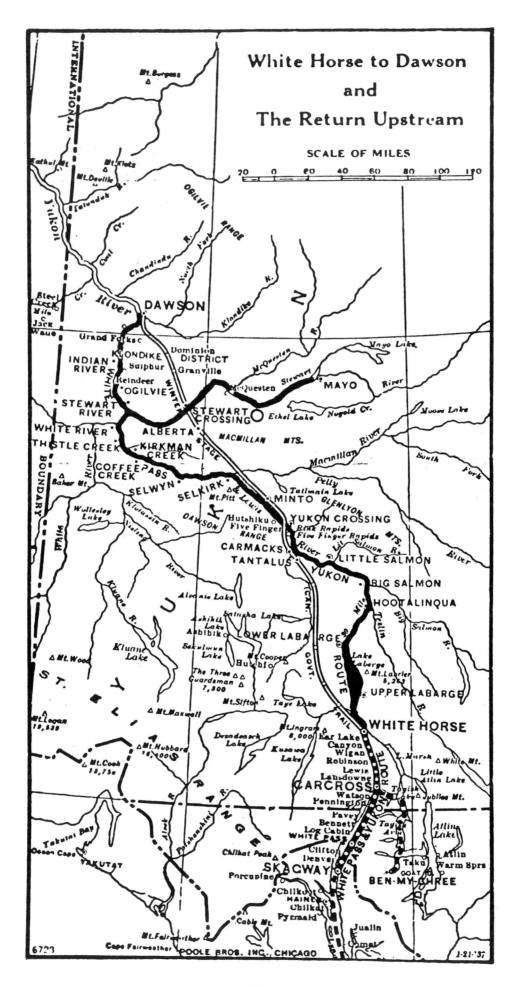

1897-1955

EARLY HISTORY

Steamboating on the Yukon River began in 1866 when the Russian-American Telegraph Company put a small boat, the **Wilder,** into service on the lower river.

Before that, the Hudson's Bay Company had been established in the area in 1842 when their company agent, Robert Campbell, built a trading post at Frances Lake, Yukon. Posts followed on the Pelly River in 1846, at Ft. Yukon in 1847 and at Ft. Selkirk in 1848.

Although there had been hints of gold in the Yukon area for years, furs were the main interest of the few hardy souls who ventured into this wilderness.

In 1873, four men who would play a large part in the development of the area--Frederick W. Hart, Arthur Harper, L. H. (Jack) McQuesten and Alfred H. Mayo--arrived in the area and eventually joined the Alaska Commercial Company (A.C. Co.), a large competitor of the Hudson's Bay Company.

McQuesten established a post in 1874, six miles upstream from a river that flowed into the Yukon, called by the Indians "Thorn-diuck."

Several steamboats made their appearance in the next several years: The A.C. Co.'s **Yukon** in 1869, the Western Fur and Trading Co.'s **St. Michael** in 1879 and the **New Racket** in 1882, eventually owned by the four previously-mentioned pioneer traders. In 1889 the A. C. Co. launched the **Arctic,** the first major boat on the river.

Gold began to supersede furs as the incentive for exploration and development of the area. A gold strike in 1886 at Fortymile River, close to the Alaska border, created the largest town along the river. Another strike at

Birch Creek, 140 miles downstream from Fortymile, established Circle City in 1893. Several other small strikes occurred in Alaska and upstream from the future site of Dawson in the 1890s.

In order to supply the growing number of settlements along the river, the North American Trading and Transportation Company (N.A.T. & T. Co.), put a boat, the **P. B. Weare,** in service in 1892.

Gradually, by trial and error, it was determined that heavy loads transported over shallow water could best be handled by the steamboat, or sternwheeler, as they were also called.

And then a series of related events, led to a momentous occurrence. The feverish activity up and down the river and all the small gold strikes culminated in one of the greatest gold strikes in history--the Klondike.

KLONDIKE GOLD RUSH

The accidental discovery of gold on Rabbit Creek (renamed Bonanza Creek), a tributary of the "Thorn-diuck" River (Klondike), in August 1896 produced one of the largest mass exoduses of people to an unknown wilderness the world has ever seen. Because the area was so remote, it took a year for word to reach the outside world, and by that time, most of the richest ground had been staked by miners already in the area.

Not knowing this, people began the arduous trip. There were several ways to get to the gold fields, all either long or difficult. The quickest way was to book passage on an ocean ship to the new towns of Skagway and Dyea at the head of the Inside Passage in Alaska, trudge

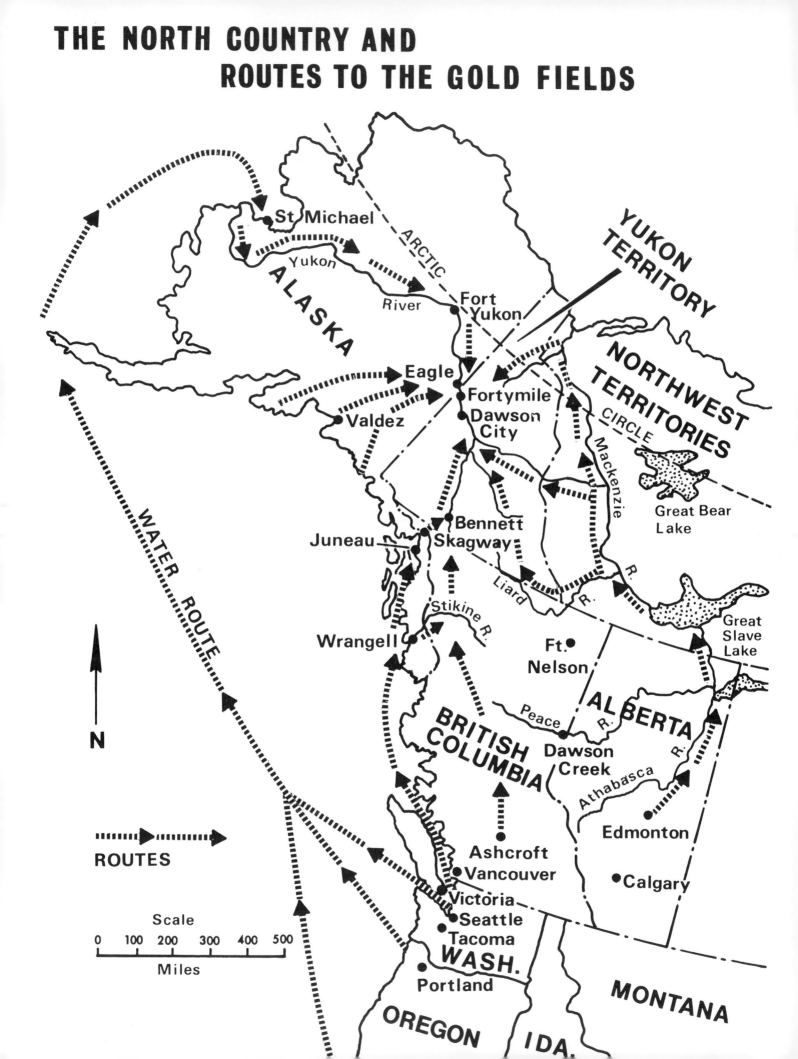

THE NORTH COUNTRY AND ROUTES TO THE GOLD FIELDS

St Michael

ALASKA

Yukon

River

Fort Yukon

ARCTIC

YUKON TERRITORY

NORTHWEST TERRITORIES

CIRCLE

Eagle

Valdez

Fortymile
Dawson City

Mackenzie R.

Great Bear Lake

Juneau

Bennett
Skagway

Liard R.

Great Slave Lake

WATER ROUTE

Stikine R.

Wrangell

Ft. Nelson

ALBERTA

N

BRITISH COLUMBIA

Peace R.

Dawson Creek

Athabasca R.

ROUTES

Ashcroft
Vancouver

Edmonton

Calgary

Victoria

Scale

0 100 200 300 400 500

Miles

Seattle
Tacoma

WASH.

Portland

OREGON   IDA.

MONTANA

THE SEATTLE POST-INTELLIGENCER.

SEATTLE, WASHINGTON, SATURDAY, JULY 17, 1897.

EIGHT-PAGE EDITION.

LATEST NEWS FROM THE KLONDIKE.
9 O'CLOCK EDITION.

GOLD! GOLD! GOLD! GOLD!

Sixty-Eight Rich Men on the Steamer Portland.

STACKS OF YELLOW METAL!

Some Have $5,000. Many Have More, and a Few Bring Out $100,000 Each.

THE STEAMER CARRIES $700,000.

Special Tug Chartered by the Post-Intelligencer to Get the News.

The Latest Reports From the New Eldorado Arrive This Morning—Interviews With Those Who Have Come Down From the North With New-Found Fortunes—The Recent Strikes Seem to Be as Rich as Reported—There Is Plenty of Gold, But Only the Hardy and Provident Can Secure It—No Man Who Is Without a Suitable Outfit Should Accept Fortune in That Remote Region—There Will No Doubt Be a Great Rush for the New Discoveries, and the Majority Will Outfit in and Leave From Seattle.

THE LAND OF GOLD.

Map Showing the Yukon Country, With Klondike and Bonanza Creeks, Where the Recent Rich Discoveries Have Been Made. The Overland Route From Seattle, by Dyea, Chilkoot Pass, the Lakes and River, Is Shown, as Well as the Outside Route by the Way of Bering Sea, St. Michaels and the Yukon River. The Dotted Line Shows the International Boundary.

over one of the passes that led into British Columbia to Lake Bennett, and then build a boat for the 500-mile trip downstream on the Yukon River to the new town of Dawson, close to the newly discovered gold fields. In the next years of 1897-1898, more than 30,000 men, women and even a few children would attempt those routes.

The easiest but longest way was by ocean ship to the port of St. Michael near the mouth of the Yukon River and then by river steamboat upriver to Dawson. This entailed a trip of more than 4,000 miles and could take months. Of course, both routes were possible only during the four-month period in the late spring, summer and early fall when the river was free of ice.

The few boats on the river could not handle this great influx of people, and the boats of 30 new companies appeared in 1897 to join those of the A.C. Co. and N.A.T. & T. Co. already in service. Shipyards worked day and night along the west coast to build enough boats to meet the demand, and by the end of the year more than 60 boats and barges were on the river.

Most of the boats operated from St. Michael to Dawson; a few went from Lake Bennett thru Miles Canyon and Whitehorse Rapids to the new town of Whitehorse. The big hurdle was getting men and supplies from tidewater Alaska over the passes to the start of the water route at Lake Bennett, a distance of nearly 30 miles.

The problem was finally solved on July 6, 1899, when the narrow-gauge rail White Pass and Yukon Route was completed from Skagway to Lake Bennett. Boats continued to operate on the lake until July 29, 1900, when the rail line was completed to Whitehorse. This railroad was a great engineering feat enabling adventurers to travel over the mountains with their supplies, avoiding the treacherous Miles Canyon and Whitehorse Rapids, and arriving at the new town of Whitehorse without having exerted themselves. From Whitehorse it was a relatively easy 400-mile downstream trip on one of the new boats to the booming mining town

*The homemade sternwheeler **May** beached on the Yukon River in 1898. She probably was built at Bennett by prospectors hoping to steam downriver 550 miles to Dawson to stake their gold claims.* UAA

4

of Dawson.

The Klondike strike had emptied out all the other towns along the river and the Klondike would remain the number one gold producing area of the North Country for many years.

THE RIVER

One of the great river systems of North America, the Yukon, rises 15 miles from the Pacific Ocean in British Columbia and then flows north and west for 2,300 miles until it empties into the Pacific Ocean at Norton Sound in the Bering Sea. The watershed of the river totals more than 330,000 square miles in Alaska and the Yukon. The Yukon flats area around Ft. Yukon is 20 miles wide but it's only 250 yards wide at the lower ramparts above Tanana. The huge delta at the mouth of the river is as much as 80 miles across, yet it is shallow enough in places to wade across. The average current is five miles per hour for most of the river's length and three miles per hour at its mouth. Elevations range from 1060 feet at Dawson, 800 feet at Eagle and 200 feet at Tanana.

Major tributaries are the Teslin, Pelly, Stewart, White and Klondike in the Yukon and the Porcupine, Tanana and Koyukuk in Alaska. Below the White River, the Yukon is discolored by glacial silt.

In the days of the steamboats, the river offered many obstacles and hazards along its way downstream from Whitehorse. Just out of Whitehorse lies Lake Laberge, which was noted for sudden, treacherous storms that boats were sometimes caught in. Thirty miles downstream at Lower Laberge at the end of the lake are the remains of some cabins and the **Casca #1.**

The stretch of river between Lower Laberge and Hootalinqua is called the Thirtymile River because that's the distance between those two points. The river winds its way here through rather steep canyons, and in this stretch several boats were wrecked in the past.

At Hootalinquia a few abandoned cabins can be seen, remnants of a small vilage and a winter storage place for boats in the past. Thirty-five miles down river is the abandoned village of Big Salmon and further down the abandoned site of Little Salmon. At mile 202 (mile 0 at Whitehorse) is the town of Carmacks where the Klondike Highway crosses the river.

The Tantalus Butte Coal Mine, which provided small amounts of fuel used by the boats, is near here.

From Carmacks it is 20 miles down river to Five Finger Rapids, perhaps the most dangerous part of the river for boat navigation. The name comes from four islands in the river that form five channels. The extreme right or east channel was the safest one, and a system was devised to get boats through it. A heavy cable was anchored in a building just above the rapids. Then when a boat got to the channel, the cable was attached to a winch on the boat, the boat was pulled through the channel if it was going upstream or it was held back if it was going downstream.

Six miles from Five Finger Rapids is Rink Rapids, the last major obstacle on the river. Although it is rather rough water, it usually presented no real problem to the boats. Nevertheless several were wrecked here through the years.

Fort Selkirk, a major ghost town, is located at mile 282. During the gold rush it was an important town and stop on the river and it thrived until the 1950s when the Klondike Highway was completed.

Stewart Island is located 70 miles up river from Dawson. It was here that boats which plied the Stewart River hauling ore unloaded their cargo onto larger boats for the run to Whitehorse.

The last stop before Dawson was at Sixtymile and Ogilvie Post, the site of the first post office in the Yukon. It was operated by John LaDue, who was to become the founder of Dawson in 1896.

From Dawson to the mouth of the river is about 1600 miles of very remote country. The towns of Forty Mile, Eagle, Circle and Fort Yukon were major stops.

Beyond Fort Yukon is the area known as Yukon Flats, which continues almost 100 miles. River steamers traveling upriver had to pick their way through the ever-changing channels. At Stevens Village the river returns to a rather well-defined channel until the Tanana River enters the Yukon near the village of Tanana.

Tanana was an important trading post operated by the N.A.T. & T. Co. Later it was the site of a U.S. Army post, Fort Gibbon, and was an important link on the central Alaska cable and telegraph system.

Many villages are strung out along the last 800 miles of river before it enters Norton Sound and the Bering Sea.

The Alaska Railroad operated two steamboats for a time on the lower river—the **Gen. Jeff C. Davis** and the **Gen. J. W. Jacobs.** They were owned by the U.S. Army's Quartermaster Corps and were used by the railroad in 1923 mainly on the Tanana River after the Alaska Yukon Navigation Company suspended service in 1922. The **Davis** was very inefficient, and both boats were taken off service in the mid 1930s and replaced by the **Nenana.**

The **Bailey, Clifford Sifton** *and* **Gleaner** *docked at Bennett in September 1899. The newly built railroad is shown in the foreground.*

YA
Macbride Museum Collection

Brochures were printed each year promoting tourism in Alaska and the Yukon. YA

ALASKA AND THE YUKON TERRITORY

WHITE PASS & YUKON ROUTE

(ca. 1916)

"THE YOSEMITE VALLEY IS BEAUTIFUL,
THE YELLOWSTONE PARK IS WONDERFUL,
THE CANYON OF THE COLORADO IS COLOSSAL,
AND ALASKA IS ALL OF THESE."

—Burton Holmes

1900 — 1955

Several shipping companies operated on the river after the railroad tracks reached Whitehorse, but the service was very poor. Competition was fierce; shipments were split up; custom papers were lost; supplies were stolen and the boats were unsafe. The White Pass Company was so disgusted with this service that in 1901 it entered the steamboat business itself. It purchased the boats of the Canadian Development Company—the **Canadian,** the **Columbian,** the **Sybil** and the **Yukoner**—and it also built a large shipyard in Whitehorse to construct its own boats.

Now a person could ride on White Pass equipment all the way from Skagway to Dawson at a cheaper fare and obtain much better service.

By the time the railroad was completed to Whitehorse, however, the gold rush was over. Large companies started moving in with hydraulic equipment and large dredges, and many individual miners were thus replaced. On the other hand, the railroad and the river boats were kept busy for years hauling the heavy machinery.

Discovery of silver-lead ore in 1915 in the Mayo district near the Stewart River, a tributary of the Yukon, provided a source of considerable additional revenue for the White Pass Company.

The steamers **Gleaner, Australian** *and* **Nora** *at the dock at the head of Miles Canyon above Whitehorse. At this point supplies were loaded onto flat cars of the Whitehorse Tram Line and taken into Whitehorse.*
UW
Hegg Collection

The ore was taken down the shallow Stewart River on small boats to the Yukon, transferred to larger boats for the trip to Whitehorse, and then shipped by rail to Skagway and waiting cargo ships. This method of transporting the ore continued until 1950 when an all-weather road made trucking possible.

The British Yukon Navigation Company (B.Y.N. Co.) was formed in 1901 by the White Pass Company to operate boats between Whitehorse and Dawson. The company also had operations on Tagish and Atlin Lake and operated the Atlin Inn at Atlin for many years. The Side Stream Navigation Company supplemented the B.Y.N. Co. from 1909 to 1919. It operated shallow draft sternwheelers on the White, Stewart, Pelly and Porcupine rivers, all tributaries of the Yukon. Its boats were the **Vidette,** the **Pauline** and the **Nasutlin.**

In 1913 the Alaska Yukon Navigation Company (A.Y.N. Co.) was formed by the White Pass Company to operate boats on the lower Yukon between Dawson and St. Michael. It also operated on the Tanana, Koyukuk and Iditarod Rivers. In 1914, the A.Y.N. Co., after a major rate war with a rival company, the Northern Navigation Company, bought out that company. Fares had dropped so much that both companies would have gone bankrupt. After 1924, the only boat operated by the A.Y.N. Co. was the **Yukon,** and in 1942 the company was dissolved.

In addition to the rapid decline in gold production in the Yukon in the early 1900s, several new forms of competition arrived on the scene to weaken the ability of the steamboat companies to stay profitable. The Alaska Railroad was completed from tidewater at Seward to Fairbanks in 1923. This basically eliminiated the need for boats to haul supplies from St. Michael up river to Tanana and then up the Tanana and Chena Rivers to the gold fields at Fairbanks (which had been discovered in 1902). Boats now could connect with the

The **Clifford Sifton** *shooting the turbulent Miles Canyon rapids on July 24, 1900.*
YA Macbride Museum Collection

Miles Canyon in 1898. A treacherous stretch of water between Lake Bennett and Whitehorse that some boats went through. A tramway was built around it to carry most of the men and supplies.   UW

Miles Canyon today is a lot less dangerous because of higher water from a hydro dam downstream at Whitehorse.   Government of the Yukon

railroad at Nenana on the Tanana River. In the 1930s the airplane was just coming into its own, and many towns along the lower Yukon, especially, could be supplied to some degree by air. Highways were starting to push into the interior of Alaska before World War II, and this further eroded the use of river transportation.

During most of the steamboat era, wood was the principal fuel used and more than 300,000 cords were burned through the years. Since a boat could burn two cords an hour going upstream, it could not carry enough wood for an entire trip.

Camps were established about 30 miles apart along the river where boats could stop to replenish their supply. Hundreds of men were hired through the years to cut the wood and stack it along the river. Normally the wood was stacked for one year to dry before it was used.

In later years, wood was much harder to get. In 1925, the **White Horse** used 1,517 cords at a cost of $8.26 a cord. This compared to $7.14 a cord in 1901. The **White Horse** could make a trip downstream from Whitehorse to Dawson without a wood stop, but going upstream it might make six to eight stops. Since time stopped for wood cost money, each stop was made as short as possible. The boat blew its whistle before getting to the stop so that the men on shore would be ready. It took a special skill and strength to load a boat without delay and get it back on the river

In later years some boats were converted to oil, but the B.Y.N. Co. resisted this because many wood cutters would have been put out of business. Coal, which would have been a good, cheap source of fuel, was not found in large enough deposits along the river to make its use feasible.

A steamboat and supplies at Canyon City just upstream from Miles Canyon. This was the start of the tramway that skirted the Canyon and Whitehorse Rapids prior to completion of the railroad to Whitehorse in 1900.					*YA*

FACTS AND FIGURES

In 1904 it took the **Susie,** one of the largest boats on the river, 15 days to make the St. Michael to Dawson run, carrying 100 tons. An upstream trip from Dawson to Whitehorse would take about four and one-half to six days while the same distance downstream could be covered in only one and one-half days.

In 1926, a river cruise from Tanana to Ruby and return on the lower river took five to six days and cost $50; a trip to Holy Cross and return, further downstream, took ten to eleven days and cost $93.

In 1917, the A.Y.N. Co. had a direct boat from Dawson to Tanana once a week. There were connections at Tanana for a boat to Fairbanks or downstream to St. Michael.

In 1937, steamers left Whitehorse every Wednesday at 7 p.m. and arrived in Dawson Friday morning. They left Dawson Saturday morning and arrived in Whitehorse on Wednesday afternoon.

*The ill-fated **Columbian** was built in Victoria, B.C., in 1898 and used on the upper river run. On Sept. 25, 1906 she was destroyed on the river between Big and Little Salmon when a crew member, shooting at some ducks from the boat, fired into the boat, which was carrying explosives. The resultant explosion and fire killed six crew members. It was the worst accident ever to occur on the river.* UW
W & S Photo

The **Yukoner** at Dawson before her first trip of the season on June 3, 1900. She was built in Victoria, B.C., in 1898 and operated until 1903. She had too much draft for the upper river run.   UW Larss & Duclos Photo

The **Bailey** was the first boat of the season to arrive at Dawson on May 23, 1901. She was built at Lake Bennett in 1899 and operated on the lake until 1900 when she was taken through Whitehorse Rapids and put on the upper river service. She was dismantled at Whitehorse in 1931.   UAA

*Canadian Development Company's steamer **Columbian** and the Yukon Flyer Line Company's **Eldorado** starting from Dawson on July 4, 1899 on a race to Whitehorse.*
UW Hegg Collection

*"In close pursuit." The **Bailey** is shown racing an unnamed steamer in the foreground on the Fifty Mile River in August 1899.* *YA Barley Collection*

*Passengers and crew line up on the decks of the **Bailey** during a wood stop on the Fifty Mile River in August 1899.*   *YA Barley Collection*

The **White Horse** *leaving Dawson in July 1901.*

YA
Goetzman Photo

The **White Horse** *docked at Dawson in the early 1900s.*   *UW Nowell Photo*

18

S. S. WHITEHORSE

C. M. COGHLAN
Master

"The table's spread. come, let us dine, my friend"

DINNER

Prohibition Cocktail

Yukon Radishes   Green Onions   Leaf Lettuce

Dawson City Tomatoes   Queen Olives

SOUPS
Consomme Clear   Cream of Oyster

FISH
Baked Marsh Lake Whitefish, Sauce au Dam

ENTREES
Boiled Brisket of Pelly River Beef, Sauce Tantalus

Macaroni au Grautin   Pineapple Fritters

ROASTS
Stuffed Haunch of Carmacks Veal
Roast Loin of Stewart River Moose with Jelly

VEGETABLES
Mashed Mooschide Potatoes   Mazie May Garden Peas

Sunnydale Spinach

DESSERT
Bonanza Plum Pudding, Hard Rock Sauce

Sourdough Blueberry Pie   Cheechaco Apple Pie

Assorted '98 Cakes   Golden Fruit

Nuggets of Cheese   Christie's Crackers

Hudsons Bay Tea   Five Fingers of Coffee

MADE IN U.S.A.

Menu of the **White Horse.**   *PABC*

Co. B, 14th Infantry arriving at Fort Gibbon, Alaska, on the Tanana River in July 1914. The steamer is pushing barges with wanigans on them. *AHL*
D. D. Pittman Collection

An excursion crowd leaving Nenana, Alaska, on board the **Reliance** on July 30, 1916. She was built at St. Michael in 1907 and wrecked and sank at Minto on the Tanana River on Oct. 6, 1917. *AHL*
Alaska Railroad Collection

The **Gen. Jeff. C. Davis** and the **Gen. J. W. Jacobs** laid up for the winter. The **Davis,** built in 1898 and originally called the **Duchesnay,** was used in Cook's Inlet. Later it was taken to St. Michael, turned over to the Quartermaster Corps of the U.S. Army and renamed the **Davis.** The **Jacobs** was built at Whitehorse for the Army. They were both turned over to the Alaska Railroad in 1923 and operated for several years on the lower river run.
AHL
Alaska Railroad Collection

Fairbanks citizens welcome home Judge Wickersham on Aug. 23, 1908.   *UAA*
Erskine Collection

*The **Monarch** with miners on the bank. She was built in the Seattle area in 1898. and towed to St. Michael. She was the first through steamer from St. Michael to Dawson in 1898.*
UW W & S Photo

Alice I *docked at Dawson in July 1898. She was built at St. Michael in 1895 and was the first steamer to arrive in Dawson in 1898.* AHL

The **Tyrrell** *in 1900. She was built in Vancouver, B.C., in 1898 and operated on the upper river run for years. She now lies in shambles on shore across from Dawson.*
YA Vogee Collection

The Casca, the White Horse and Keno, three boats that survived many years on the river are shown at the shipyards at Whitehorse possibly in the 1930s. DP

Yukon River Steamers at Shipyards

Whitehorse, Y.T.

*The British Yukon Navigation Company fleet laid up at Whitehorse in 1901.   YA
Scharschmidt Collection*

*The **Casca #2** on the right and the **Dawson** on the left at the Whitehorse dock
in 1916.*
*YA
Macbride Museum Collection*

The **Gen. J. W. Jacobs** *is shown docked at Manley Hot Springs, Alaska, in the 1920s.* UW Larss & Duclos Photo

The **Tanana** *at the Northern Commercial Company's dock in Fairbanks. She was built at St. Michael in 1904 and operated mainly on the sidestreams until she was sunk in the Thirtymile River in 1915. She was raised and repaired but sank again near Minto on the Tanana River in 1921.* UAA
Erskine Collection

*The **Bonanza King** laden with passengers on the first excursion to Forty Mile on May 28, 1899.*
Vancouver Library Collection

ORIGINAL. | DOMINION OF CANADA, DEPARTMENT OF MARINE AND FISHERIES. | FORM A.

CERTIFICATE of the Inspector of Hulls & Equipment for a Steamboat to carry Passengers, or for a Freightboat of or over 150 tons gross.

Having examined the hull and equipment of the steamboat *Australian* of *Victoria* whereof *C. D. C.* of *Victoria* owner on this 23rd day of *Aug* A.D. 1900.

The particulars of her gross and register tonnage as shewn on her certificate of registry, being as follows:

Tonnage under tonnage deck 95.08 Tons   Houses on deck: 329.40 Tons
Total gross tonnage 420.43 ..   Deduct for engine room 114.
Register tonnage 318.44

I, F. M. Richardson, Inspector of hulls and equipment, do hereby certify that her hull is in all respects staunch, seaworthy and in good condition for navigation; that the equipment of the vessel throughout is in conformity with the requirements of the "Steamboat Inspection Act, 1898," the said steamboat having on board, properly placed and in good order for immediate service:— 1 boats, having (together) a carrying capacity for 24 persons; life boats having (together) a carrying capacity for persons, 220 life preservers, wooden floats; 25 fire buckets; 6 axes, 6 lanterns, 2 life buoy, having a proper bearing line attached, and that she has the fire pumps, hose, and other appliances for extinguishing fire required by the said Act, and placed as therein provided and in every way efficient and according to the requirements of the said Act, and I further certify that the said steamboat is permitted to run on the waters between *Bennett* and *Taku* from this 23 day of *Aug* to the 23rd day of *Aug* 1901 and that she is adapted and fit to carry 200 passengers and no more.

Dated at VANCOUVER this 5th day of Sept. 1900

F. M. Richardson,
Inspector of Hulls and Equipments

CERTIFICATE of the Inspector of Boilers and Machinery for the same boat.

And I, F. M. Richardson, Inspector of boilers and machinery, do hereby certify that the engine, boiler and machinery of the steamboat *Australian* are sufficient and suitable to authorize her being lawfully employed *in carriage of Freight and Passengers*, without hazard to life on the route between *Bennett* and *Taku* from this 23rd day of *Aug* to the 23rd day of *Aug* 1901 that the engine of the said steamboat is of 66 nominal horsepower and that her boiler can carry with safety 200 pounds of steam pressure per square inch, and no more.

Dated at VANCOUVER this 5th day of Sept. 1900

F. M. Richardson,
Inspector of Boilers & Machinery.

Here insert "in carriage of passengers" or "as a freight boat" or "as a ferry boat" as the case may be.

28

Form 138_ 2-6 04 2M.

#1

THE WHITE PASS & YUKON ROUTE
River Division

MASTER'S TRIP REPORT TO THE SUPERINTENDENT

Steamer **Bonanza King.**   Voyage 11

Barge **Klondike**

NORTH BOUND   **SOUTH BOUND**

DATE	Time Arrived	Time Departed	Cords wood taken	PORTS OF CALL	DATE	Time Arrived	Time Departed	Cords Wood taken
				Dawson	Octo. 9		2 40 p	
				Sweed Creek		4 25	4 30	
				Stop a/c Fog	10	12 40 a	2 30 a	
				Ogilvie		4 00 a	4 30 a	
				Stewart River		1 00		5
				White River		2 00 a	2 10 a	
				Str. Dawson		4 p		
				Thistle Creek		4 35 p	5 45 p	
				Selkirk		6 45 p		
				Kirkman		6 45	7 35	7
				Coffee Creek		11 00 p	11 05 p	
				Martins Ldg		11 30 p	11 30 p	
				Wood Camp #27	11	3 00 a	4 10 a	10
				" " 24		3 30 p	3 45	2
				Selkirk		4 20 p	4 30 p	
				Str. White Horse		6 22	6 25 p	
				Wood Camp #21		6 40	7 40	10
				Landed passenger		10 55	11 10	
				Minto post	12	1 00 a	2 00 a	
				Wood Camp #20		5 10 a	6 10 a	10
				" " #16		4 25 p	4 55 a	6
				Myers Road House		5 25	5 45	
				Tantalus Mines		9 00 PM	10 00 PM	15 Tons
				Stop Myers		2 10 a		
				drop scow in slough				
				1 mi above Moorsides				
				old wood Camp				
				water 5 ft. head				
				of slough dry			3 00 am	

NOTE.—*This report must be made and handed into the office of the Superintendent on completion of each voyage.*

Time of arrival and departure from all places, where stops are made, must be shown.

In addition to this, show time passing the following principal points as follows: Lower Le Barge, Hootalinqua, Big Salmon, Five Fingers, Selkirk, Selwyn, Stewart River, Ogilvie, *whether stop is made or not. Also show arrival and departure from* White Horse *and* Dawson.

(OVER)

*The **Sarah** at Dawson in 1900.*   *UW W & S Photo*

*The **Hannah** taking on a supply of oil along the Andreafsky River in Alaska. She was built in Unalaska in 1898 and was a sister ship of the **Sarah** and **Susie**. They were the queen ships of the lower Yukon run for many years.   UAA Erskine Collection*

Disembarking passengers and freight at Dawson.   UW Hegg

Thirty miles below Lake Laberge at the confluence of the Yukon and Teslin Rivers was Hootalinqua, another stop on the prospectors' route down the Yukon. A North-west Mounted Police post was established here in 1898.   UW

31

A barge with dancing couples is pushed by the **Casca**. *There is no description of the occasion, but it looks like an elaborate celebration.* *UW Ellingsen Photo*

Horses and gas drums being transported up the Stewart River. The trip from Stewart to Mayo took three days and two nights. There were 14 rapids on the river where boat and barge had to be winched through. The trip down river took only 12 hours.
YA Dennett Collection

Five Finger Rapids was the last major obstacle on the river before Dawson. The east channel was the most used by boats going upstream and downstream.   YA

Thousands of bags of silver-lead ore stacked at Mayo and awaiting shipment to Whitehorse by sternwheeler.   YA Schellinger Collection

No. 814.—Capt. and Officers of Steamer "D. R. Campbell," Dawson, Y. T.

Crew members of the **Susie** *and the* **D. R. Campbell** *at Dawson.*
Author's Collection

No. 801.—Capt. and Officers of Steamer "Susie," Dawson, Y. T.

Crew members of the **Jennie M** inside a cabin.   UAA

Officers and crew of the **Bailey** pose for a group picture on the top deck of the sternwheeler in August 1899.   YA Barley Collection

The Forward Saloon (top) and the Dining Saloon (bottom) of the steamer **Alaska.**
AHL
R. N. DeArmond Collection

The dining room of a sternwheeler.   *Vancouver Public Library*

*Passengers on the **Susie**.*   *UAA*

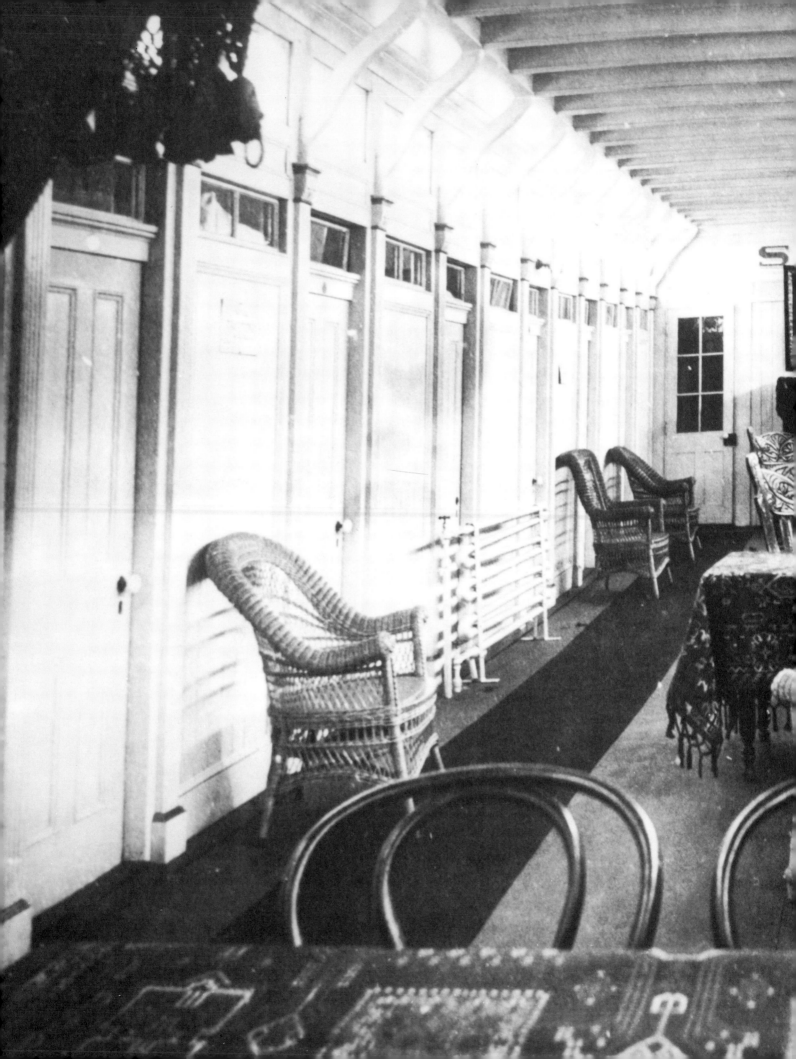

The "social hall" or sitting room of the Suzie.

"Wooding up" on the **Julia B.** *The men appear to be soldiers, possibly from Fort Gibbon.* AHFAM

The **Casca** *ready to sail from Dawson on Oct. 11, 1908. Wood is stacked up to be loaded on board.* YA

Loading up with wood on the Fifty Mile River.

Loading cord wood. In the early days the sternwheelers were fueled by wood, and stops had to be made frequently to resupply the hungry boilers. A steamer could burn 120 cords of four-foot wood on a trip from St. Michael upriver to Dawson.
YA

Loading wood on the **Aksala.** *Twenty cords of wood were burned every eight hours on the upriver run and many fuel stops had to be made along the way. YA*
Dennett Collection

The **Casca** and the **White Horse** beached on the banks of the Yukon River at Whitehorse before they were burned in 1974. Government of the Yukon

The **Dawson** "wooding up" in 1901. She was built at Whitehorse in 1901 and wrecked at Rink Rapids in 1926. YA Barley Collection

WHITE PASS & YUKON ROUTE

HERMAN WEIG, GENERAL AGENT
1016 CHAMBER OF COMMERCE BUILDING
CHICAGO

I send you herewith booklets describing the trip to Alaska, Atlin and White Horse, Dawson and Nome.

If you are undecided as to where to go this summer, and, especially, if you are contemplating a trip to Alaska, you will find a perusal of these booklets decidedly worth while. But in taking a trip to Alaska do not overlook the fact that if you limit your trip to a cruise along the shores you will miss seeing the most interesting part of this Northland. That this is a fact, is, we believe, evidenced by the many letters received from tourists who have taken a trip from Skaguay into the interior over our lines. We have published a few of these letters in our booklet "Opinions" (copy of which is enclosed), and they are worth reading.

It is a fact worth noting that there are more women than men who take the tourist trip to Atlin and Dawson.

From June 16th to August 22nd the Alaska S. S. Co. and the Pacific Coast S. S. Co. will each operate two steamers on an excursion itinerary, sailing from Seattle every third day and stopping at all the interesting ports between Seattle and Skaguay, including the glaciers. Southbound, these steamers will stop at Sitka.

The Canadian Pacific Railway will operate two steamers from Victoria and Vancouver, sailing from these ports every Friday and Saturday, respectively. They will also make special stops during the summer season, but they will not call at Sitka. Passengers can, of course, take any steamer they like from or to Seattle, Victoria or Vancouver, except the S. S. "Spokane" of the Pacific Coast S. S. Co., which carries only continuous round trip passengers and does not permit any stop overs.

The round trip excursion rates are as follows:

ATLIN

From Skaguay, Alaska, to Atlin and return, including side trip from Caribou to White Horse and return, effective June 15th to Sept. 30th - - - - - - - - - - - $40

Tickets will be limited to 20 days with October 10th as the final limit.

DAWSON

From Skaguay, Alaska to Dawson and return, effective June 20th to August 31st - - - - $100

Tickets will be limited to 30 days with September 15th as the final limit.

SIDE TRIP TO ATLIN

Passengers holding Dawson or Nome round-trip tickets, who desire to make the side trip from Caribou to Atlin and return, can do so for $15.00 extra. This includes meals and berth on the lake steamers. The trip can be made either on the way to or from Dawson, and a 7-days' extension of time will be allowed for this side trip.

NOME

From Skaguay, Alaska, to Nome, Alaska, and return to Seattle, effective June 15th to August 15th - $170
(Via Dawson and St. Michael, returning direct from Nome to Seattle)

Limit of return from Nome, Alaska, September 15th. Passengers holding tickets to Nome, who desire to make a side trip from Tanana to Chena or Fairbanks, can arrange with the river lines (beyond Dawson) for necessary stop-over to make this trip, limited to 14 days (within the limit of the ticket) on payment of $40.00 extra.

Reservations cannot be guaranteed on stop-over privileges.

The rates named above include meals and berth while on the ocean, lake and river steamers, but do not include the maintenance of passengers while awaiting connections at any point.

Children between the ages of 5 and 12 will be carried at one-half fare.

To the above mentioned rates, except that to Nome, should be added the cost of steamship ticket which is $30.00 each way. This is for first-class passage and includes meals and berth. As the rate to Nome includes the steamship fare to Seattle, the fare from Seattle or Vancouver to Skaguay one way only is added.

Thus, the through round trip excursion rates from Seattle, Victoria or Vancouver will be as follows:

To Atlin-White Horse and return - - - - - - - - - - - - $100
To Dawson and return - - - - - - - - - - - - $160
To Nome and return - - - - - - - - - - - - $200

One hundred and fifty pounds of baggage will be carried free on each full ticket and 75 pounds on each half ticket via the White Pass & Yukon Route and its connecting lines. All weight in excess of these amounts will be charged for at current excess baggage rates.

As to clothes, it is advisable to be provided with a medium weight wrap or overcoat, underclothing such as you would wear during the late spring in the east, walking boots or rubber overshoes for use in climbing the mountains and glaciers. While you might have some showers along the coast, it is nearly always dry in the interior, but to provide for emergencies a waterproof garment or umbrella should be taken along; the former is preferable.

If you like fishing, bring your trout rod and a few flies and a heavier rod for salmon and halibut fishing. The bay at Skaguay will afford you a splendid opportunity for salmon and halibut fishing.

By all means bring your camera and plenty of films or plates. A field or opera glass will help you enjoy the scenery that is more distant.

If there is any information that you desire that is not given herein, please do not hesitate to ask for same.

Trusting the enclosed booklets will awaken in you a desire to see this wonderland of nightless days, I am,

Yours faithfully,
Herman Weig,
General Agent.

SEE ALASKA—but don't be content with merely seeing the shores—see the land beyond—you will never regret it.

CONSTRUCTION

A look at the appendix of this book will show that most of the boats that were in service prior to or during the Klondike Gold Rush were constructed in shipyards along the Pacific Coast--Victoria, B.C., Seattle, Portland or San Francisco. A few were constructed at Unalaska in the Aleutian chain, at St. Michael, Alaska or Lake Bennett, B.C.

Until the railroad was connected to Whitehorse in 1900, the only way to get a large boat on the Yukon River was to sail or tow it from the west coast shipyards, 2,500 miles by open sea, to St. Michael and then up the river over 2,000 miles to Whitehorse.

Once the railroad was completed, heavy machinery and material could be transported to Whitehorse, and a large shipyard was established there after 1900. Boats were not only constructed there, but were stored on ways (storage ramps) for the winter. Repairs could be made on the boats before they were put back in the water for the river season. It was a big business in the early days.

Most of the early boats brought up from the west coast or constructed at Unalaska were the Mississippi river-boat type, designed for a sluggish, slow moving river but not suitable to the fast current and narrow channels of the

*Partial view of the sternwheeler **Australian** under construction at Lake Bennett in May 1899. The superstructure is almost completed.* YA
MacBride Museum Collection

45

Yukon River. It was soon learned that boats on the Yukon would have to be designed to meet the problems peculiar to that river.

Three of the biggest boats to ever ply the Yukon were typical of those on the Mississippi-- the **Susie, Sarah** and **Hannah.** They were all constructed in Louisville, Ky. in 1897, shipped in sections to Unalaska where they were completed and then towed to St. Michael for service on the lower river run.

These magnificent boats were rated at 1,130 tons, could haul up to 300 tons of freight, and had a cabin capacity of 150 passengers. For a fast, rush trip to the gold fields, up to 500 people could cram aboard.

Since the river had a fast current (5-6 miles per hour), the boats had to be constructed with an enormous backing power in order to safely carry the heavy loads downstream. They had a draught of about four feet loaded and 18 inches unloaded. Fifteen miles per hour was an average speed downstream.

Most of the steamers constructed for the river were designed for freight hauling with passenger accommodations only as an afterthought. They were made of wood. The cargo deck was on the first level, close to the water line, to facilitate loading freight and wood. The boiler and machinery were also at this level.

The deck above was called the passenger or saloon deck. Here were the passenger cabins, dining area, galley, toilets and some crew quarters. There was normally no running water in the cabins, only a wash basin and water pitcher. The galley stove was usually fueled by wood, and the hot water used in cooking came from the boiler on the lower deck. An icebox was provided for storage of perishable items. Ice was bought from ice houses in the major river towns.

Sternwheeler **White Horse** *with workmen posing on all decks after construction was completed on May 25, 1901, only 43 days after the keel was laid in the Whitehorse shipyard. In the background are the sternwheelers* **Dawson** *and* **Selkirk.** *YA Barley Collection*

Above the passenger deck was the "Texas Deck," called that because the biggest and best cabins were there. These were usually reserved for the captain and officers of the boat. The term originated on the Mississippi riverboats where passenger cabins were named after states--thus the word "stateroom."

On top of the "Texas Deck" was the pilot house where the main controls for operating the boat were located. The captain or pilot commanded the boat from this vantage point.

Steam to power the large paddlewheels at the rear of the boat was generated in a large boiler on the freight deck. For most of the steamboat era, wood was the main source of fuel for the boilers. Some were converted to oil burners in later years, and some at times burned coal, but there was no large coal deposit close to the river to provide a steady source of this fuel.

The paddlewheels were huge wooden contraptions, some up to 20 feet high and more than 20 feet across. They were turned by large pitman arms attached to the steam engines that received steam from the boilers. These powerful engines produced hundreds of horsepower and when the engine on one side pushed the pitman arm, the engine on the other side pulled the other arm. This prevented the engines from stalling and gave constant power to the wheel.

Rudders at the back steered the boat. Later, hydraulic rudders were used for sharp turns when the boat was in reverse.

The last boat constructed on the river was the **Klondike #2,** built at Whitehorse in 1937.

Sternwheeler **Tanana** *in dry dock at St. Michael. Her paddlewheel has been removed and repairs are being made. Built in 1904, she operated on side streams in Alaska and sank in 1921.*

UAA
Erskine Collection

Construction views of a sternwheeler, probably in Whitehorse.　　　　　*YA*
Puckett Collection

Construction view along the Yukon River.

YA
Puckett Collection

Sternwheeler **M. L. Washburn** in dry dock at St. Michael in 1911, the year she was built by the Northern Navigation Company. She was sold to the Alaska-Yukon Navigation Company in 1914, and in 1920 she struck a rock and sank near Little Salmon, Yukon.

UAA
Erskine Collection

*Sternwheeler **Susie** in dry dock at St. Michael. The boats were pulled up the ways by large winches and were docked there for repair or winter storage. UAA Erskine Collection*

Sternwheelers owned by the Alaska Railroad on the bank of the Tanana River in 1948. AHFAM Alaska Railroad Collection

TOWNS ALONG THE RIVER

In the early part of the century, many towns along the Yukon River depended on the steamboat to provide their main source of contact with the outside world. And for many years after the Klondike Gold Rush, many towns had no other means of communication except for the occasional dog sled driver who came through in the winter.

The airplane opened up the entire country in the 1920s, but the large quantity of supplies needed by some communities could not be brought in by plane. Only when the highways began penetrating the wilderness did the dependency on river boats decrease.

Highways to Fairbanks, Circle and Eagle, Alaska, opened up access points to the Yukon and its tributaries. The Alaska Highway, constructed during World War II, provided the stimulus for continued road building in the Yukon, and with the completion of the road to Mayo in 1950 and to Dawson in 1955, the steamboat era passed into history.

Dawson was the principal town on the river through most of the boat era. During the gold rush, from 1897-99, it provided the business for dozens of boats, and in 1901 more

A view of Caribou Crossing (Carcross) at the head of Lake Bennett before the railroad reached here. The town became an important shipping point for the Yukon lakes.   YA

51

than 60 boats docked there. In the early years, the only means of getting large mining machinery and other commodities to Dawson was by boat, during the months that the river was free of ice. For the rest of the year, the town was virtually isolated from the outside world. There was a crude winter and summer trail from Whitehorse, but it could not handle the large quantities of items needed. With the completion of the Klondike Highway in 1955, Dawson was no longer isolated eight months of the year.

Whitehorse started out as the northern terminus of the White Pass and Yukon Route and the southern terminus of the riverboat system. It grew more important as the years went by and was the focal point for construction of the Alaska Highway during World War II. As the highway system increased and the boat business decreased, Whitehorse became increasingly important. In 1953 the capital of the territory was moved from Dawson to Whitehorse, and shortly thereafter the boat era ended.

The other towns downstream from Dawson—Eagle, Circle, Ft. Yukon, Tanana, Ruby and Marshall were important riverboat stops through the years, but only Eagle and Circle were eventually connected by road to the Alaska Highway system.

Sixty miles up the coast from the mouth of the river is St. Michael, located on an island with the same name. It was founded by the Russians and used by them as a shipping point for exploration of the river. At the time of the gold rush, it became an important transfer point from ocean ships to riverboats, and a military post and post office were established. Several boats were constructed here, and it became a major winter storage site. After the White Pass Railroad was completed in 1900, the town became less important, and the opening of the Alaska Railroad in 1923 ended any need for an all-water route to Dawson.

Many of the boats that plied the lower Yukon were left abandoned on the ways at St. Michael, since there was no further need for their services on this part of the river.

A major highlight of the year in each town along the river was the arrival of the first boat in the spring. In the early years, most of the towns were completely cut off from the outside world until the river opened up in the spring.

As the boat whistle sounded and the boat came into sight, the townspeople turned out to welcome it. The first boat brought in much needed supplies, news from the outside world, and, most importantly, the first touch of reality after a long eight-month hibernation. Later, the radio, telephone, airplane and roads kept these formerly isolated communities in touch with the outside world.

Whitehorse about 1898.   *UAA*

Panoramic view of the British Yukon Navigation Company's fleet dry-docked for the winter at the Whitehorse shipyards in 1901. At least twelve sternwheelers are shown. UW

CITY OF WHITE HORSE Y.T.

ADAMS & LARKIN PHOTO.
DAWSON Y.T.

The waterfront of Whitehorse early in the twentieth century. Many tents are still in evidence and the train station is not yet completed. YA

The waterfront of Whitehorse in the early 1900s. By this time the town had become a major shipping point on the Yukon River.

YA
Dennett Collection

The waterfront of Whitehorse in 1944. Only a few sternwheelers were still in service on the river. The population of Whitehorse had increased during the war from 500 to many thousands because of the construction of the Alaska Highway and the Canol pipeline project.

USA

The waterfront at Dawson--a busy place in the spring of 1898. The Klondike Gold Rush was at its height, and thousands were converging on the town.   UW

The wharf at Dawson in the early 1900s.

The **Bailey** *docked along side of the* **Yukoner** *and astern of the* **Gold Star** *at Dawson in June 1900.*
PAC
Woodside Photo

The **Lotta Talbot** *docked at Dawson on Aug. 12, 1899. She was built in Seattle in 1898 by the Pacific Cold Storage Co. and operated on the St. Michael to Dawson run. She was wrecked by ice at the Fairbanks waterfront.*
UAA
Selid Collection

Waterfront view of Eagle, Alaska on the Yukon River just west of the international border in the late 1890s.   *YA*

Circle City, Alaska in the 1890s. This was an important mining and trading camp on the Yukon River before the gold rush, and was the starting point for many of the early claim stakers in the Klondike. It was built by Jack McQuesten, a leading trader in the Yukon area for many years.   *UW*

*The **Sarah** is shown unloading freight at Fort Yukon, Alaska.* *UAA*
Alaska Agriculture Exp. Station Collection

Chena, Alaska in 1905, on a major tributary of the Yukon River. *AHFAM*

Ruby, Alaska on May 5, 1912. The ice is breaking up and the boat season is just starting. AHL
Clemons, photographer

Meeting the boats at Ruby, Alaska in 1912. AHL
Clemons, photographer

Nulato, Alaska on the lower Yukon in the early 1900s. UAA
Alaska Historical Society Collection

St. Michael and the Northern Commercial Co.'s plant in September 1908. UW

WINTER

Operation of steamboats on the Yukon River was, of course, a seasonal business; at this latitude, winter comes early and stays late. The dates of the final freezing and breakup of the river meant quite a bit to the economic stability of the boat companies.

The earlier the river broke up in the spring, the earlier the boats could haul supplies and passengers to the river towns and carry ore from the Yukon mines to Whitehorse. And the reverse was true in the fall. The later the river stayed ice-free, the longer the companies had to operate.

The season usually started in mid- to late May and ran to early October. Lake Laberge was one of the last stretches on the river to thaw and Herbert Wheeler, then president of the

White Pass Company devised a unique method to speed the breakup. Using a Model T truck, he spread a mixture of carbon black, old crankcase oil and diesel oil in a 60-foot-wide path across the length of the lake. The mixture absorbed the sun's rays and rotted the ice. Steamers pushing barges could break up the ice and add perhaps several weeks to the season.

Ice was the greatest hazard to navigation. In the spring the boats would encounter large floating chunks; in the fall the river could freeze overnight, trapping a boat for winter. Floating chunks of ice were large enough to puncture the hull of a boat if it was not protected by iron plates. And in the fall, ice pushing against a boat could even pitch it

Ice breaking on the Yukon River at Circle City, Alaska, on May 21 1897. AHFAM

ashore or against another boat or obstacle in the river. When the spring breakup came, ice could move as much as 100 miles a day, crushing everything before it. Many boats locked in the ice for the winter were destroyed in this way.

Sometimes on the last run of the season, a boat would have to race against the river to return to its winter quarters and be taken out of the water before freeze-up. Boats that lost the race had to be abandoned in the river for the winter.

Boats that made it to their home base were hauled up on ways for the winter. These dry docks also gave the maintenance crews a chance to inspect and repair any damage to the hull before the next river season.

Boats on the upper river were either docked at the shipyards at Whitehorse, at Dawson, or at a few other spots on the river. Some of the boats, at one time, were left in the river along the Dawson slough just south of the town.

On the lower river in Alaska, boats were stored at St. Michael, Nenana and a few other sites.

Lake Bennett in winter, about 1901. When the railroad was connected to Whitehorse on July 29, 1900, sternwheelers were no longer needed to haul freight down Lake Bennett, and all river traffic could originate at the end of the line at Whitehorse. Bennett quickly became a ghost town, and Whitehorse became the important transfer point.   *UW*

The **Jennie M** *caught in the ice.*

The **Leah** *and the* **Louise** *caught in the ice.*

*The sternwheeler **Nora** landing in the ice at Dawson on Nov. 8, 1901.*   *UAA Selid Collection*

At least six sternwheelers are shown wintering at the "Dawson Slough" across from Dawson in 1905-06.   *YA*

The **Prospector** *arriving in Dawson covered with ice and snow. She was the last sternwheeler to arrive from Whitehorse on Oct. 20. 1903.* YA

The sternwheeler **Alice,** *snowbound below Fort Yukon, Alaska in the winter of 1897-98.* AHFAM

B. Y. N. Fleet in Winter Quarters
Whitehouse 1905 - 6.

Watchman J. G. Roberts & Wm Shulburg

Courtesy of the White Pass and Yukon Route.

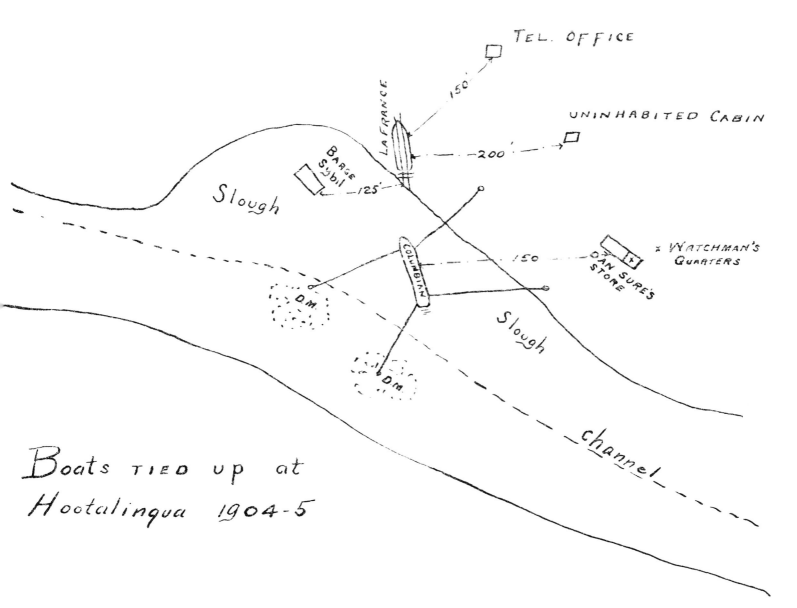

TEL. OFFICE

UNINHABITED CABIN

LAFRANCE

BARGE Sybil

Slough

150'

200'

125'

COLUMBIAN

DM

DM

150

DAN SURE'S STORE

x WATCHMAN'S QUARTERS

Slough

channel

Boats TIED up at Hootalinqua 1904-5

Courtesy of the White Pass and Yukon Route.

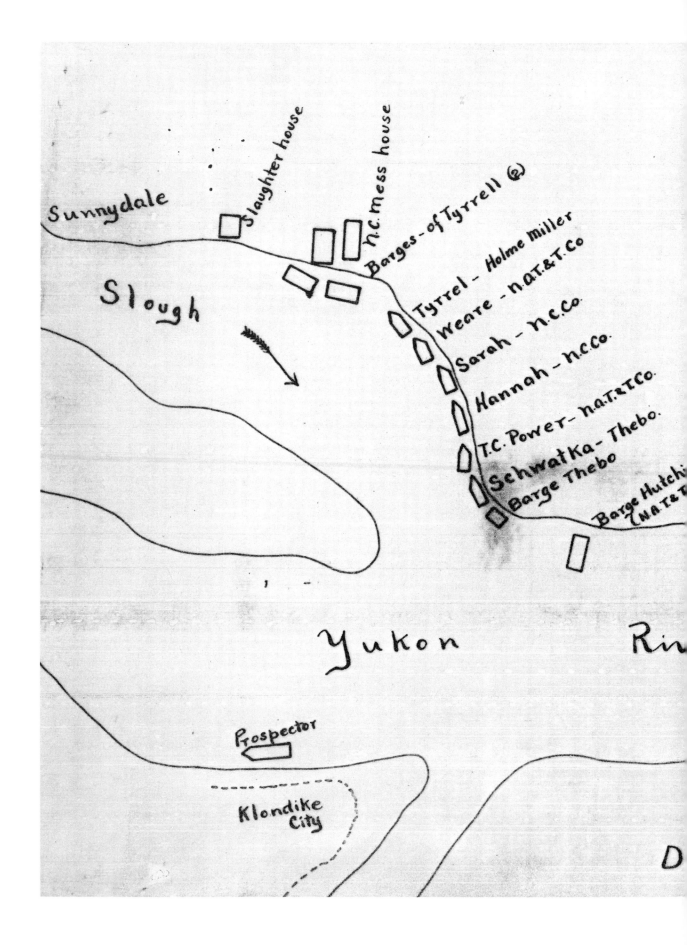

Sunnydale

Slaughter house

n.c. mess house

Barges - of Tyrrell @

Slough

Tyrrel - Holme miller

Weare - n.a.T.&T.Co

Sarah - n.c.Co.

Hannah - n.c.Co.

T.C. Power - n.a.T.&T.Co.

Schwatka - Thebo.

Barge Thebo

Barge Hutchi
(NA T & T

Yukon   Ri

Prospector

Klondike
City

D

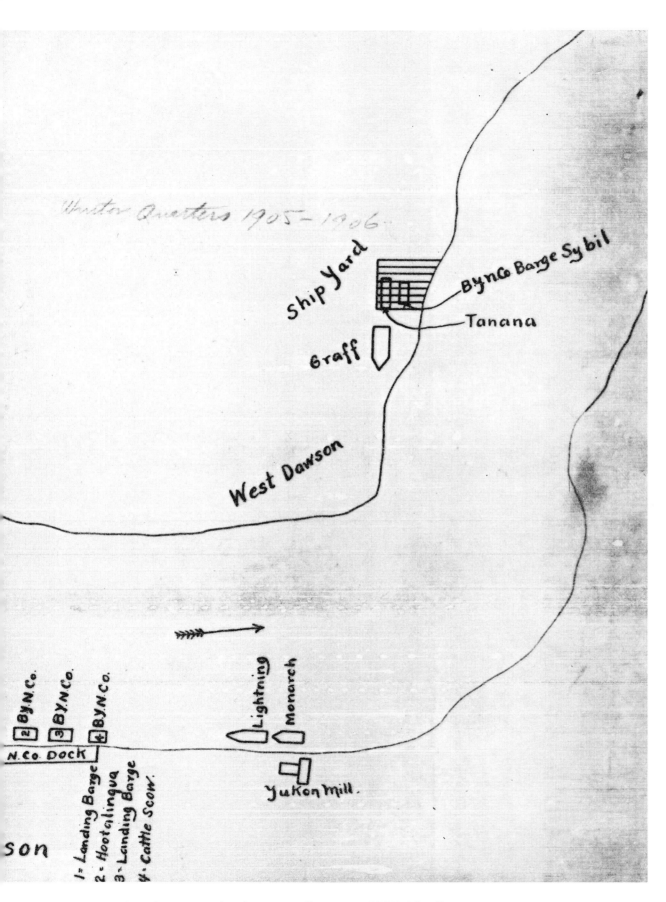

Winter Quarters 1905-1906.

Ship Yard

BYnCo Barge Sybil

Tanana

Graff

West Dawson

Lightning

Monarch

Yukon Mill.

2 B.Y.N.Co.

3 B.Y.N.Co.

4 B.Y.N.Co.

N.Co. Dock

1 - Landing Barge

2 - Hootalinqua

3 - Landing Barge

4 - Cattle Scow.

son

Winter headquarters for boats at Dawson, 1905-06. Courtesy of the White Pass and Yukon Route.

The **W. S. Stratton,** *which was wrecked in ice jams on the Yukon on Oct. 24, 1899. UW*
Larss & Duclos Photo

*The **Vidette** was beached for the winter at Indian River, 35 miles south at Dawson, on Nov. 3, 1912. Twenty-six passengers from the boat, which is in the background, are preparing to pull something up and onto the river bank.* *YA*
Schellinger Collection

WRECKS & FIRES

Steamboating on the Yukon River was never easy. The river is swift (5-6 miles per hour), very shallow at certain times of year and dotted with all kinds of obstacles from narrow channels to rapids. In addition, in the lower river, the channels shifted from year to year, necessitating skill and concentration on the part of the captain. This was especially true in the Yukon delta where an immense area was scarcely above the level of the tides, and many channels led to a dead end.

Ice was a major problem in the spring and fall and many boats were wrecked from floating chunks or fall freeze up.

Shifting sandbars were probably the most annoying obstacles in the river, and even experienced and competent captains and pilots got stuck on them.

There were several ways for a boat to get free. The easiest, if the bar was loosely compacted, was simply to back up intermittently as hard as possible, letting the stern wheel wash

*A view of the wreckage of the **Columbian** on Sept. 25, 1906. The explosion and fire occurred at Eagle Rock between Big and Little Salmon.*   *YA*
Sharschmidt Collection

away the sand and gravel. The boat would slowly drag itself across.

If backing up did not work, "lining" or "sparring" was tried. "Lining" was simply stringing out a wire cable from the boat to a solid object or "dead man" on shore. The steam capstan on board would slowly pull on the cable and attempt to winch the boat toward shore and off the bar. This worked sometimes.

"Sparring" involved the two huge spars or legs which were carried on each side of the boat. Swinging derricks set the spars in the water, touching bottom. Blocks were attached to the tops of the spars, and ropes were fastened to the steam capstan. Moving slowly, the capstan was able to transfer a large part of the weight of the boat and cargo to the spars. Then the engines were moved ahead, and the boat jumped or "leaped" forward. This action was repeated until the boat cleared the bar. Sometimes this "sparring" was done in conjunction with

"lining" and the boat could be jumped forward, backward, or even a bit sideways.

If all these methods failed, the crew could unload some or all of the cargo or wait until another boat came along and hope that it would help pull the stranded boat off the bar.

Through the years many boats were lost to fire, were sunk because of hitting obstacles, or were crushed by ice.

The **D. E. Goddard** and the **Thistle** sank in Lake Laberge. The **Vidette** left Dawson in November 1912 with 125 people on board bound for Whitehorse. One week later at Indian River the boat had to be abandoned because the river suddenly froze. The passengers had to walk the 35 miles back to Dawson.

Rink Rapids, below Five Finger Rapids, claimed several boats. In October 1926, the **Dawson,** wrecked there, was a total loss. In July 1936, the **Casca #2,** flagship of the B.Y.N. fleet, hit a rock and sank in 10 to 15 feet of water in two minutes. The passengers were taken off and

*The **Yukoner** on fire at the Dawson waterfront on May 2, 1900.*   YA
Vancouver Library Collection

72

flown back to Whitehorse.

The **James Domville** was wrecked in the Thirtymile River in 1899; the **Reliance** sank at Minto on the Tanana River in 1906; the **Rock Island #1** sank at Chena, Alaska, about 1906; the **Selkirk** was wrecked at the mouth of the Stewart River in 1920. The **M. L. Washburn** sank at Little Salmon while on her way to help the **Selkirk**. The **Tanana** sank twice, the first time in the Thirtymile River in 1915, the second time at Minto on the Tanana River in 1921. The **Willie Irving** and the **W. S. Stratton** were both caught in ice 35 miles from Selkirk in 1899 and were total losses. The **Pauline** was wrecked by ice at Dawson in 1916. The original **Klondike** sank below Hootalinqua in 1936, but her machinery was salvaged and installed on the present **Klondike #2**.

Several boats had disastrous fires or explosions. The most serious occurred on Sept. 25, 1906, at Eagle Rock between Big Salmon and Little Salmon, when the **Columbian** blew up. The boat was carrying three tons of explosives. A member of the crew picked up a gun to shoot some ducks on the river edge, but he stumbled and shot into the explosives. The resultant explosion and fire killed six crew members and destroyed the boat. It was the worst accident to ever occur on the river. The **Mona** or **Muno** burned at Dawson in 1902; the **Canadian** burned north of Whitehorse.

In June 1974, a destructive fire in Whitehorse burned the **Casca #3** and **White Horse** to the ground. They had been docked along the river for possible restoration as tourist attractions when an arsonist destroyed these two proud old ladies of the river.

The **Yukoner**, *last operated in 1900. She proved to have too much draft for the upper Yukon River run and sat at Whitehorse for years as a derelict and a lumber storage place.*

YA
Kamloops Museum Collection

Steamer **Dawson** wrecked at Rink Rapids just below Five Finger Rapids in October 1926. She was built at Whitehorse in 1901 for the British Yukon Navigation Company.
DP

Wrecked steamer **James Domville** at Whitehorse Rapids in 1899. Built in North Vancouver, B.C., in 1898, she was a total loss. The riffle where she struck was known for years as the Domville Bar.
DP

*The **Klondike #1** with just its superstructure visible above the waterline.   YA
Irvine Collection*

*View of the battered foredeck of the sternwheeler **Klondike #1** after its accident
below Hootalinqua in the spring of 1936. The mail launch **Shamrock** is visible
to the left. The **Klondike #1** was built in 1929.   YA
Irvine Collection*

*Two views of the **Casca #3** and the **White Horse** burning at Whitehorse on June 21, 1974. The fire was the work of an arsonist and resulted in a great historical loss to the citizens of the Yukon.*   Whitehorse Star

WAR YEARS

Like the other transportation systems in Alaska and the Yukon--trains, airplanes, and vehicles--the remaining boats on the Yukon River were called on to contribute to the war effort. But like the other conveyances, the boats were overworked and under-maintained. By 1942, when the huge war-related construction projects were just beginning, the steamboat era was coming to an end. Airplanes and trucks were making inroads into the freight and passenger hauling business on the river.

The U.S. and Canada instituted a massive construction program in response to the growing menace of the Japanese in the Pacific area and specifically to their occupation of several islands in the Aleutian chain in June 1942. Larger and better airfields also had to be built to accommodate the ferrying of lend-lease airplanes to Russia through Canada and Alaska.

The Alcan (Alaska) Highway project was begun in early 1942 to connect Dawson Creek, British Columbia, the end of the road and railroad, with Fairbanks, Alaska, 1,500 miles to the north and west. The route traversed a no-man's-land which was largely unmapped and only slightly explored.

At about the same time a massive pipeline construction project (Canol Project) was begun to bring oil from Norman Wells, Northwest Territories, south and west nearly 500 miles to a refinery at Whitehorse. This route was also through largely unexplored country.

These construction projects had to rely on very inadequate transportation systems serving both countries. Two main transportation arteries served the interiors of Alaska and the Yukon. The Alaska Railroad stretched from Seward on the Kenai Peninsula to Fairbanks

*The **White Horse** is shown in 1942 pushing a barge of U.S. Army trucks to be used in constructing the Alaska Highway.*   USA

in the interior, a distance of more than 400 miles. The White Pass and Yukon Route connected tidewater at Skagway, Alaska, to Whitehorse, Yukon, a distance of 110 miles. Both of these railroads were totally inadequate for the volume of freight that had to be transported on them.

The remaining steamboats on the Yukon were pressed into service for the war effort as much as possible. Several were used extensively to haul men and supplies on the Yukon lakes to points along the Alaska Highway construction route. Some material was hauled by rail to Whitehorse, put on barges and pushed downriver to Dawson and to Tanana, Alaska, where other boats took over and pushed the barges to Fairbanks, the northern terminus of the highway.

The **Yukon** was used to carry men and supplies for the proposed Trans-Canadian, Alaska and Western Railroad project up and down the lower Yukon River. The **Nenana** hauled freight to several auxiliary air bases along the lower Yukon River.

In November 1942, a rough pioneer road was completed from Dawson Creek to Fairbanks, and another year was spent upgrading it. The Canol pipeline project was completed in 1944, and oil began flowing into Whitehorse.

The steamboats had served the war effort well but the end of the river boat era was in sight by 1945.

The **Aksala** *and the* **Casca** *sit in drydock in 1942 at Whitehorse. These boats were used to transport material for constructing the Alaska Highway in 1942. USA*

The **Keno** is shown landing equipment on the Teslin River. It also transported men of the 340th Regiment of the U.S. Army who were building the Alaska Highway between Teslin and Watson Lake. *Glenbow-Alberta Institute Calgary, Alberta*

The **Yukon,** which, during the war, was used to transport men and equipment for the Trans-Canadian, Alaska and Western Railroad Study. The purpose of the study was to explore the feasibility of building a railroad from Prince George, British Columbia, to the Bering Straits to help in the war effort. *UAA Edby Davis Collection*

The dry dock area and White Pass and Yukon tracks at Whitehorse in 1944. The **Casca,** *the* **Keno** *and several other boats are shown.* USA

Heavy equipment was transported to Nenana via the Alaska Railroad, transferred to river barge and pushed by sternwheeler to Galena, Alaska and other points on the lower river. This picture was taken in August 1944. USA

Another view of the Whitehorse dry docks. The fuel drums are for use by U.S. Army troops.
Richard Finnie
Belvedere, California

Army vehicles and equipment loaded onto barges at Dawson. Military equipment was brought up the Inside Passage to Skagway, taken by rail to Whitehorse, by barge down the Yukon to Nenana, and then taken to Fairbanks for use on the Alaska and Richardson Highways. A very long trip!
YA
C. Haines Collection

Steamboats were kept busy along the Yukon River and lakes, hauling supplies and men for construction of the Alaska Highway. USA

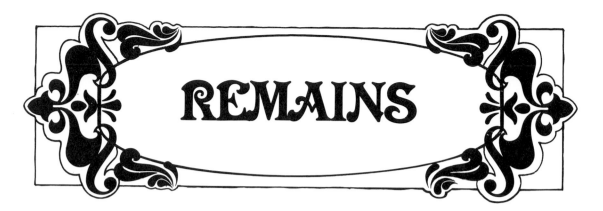

REMAINS

Of the approximately 250 boats that plied the river in the 90-year period, only a very few remain in Alaska and the Yukon. As shown in the appendix of this book, most of the boats were either wrecked, burned, abandoned, converted to other uses, or, as the years went by and the economics of the area changed, were simply phased out for more cost-efficient and faster means of travel and transport.

Only four boats are preserved in one form or another for public view. The **Klondike #2** has been faithfully restored to its 1937 appearance by Parks Canada and is on display at Whitehorse. The **Keno** likewise has been partially restored by Parks Canada and is on display at Dawson. The **Tutshi** sits forlornly on the beach at Carcross, still in reasonably good shape, but not open to the public. The

An old derelict sits on the beach, only a shadow of its former self. Richard Finnie
Belvedere, California

83

Nenana was donated to the Fairbanks Chamber of Commerce and moved in 1967 to Alaskaland, where part of it was converted to a bar and restaurant. It is now (1982) undergoing restoration.

Part of the **Alaska** (or **Aksala**) was placed on a site along the Alaska Highway, just east of Whitehorse, for use as a restaurant. It is now abandoned.

The remains of several boats can still be seen in the river itself. Parts of the **Casa #1** are still visible at Lower Laberge, 58 miles below Whitehorse. The boat was beached here many years ago. Immediately downstream from Hootalinqua, 90 miles below Whitehorse, are the remains of the **Evelyn** on Shipyard or Hootalinqua Island. Further downstream are the remains of the **Klondike #1,** which was wrecked in the Thirtymile River in 1936 and has drifted to its present location. It can be seen at periods of low-water.

The largest boat graveyard is located just downstream from Dawson on the opposite, or west side, of the river. Sitting along the river are five once-proud and elegant river boats that are slowly "going back to nature." The **Victorian, Schwatka, Tyrrell, Julia B** and **Seattle #3** were put up on ways years ago, and each year they deteriorate more and more.

Two proud old ladies, the **Casca #2** and **White Horse,** were put on display near the White Pass station at Whitehorse in the early 1970s. They were not restored but were some of the last reminders of another age. In 1974, an arson fire destroyed both boats in a spectacular blaze.

Let us appreciate the work of the restoration crews on the remaining boats; it provides one of our last links with another era.

Remains of the **Evelyn (Norcun),** *slowly decaying on Shipyard Island just downstream from Hootalinqua.*
Government of the Yukon

An old barge abandoned on shore at Minto, Yukon.   SC

Remains of the first **Casca** *at Lower Laberge. It was beached here after being used as a barge for many years.*   Government of the Yukon.

Steamboat remains at the old boat yard just downstream from Dawson.   *SC*

More scenes at the old boat yard near Dawson.
SC

87

More scenes at the old boat yard near Dawson. *SC*

KENO, KLONDIKE, NENANA, TUTSHI

KENO

One of the newer boats on the river, the **Keno,** was built at Whitehorse in 1922 as a side steam freight hauler. In 1937 she was made ten feet longer to accommodate more freight. She mainly worked the shallow Stewart River, hauling silver-lead-zinc concentrates from Mayo to Stewart City, a distance of 180 miles. There, larger boats picked up the freight for the final trip upriver to Whitehorse.

The **Keno's** draft was only three feet, making it easy to navigate the shallow river. The boat worked the river from 1922 to 1951, and also made many trips to Dawson early each season.

When there was a large ore load to transport, the boat pushed a barge and both were loaded with ore. The **Keno** could haul 120 tons, the barge an additional 225 tons.

A crew of approximately 21 men plus the captain and the pilot were needed to operate the boat. The crew included two mates, five or six deck hands, three firemen, two engineers, four waiters, one mess boy, one pantry man and two cooks.

The freight deck consisted of the area from the back end of the boiler to near the engine room. Bags of ore, each weighing 125 pounds, were stacked in this area along with other general freight.

*The **Keno** aground on a gravel bar on the Stewart River. Preparations are being made to spar off the bar.*
                                                                    YA
                                                        Dennett Collection

Above the freight deck was the passenger deck, which could accommodate up to 32 passengers. Above this was the Texas deck which housed the captain and his officers.

In 1951, the **Keno** was retired from the river and was laid up in dry dock at Whitehorse. Then in 1960 she was donated by the B.Y.N. Co. to the Canadian government and made the last downstream run of any boat to its permanent dry land home at Dawson.

To accomplish this run, several obstacles had to be overcome. The bridge across the Yukon River at Carmacks had been constructed after the boats were taken off the river, and the **Keno** was too high to go under it without alterations. So the pilot house was taken off and placed on the Texas deck, and the hydraulic steering system was set up in the observation room of the passenger deck. The front mast had to be shortened, and the smoke stack had to be laid on the Texas deck. Even so, there was only an 11-inch clearance when the boat went under the bridge.

The **Keno** has been partially restored by Parks Canada and now sits proudly on the river bank at Dawson.

*Bow shot of the **Keno** at Whitehorse with some passengers and crew on deck just before she left for Dawson on her last voyage in 1960. The wheelhouse has been removed and the smokestack put on hinges to enable the boat to clear the Yukon River bridge at Carmacks.*
YA
Alaska Historical Library Collection

The **Keno** *docked on the river bank at Dawson.*   *SC*

Top deck of the **Keno.** *SC*

Paddlewheel of the **Keno.** *SC*

KLONDIKE

Two steamboats on the Yukon River were named **Klondike.** To solve the problem of increased loads of ore from Mayo, loads that the smaller boats could not handle efficiently, the British Yukon Navigation Company designed a larger boat that could carry more than 300 tons and still maintain the same time schedule as the smaller boats. This was the original **Klondike,** built at the Whitehorse shipyards in 1929. She proved to be a very durable and fast boat on the ore run to Whitehorse. However, in June 1936, she ran into the river bank below Hootalinqua when the captain attempted to run a bend and misjudged the current and distance.

Only the engine was salvaged from this wreck, and the company immediately began construction on a new boat, the **Klondike #2,** which went into operation in June 1937. This is the boat that is now on display at Whitehorse.

Her schedule consisted of a 40-hour trip from Whitehorse downstream to Dawson with a load of general freight and then the return trip to Whitehorse, with a stop enroute at Stewart, where ore was picked up. This upstream trip could take up to four days because of the swift five- to six-mile current.

By the late 1930s, the cost of operating sternwheelers was becoming increasingly high. An estimate of $11,000 was given for a month's operation of the **Klondike** along with an initial investment of over $105,000 to build her.

Passenger rates reflected these costs in 1926:

	NORTHBOUND		SOUTHBOUND	
	1st Class	2nd Class	1st Class	2nd Class
Whitehorse-Dawson	$35.00	$25.00	$55.00	$40.00

High rates also had to be charged for the commodities delivered to Dawson.

With the seasonal economy of the Treadmill mine at Keno in the late 1930s and 1940s, the days were numbered for the ore-hauling boats. In 1947 the **Klondike** and other boats could not keep up with the increased ore production, and in 1950 a road was built connecting Mayo with Whitehorse so that ore could be hauled by truck year-round. This road, along with the completion in 1955 of the Klondike Highway connecting Dawson to Whitehorse, sounded the death knell for river boats. The **Klondike's** service, however, was not yet at an end. She was transformed into a tourist boat in 1953-54. This joint venture of the White Pass Company (B.Y.N. Co.) and Canadian

Klondike #1 *docked at the Whitehorse shipyards either just after construction or after being launched from dry dock. She was built in 1929 and wrecked near Hootalinqua in 1936.* YA

93

dian Pacific Airlines cost $100,000. The airlines chartered the boat to connect with its air service to Whitehorse.

The boiler was converted to an oil burner, additional cabins and a new lounge and bar were added, and the dining room was enlarged. Additional crew members were added to cater to the tourist trade.

For two seasons the **Klondike** operated between Whitehorse and Dawson with capacity crowds, but even this could not offset the high operating costs. So in 1955 the **Klondike**, the last of the operating boats on the Yukon River, was put on ways at Whitehorse never to enter the water again.

In 1966 she was hauled through town to her final resting place near the Robert Campbell Bridge along the river she plied for so many years. Parks Canada took over administration and restoration, and on July 1, 1981, the project was completed. The **Klondike** today looks exactly as she did in the summer of 1937, from the freight on board to the hand towels and blankets monogrammed BYN (British Yukon Navigation Company).

It is a real credit to the Parks Canada personnel that they have created a faithful reproduction of the 1937 steamer.

*The **Klondike** at Whitehorse in July 1944.*

USA

*The **Klondike,** the last active sternwheeler on the Yukon River, being moved in 1966 along First Avenue in Whitehorse to its new home where it would be put on display.*
YA
Vancouver Library Collection

The Klondike, *the* **Aksala** *and the* **Keno** *at Stewart City in the 1930s. Ore bags are piled up on a barge in the foreground.* *YA Dennett Collection*

The **Klondike** at 11:00 a.m. on June 30, 1981. Last minute details in preparation for the July 1 Canada Day opening ceremony. PC

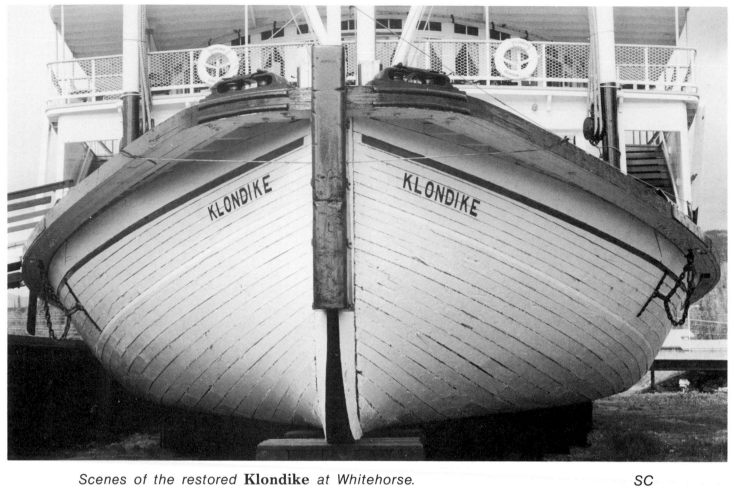

Scenes of the restored **Klondike** *at Whitehorse.*   SC

*Rudders on the **Klondike**.* SC

*The captsan of the **Klondike**. It was used to maneuver the boat through Five Finger Rapids, to bring aboard heavy freight and to winch up to the barges.* SC

Smokestack and upper deck of the **Klondike**.
SC

Observation room, looking forward (top) and dining room, looking aft (bottom) on the saloon deck of the **Klondike.** *PC*

Wheelhouse (pilothouse) and cargo deck of the **Klondike.** *PC*

Galley (pantry stores) (top) and galley looking forward of the **Klondike.** PC

Master's quarters on the Texas deck of the **Klondike.** *PC*

Typical passenger cabin, 1st class, upper single bunk of the **Klondike.** *PC*

NENANA

One sternwheeler still remains in Alaska. It is the **Nenana,** built in the town of the same name in 1922. It was acquired by the Alaska Railroad the following year for service on the Tanana and Yukon rivers.

After 22 years of service on the rivers, including heavy duty hauling during World War II, the boat was retired in 1954 and donated to the Fairbanks Chamber of Commerce.

It was moved to Alaskaland Park in Fairbanks in 1967 and put on permanent display. The upper deck was turned into a restaurant and bar.

In 1981 a cover was placed over the boat to protect it from the weather, and restoration work was begun.

The **Nenana** *leaves Nenana on the Tanana River for Galena on the Yukon River on Aug. 19, 1944 with a load of supplies for the military airstrip.* USA

The **Nenana** *and barge on the lower river on Oct. 1, 1949.* *AHFAM*
Alaska Railroad Collection

The **Nenana** *dock at Alaskaland in Fairbanks.* *UAA*

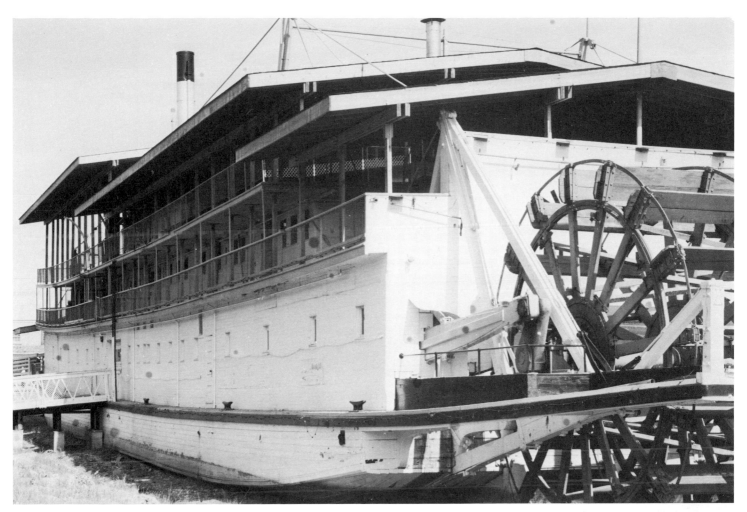

*A view of the **Nenana** covered in 1981 for protection and restoration.*   SC

TUTSHI

At 1,040 tons, the **Tutshi** was one of the larger boats in the Yukon. She was built at Carcross in 1918, and her original run was between Carcross and Grahame Inlet on Tagish Lake. She was later converted to an oil burner and carried tourists to Ben-My-Chree at the southern tip of Taku Arm.

Ben-My-Chree was the site of a mine in the early 1900s, but the mine caved in, and the owners, Mr. & Mrs. Otto Partridge, never

reopened it. Instead they imported plants and trees from around the world and converted the area to a beautiful garden spot. The **Tutshi** brought tourists here to view the gardens, and after the deaths of the owners in the 1930s, the White Pass Company, which then owned the site, operated the boat until 1955.

In her day the **Tutshi** had a crew of 29 and could carry 135 passengers. She was beached on the shore of Lake Bennett at Carcross in 1972, repainted in 1977, and is still waiting a decision on further restoration.

Passengers boarding the **Tutshi** *at Carcross for a trip down Tagish Arm to Ben-My-Chree.*   *DP*

The **Tutshi** *at Ben-My-Chree.*   *DP*

The **Tutshi** and **Gleaner** docked at Carcross in the 1920s.

YA
Dennett Collection

Three forms of transportation on view at Carcross--river, road and railroad.

Government of the Yukon

APPENDIX

The following list of steamboats on the Yukon River system is a compilation of a report that Mr. William D. McBride of Whitehorse did in 1949 for the **Caribou and Northwest Digest** magazine. Information on all 250 boats on the river is incomplete or non-existent. Additional information was collected by the author.

McBride was born in Butte, Montana, and attended Oberlin College in Ohio and Blair Business College in Spokane, Washington. He first saw the Yukon country in 1899, a year after his father took the "Trail of '98." He worked for several railroads in the lower 48 before moving to St. Michael, Alaska, to work for the Northern Navigation Company.

In 1914 he joined the White Pass and Yukon Route's river division in Whitehorse and worked there for the rest of his career. He became very knowledgeable about Yukon and Klondike history and was a founder of the museum in Whitehorse that was to bear his name--the McBride Museum.

1. **A. J. Goddard** - 15 tons, the hull was built in San Francisco but assembled at Lake Bennett. It was the first boat from the upper Yukon to arrive at Dawson on June 21, 1898. It sank in 1899 at Goddard's Point on Lake Laberge.
2. **Agnes E. Boyd** - 731 tons, no other information.
3. **Aksala** - 642 tons, built at Whitehorse in 1913 by the A.Y.N. Co. as the **Alaska.** Name changed to **Aksala** when it was owned by the B.Y.N. Co. It operated until 1952 and now sits at Mile 913 on the Alaska Highway. At one time it was used as a dining lounge.
4. **Alice I** - 400 tons, built at St. Michael for the A.C. Co. in 1895. First arrived at Dawson on July 6, 1898.
5. **Alice II** - 262 tons, built in Seattle in 1909 for the N.C. Co. Purchased by the Alaska Railroad from the A.Y.N. Co. in 1927 and placed in service on the lower river run. Retired after World War II.
6. **Anawanda** - 31 tons, built in Portland, Ore. and rebuilt in 1898 at St. Michael.
7. **Anglian** - 162 tons, built at Teslin Lake in 1898 after the machinery was taken up the Stikine River to Telegraph Creek and then overland to Teslin. First arrived at Dawson on July 28, 1898 with 40 members of the Royal Northwest Mounted Police aboard. It was dismantled in 1931 at Whitehorse.
8. **Arctic** - built at St. Michael in 1898 by the A.C. Co. It was the first steamer to arrive at Dawson on Oct. 17, 1896. Caught in an ice jam near Forty Mile in 1897 and demolished. Its machinery was installed on a barge.
9. **Arnold** - 692 tons, built at Unalaska in 1898 for the Alaska Exploration Co. It was towed to St. Michael and arrived in Dawson on Oct. 4, 1898. Later it was beached at St. Michael.
10. **Australian** - 422 tons, built in Victoria, B.C. for the C.D. Co. in 1899 and later owned by the B.Y.N. Co. It was operated on the Bennett-Canyon City run before 1900 and later on the Carcross-Atlin run. In 1942 it was rebuilt as a barge for use on the Alaska Highway project.
11. **Bailey** - 193 tons, built at Lake Bennett in 1899 and operated on the Bennett-Canyon City run and later on the Whitehorse-Dawson (upper river) run. Demolished at Whitehorse in 1931.

12. **Bonanza King** - 466 tons, built in Dutch Harbor in 1898 and arrived in Dawson on Sept. 24, 1898. Sister ship of the **Eldorado.** It was later used as a lumber store room in Whitehorse.

13. **Bella** - 370 tons, built at St. Michael in 1896 for the A.C. Co. It ws the second boat to arrive at Dawson in July 1897. Later beached at St. Michael.

14. **Bellingham** - built at Lake Bennett in 1897. It was the first boat to arrive from Bennett in 1898 through Whitehorse Rapids.

15. **Canadian** - 716 tons, built in Victoria, B.C. in 1898 and sailed from there to Dawson arriving on Aug. 24, 1898. It was called "The Bull of the Woods" on the upper Yukon run. Sank south of Whitehorse.

16. **Casca #1** - 590 tons, built in Victoria, B.C. and sold to the B.Y.N. Co. Operated on the upper river run. It was dismantled at Whitehorse in 1911 and the hull was used as a landing barge at Lower Laberge.

17. **Casca #2** - 1,079 tons, built at Whitehorse in 1911 for the B.Y.N. Co. and used as the company's flagship on the upper river run and on Midnight Sun excursions to Ft. Yukon. It was wrecked at Rink Rapids on July 9, 1936, a total loss.

18. **Casca #3** - 1,300 tons, built at Whitehorse in 1937 for the B.Y.N. Co. The machinery from **Casca #2** was salvaged and used to build the **III.** It was the plushest tourist boat on the Whitehorse-Dawson run. The last year of operation was 1952. It sat on the bank of the Yukon River at Whitehorse until 1974 when it burned to the ground.

19. **Charles H. Hamilton** - 595 tons, built in 1897 at St. Michael by the N.A.T. & T. Co., N.N. Co., and A.Y.N. Co. Beached at St. Michael.

20. **City of Paris** - built in 1898 and used on the lower river run. Sold to the Northern Commercial Co. in 1901. It supposedly carried a quantity of liquor aboard and it was accidentally set on fire by a party who was searching for the illicit cargo and became a total loss.

21. **Clara Monarch** - built in San Francisco. Operated mainly on the Whitehorse-Dawson run. Reputed to be the ship "Sea Wolf" in Jack London's novel. Sank in the slough below Whitehorse.

22. **Clara** - 144 tons, built in San Francisco in 1898. Dismantled at Dawson in 1901.

23. **Clifford Sifton** - built at Lake Bennett in 1898 by a syndicate of Kansas women. Operated on the Whitehorse-Dawson run. Converted to a barge and wrecked in a slough near Dawson.

24. **Columbian** - 206 tons, built in Victoria, B.C. in 1898. Operated on the upper river. On Sept. 25, 1906, a crewman accidentally fired a shot into explosives carried on board. The resulting explosion killed six crew members and destroyed the boat. It was the worst accident involving steamboats on the river.

25. **Dawson** - 779 tons, built at Whitehorse in 1901 for the B.Y.N. Co. Operated on the Whitehorse-Dawson run. Wrecked at Rink Rapids in 1926.

26. **Delta** - 293 tons, built at St. Michael in 1905. Operated on side streams and to Fairbanks. Beached at St. Michael.

27. **Dusty Diamond** - 101 tons, built at St. Michael in 1898. Operated on side streams on the lower river.

28. **Dorothy** - built in Seattle in 1898.

29. **D. R. Campbell** - 718 tons, built in Seattle in 1898. Operated on the St. Michael-Dawson run and to Fairbanks.

30. **Ella** - operated from Whitehorse to Fairbanks in 1905. No other data.

31. **Emma Nott** - 48 tons, built at Lake Bennett in 1898.

32. **F. K. Gustin** - 718 tons, built in Seattle in 1898.

33. **Flora** - 63 tons, built at Lake Bennett in 1898 for the Bennett Lake and Klondyke Navigation Co. Taken through the Whitehorse Rapids and put on the Dawson run. Converted to a barge in 1903.

34. **Florence S** - 90 tons, built in St. Michael in 1898 as an iron hull boat. Operated on the upper river run. Sank in the Thirtymile River about 1900 with the loss of three lives. Raised in 1901 and operated on the lower river. Later used as a barge.

35. **Gleaner** - 241 tons, built at Lake Bennett in 1899. Operated on the Carcross-Atlin run.

36. **Glenora** - 542 tons, built in Tacoma, Wash. in 1898. Burned at Dawson in 1902.

37. **Golden Crown #1** - 114 tons, built at Whitehorse in 1902. Used as a dredge on the Stewart River.

38. **Gold Star** - built at St. Michael in 1898. Wrecked at Five Finger Rapids in 1900 and again in the Tanana River 15 miles below Chena.

39. **Hannah** - 1,130 tons, built at Unalaska in 1898 by the A.C. Co., N.N. Co. and the A.Y.N. Co. Operated on the St. Michael-Dawson-Fairbanks run. Sister ship of the **Sarah** and **Susie.** These were the most elegant boats on the river but were abandoned at St. Michael when the all-water route was no longer needed.

40. **Herman** - 456 tons, built at Dutch Harbor, Alaska in 1898. Used for towing barges to the mouth of the Yukon River and along the lower river run. Abandoned at St. Michael.

41. **Ida May** - 278 tons, built at Stockton, Calif. in 1898. Operated on the upper river during the gold rush and on the lower river in the early 1900s. Abandoned at St. Michael.

42. **Idler** - 61 tons, built at Fairbanks in 1911. Later converted to diesel engines.

43. **Iowa** - built at Lake Bennett in 1898. Went through Whitehorse Rapids to Dawson in June 1898.

44. **Isabelle** - 162 tons, built at St. Michael in 1899 and operated on the lower river run. Abandoned at St. Michael.

45. **John Cudahy** - 819 tons, built at Unalaska in 1898. It was the fastest boat of the N.A.T. & T. Co.'s fleet on the lower river run.

46. **John J. Healy** - 450 tons, built at St. Michael in 1898. Named after the general manager of the N.A.T. & T. Co. Operated on the lower river run.

47. **Joseph Clossett** - 147 tons, built at Lake Bennett in 1898. Operated on the Whitehorse-Dawson run. Dismantled at Whitehorse in 1931.

48. **Julia B** - 835 tons, built at Ballard, Wash. in 1908. Operated mainly on the lower river run. Beached on the river bank just downstream from Dawson.

49. **J. P. Light** - 785 tons, built at Seattle in 1898. Operated on the lower river run.

50. **J. W. Jacobs** - built at Whitehorse for the U.S. Army Quartermaster Corps. Turned over to the Alaska Railroad in 1923. Operated on the lower river for the railroad until retired in 1933.

51. **James Domville** - built at North Vancouver, B.C. in 1898. Sailed from there via the ocean to St. Michael and then to Dawson. Wrecked in the Thirtymile River in 1899 as a total loss.

52. **Jeff C. Davis** - built in Port Blakely in 1898 as the **Duchesnay.** It was used in Cook Inlet and later by the U.S. Army to supply its military outposts. The army renamed it the **Jeff C. Davis.** Transferred to the Alaska Railroad in 1923 and dismantled at Nenana in 1933.

53. **John C. Barr** - 546 tons, built at Unalaska in 1898.

54. **Katie Hemrich** - 248 tons, built at Seattle in 1898. Bought by the U.S. Army in 1900. Later sank at Nulato on the lower river.

55. **Kilburn** - built at Lake Bennett in 1898. Beached at Carcross.

56. **Kluahne** - built at Whitehorse, date unknown, by Taylor & Drury Co. Used on many of the upper river tributaries.

57. **Klondyke** - 406 tons, built at Dutch Harbor in 1898. Used as a harbor tug at St. Michael and and later as a barge.

58. **Klondike #1 -** built at Whitehorse in 1929. Operated on the upper river. Sank below Hootalinqua in 1936.

59. **Klondike #2** - see chapter 8.

60. **Koyukuk #1 -** built at St. Michael in 1902. It was wrecked and the machinery installed in the **Koyukuk #2.**

61. **Koyukuk #2 -** 254 tons, built at St. Michael in 1906. It was wrecked and its machinery was installed in the **M. L. Washburn.** Operated on the lower river run.

62. **La France** - 201 tons, built at Lower Laberge in 1902. Operated on the upper river run until she sank in the Pelly River. She was raised and repaired, but sank in 1911 in the Thirtymile River.

63. **Lavelle Young** - 506 tons, built in Portland, Ore. in 1898. Sailed via the ocean to St. Michael and operated on the lower river. Dismantled in 1920.

64. **Leah** - 477 tons, built at St. Michael in 1898 by the Alaska Commercial Co. Wrecked below old Kaltag on the lower Yukon. Operated on the lower river run, 1905-07.

65. **Leon** - 638 tons, built at Unalaska in 1898. Abandoned at St. Michael.

66. **Leota** - 36 tons, built at Alameda, Calif. in 1898.

67. **Lightning** - 557 tons, built at Vancouver, B.C. in 1898. Operated on the upper river run until

1914. Dismantled at Dawson in 1919.

68. **Linda** - 692 tons, built at Unalaska in 1898. Abandoned at St. Michael.
69. **Linderman** - built at Lake Bennett in 1898. Sister ship of the **Kilburn.** Beached on the Thirty-mile River.
70. **Lorellei** - built at Lake Bennett in 1898.
71. **Los Angeles** - 29 tons, built at St. Michael in 1898.
72. **Lotta Talbot** - 242 tons, built in Seattle in 1898. Operated on the lower river run. Abandoned at St. Michael.
73. **Louise** - 717 tons, built at Unalaska in 1898. Operated on the lower river run. Abandoned at St. Michael.
74. **Luelle** - 52 tons, built at Stockton, Calif. in 1898. Operated between Fairbanks and the Koyukuk River.
75. **Lully C** - built and operated on Lake Bennett in 1898.
76. **Marjorie** - 278 tons, built at New Westminster, B.C. in 1898. Abandoned in 1914.
77. **Margaret** - built at St. Michael in 1897. Operated on the lower river run. Abandoned at St. Michael.
78. **Mary F. Graff** - 864 tons, built in Seattle in 1898.
79. **Martha Clow** - 98 tons, built at Stockton, Calif. in 1898. Operated on the lower river run.
80. **May West** - 134 tons, built at St. Michael in 1896. First steamer into Dawson on June 8, 1898. Bought by the R.N.W.M.P. and renamed the **Vidette.** Later ressold and operated on the Stewart River. Sunk in Lake Laberge in 1917.
81. **Milwaukee** - 396 tons, built in Ballard, Wash. in 1890. Finished on the Kuskokwin River in Alaska.
82. **Minneapolis** - 236 tons, built in Tacoma, Wash. in 1898. Sold to the Alaska Railroad in 1927. Operated on the lower river run.
83. **Mocking Bird** - 82 tons, built in Tacoma, Wash. in 1898.
84. **Mona** or **Muno** - 289 tons, built on the Stikine River in 1898. Burned at Dawson in 1902.
85. Monarch - 463 tons, built at Ballard, Wash. in 1898. It was towed from Seattle to St. Michael. Abandoned at St. Michael.
86. **M. L. Washburn** - 284 tons, built at St. Michael in 1911 by the N.N. Co. Machinery was taken from the **Koyukuk #2.** Operated mainly on the St. Michael-Iditarod run. Sold to the A.Y.N. Co. in 1914. Sank near Little Salmon, Yukon in 1920 while enroute to assist the **Selkirk** which had wrecked at the mouth of the Stewart River.
87. **Nasutlin** - 405 tons, built at Whitehorse in 1912 by the B.Y.N. Co. Cut in half at Dawson as it was being towed out.
88. **Nenana** - see chapter 8.
89. **Nora** - 67 tons, built at Lake Bennett in 1898. Operated on the upper river run. Dismantled in 1903 and converted to a barge.
90. **Norcum** - 508 tons, built in Seattle in 1908 as the **Evelyn.** Wrecked in the Tanana River. Rebuilt at St. Michael. Remains on Shipyard Island.
91. **Northern Light** - 12 tons, built at St. Michael in 1896. Sank in the Koyukuk River.
92. **North Star** - 28 tons, built at St. Michael in 1898.
93. **Ora** - 69 tons, built at Lake Bennett in 1898. Operated on the upper river run. Dismantled in 1903 and converted to a barge.
94. **Oil City** - 718 tons, built in Seattle, Wash. in 1898. Abandoned at Holy Cross, Alaska.
95. **Olive May (Dora)** - 54 tons, built at Whitehorse. Operated on the upper river run. Sank in the Thirtymile River. Thought to be the inspiration for the boat "Alice May" in Robert Service's poem, "The Cremation of Sam McGee."
96. **Pauline** - 145 tons, built at Whitehorse in 1907. Wrecked by ice at the Sunnydale Slough, Dawson in 1916.
97. **Pelly** - thought to be the first boat to travel upstream from Dawson. Later operated on the lower river during the Nome gold rush.
98. **Philip B. Low** - 466 tons, built in Seattle in 1898. Operated on the upper river run. Sank several times. Named changed to **Eldorado.** Dismantled in 1903.
99. **Pilgrim** - 718 tons, built in Seattle in 1898. Abandoned at St. Michael.
100. **Portus B. Weare** - 400 tons, built at St. Michael in 1892. The first boat owned by the N.A.T. & T.

Co. One of the first boats to reach Dawson in 1898. Abandoned at St. Michael.

101. **Prospector** - 165 tons, built at Whitehorse in 1901. Used on the side streams. Machinery was taken out of the boat and installed in the **Nasutlin.**

102. **Quick** - 67 tons, built at Dawson in 1900. Later used as the Dawson ferry.

103. **Quickstep** - 343 tons, built in Seattle in 1898.

104. **Reliance** - 291 tons, built at St. Michael in 1907. Operated on the lower river run and Koyukuk River. Sank at Minto on the Tanana River in 1917.

105. **Robert Kerr** - built in Seattle in 1898. Hauled meat between St. Michael and Dawson.

106. **Rock Island #1** - 535 tons, built in Seattle in 1898. Sank at Chena, Alaska about 1906.

107. **Rock Island #2** - built at St. Michael; date unknown.

108. **Samson** - 272 tons, built at Fairbanks in 1910.

109. **Sarah** - 1130 tons, built at Unalaska in 1898. A sister ship of the **Hannah.**

110. **S. B. Mathews** - 200 tons, built in San Francisco in 1895.

111. **Schwatka** - 484 tons, built at Port Blakeley in 1898. Named after Lt. Frederick Schwatka of the U.S. Army who made a trip down the Yukon River in 1883 naming many of the lakes and tributaries. Beached on the river bank just downstream from Dawson.

112. **Seattle #1** - built at St. Michael in 1898.

113. **Seattle #2** - 718 tons, built in Seattle in 1898. Abandoned at St. Michael.

114. **Seattle #3** - 548 tons, built at Dutch Harbor in 1898. Beached on the river bank just downstream from Dawson.

115. **Selkirk** - 777 tons, built at Whitehorse in 1901. Operated on the upper river run. Wrecked at mouth of the Stewart River in 1920.

116. **Shusana** - 49 tons, built at Fairbanks in 1913.

117. **Sovereign** - built at Ballard, Wash. in 1898. Towed from Seattle to St. Michael and operated on the lower river until 1904. Abandoned on the beach at Nome, Alaska.

118. **St. Michael #2** - 718 tons, built in Seattle in 1898.

119. **Susie** - 1,130 tons, built at Unalaska in 1898. Sister ship of the **Hannah.** Abandoned at St. Michael.

120. **Sybyl** - 654 tons, built at Victoria, B.C. in 1898. Converted to a barge in 1904.

121. **Tacoma** - 718 tons, built in Tacoma, Wash. in 1898.

122. **Tana** - 234 tons, built in Seattle in 1905. It was originally gasoline-powered, but was towed to Lower Laberge in 1906 and converted to steam. Operated out of Fairbanks until 1916 when she was taken to the Kuskokwin River.

123. **Tanana** - 495 tons, built at St. Michael in 1904. Operated on the side streams. Sunk in the Thirtymile River in 1915 but was raised and repaired. She sank again in 1921 near Minto on the Tanana River, her final resting place.

124. **Tanana Chief** - 72 tons, built at Unalaska in 1898. Beached at Chena.

125. **T. C. Power** - 819 tons, built in Alaska in 1898. Operated on the lower river run. Abandoned at St. Michael.

126. **Teddy H** - 153 tons, built at Fairbanks in 1910. Sank near Nenana.

127. **Tutshi** - see chapter 8.

128. **Tyrrell** - built in Vancouver in 1898. Operated on the upper river run. Beached on the river bank just downstream from Dawson.

129. **Victoria** - 55 tons, built at St. Michael in 1897. Second boat to dock at Dawson on June 11, 1898. Abandoned at St. Michael.

130. **Victorian** - 716 tons, built at Victoria, B.C. in 1898. Operated on the upper river run. Beached on the river bank just downstream from Dawson.

131. **Viola** - built at Lake Bennett. It was 30 feet long and was the smallest steamer to go through the rapids to Whitehorse from the lake.

132. **W. H. Evans** - built at Ballard, Wash. in 1898. Grounded on the Yukon Flats on its first trip.

133. **White Horse** - 1,120 tons, built at Whitehorse in 1901 by the B.Y.N. Co. Rebuilt in 1930, She was beached at Whitehorse and burned to the ground in 1974.

134. **White Seal** - 194 tons, built at Fairbanks in 1905. Bought by the Alaska Railroad in 1905.

135. **Wilbur Crimmins** - 124 tons, built at Coupeville, Wash. in 1898. Operated on both upper and lower river runs.

136. **Will H. Isom** - 983 tons, built at Ballard, Wash. in 1901 by the N.A.T. & T. Co. Operated on the lower river run until about 1907. Abandoned at St. Michael.

137. **Willie Irving** - built at Lake Bennett in 1898. Thought to be the first boat to go through the Whitehorse Rapids in 1899. Caught in the ice, 35 miles from Selkirk in 1899, a total loss.

138. **William Ogilvie** - built at Lake Bennett in 1899. Abandoned at Taku, B.C.

139. **W. J. Mervin** - 229 tons, built in Seattle in 1883. Sank in a storm off Nome, Alaska.

140. **W. S. Stratton** - 93 tons, built in Seattle in 1898. Operated on the upper river run. Caught in the ice, 35 miles from Selkirk in 1897, a total loss.

141. **Yukon** - built in 1883. Operated on the lower river in 1898. Wrecked on the Koyukuk River.

142. **Yukon** - 651 tons, built at Whitehorse in 1913. Sister ship of the **Alaska.** Operated between Dawson and Nenana. It was rebuilt in 1936 and sold to the Alaska Railroad in 1942.

143. **Yukoner** - 781 tons, built in Victoria, B.C. in 1898. Rebuilt at St. Michael the same year and burned at Dawson in 1902. It last operated in 1903 on the upper river run because it had too much draft to continue operating on the river. It was beached at Whitehorse and used for lumber storage for years.

144. **Zealandian** - 180 tons, built at Lake Bennett in 1900. Operated on the upper river run. Demolished in Whitehorse in 1931.

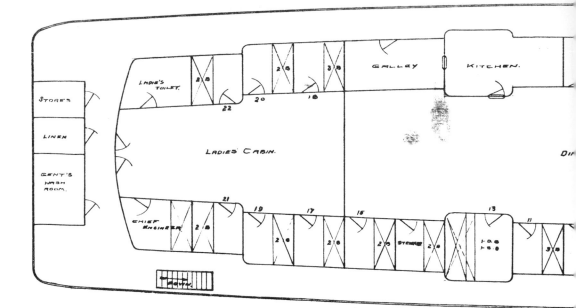

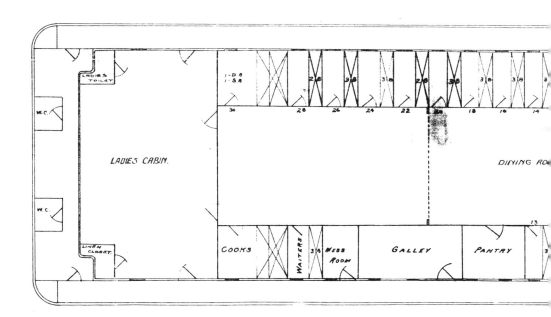

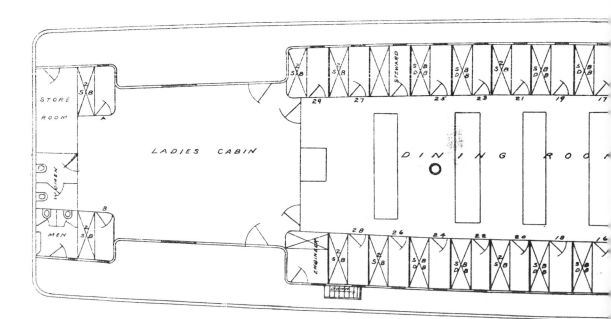

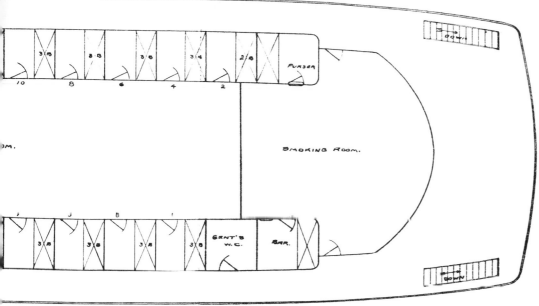

*Saloon deck plan of the **Yukoner**.*

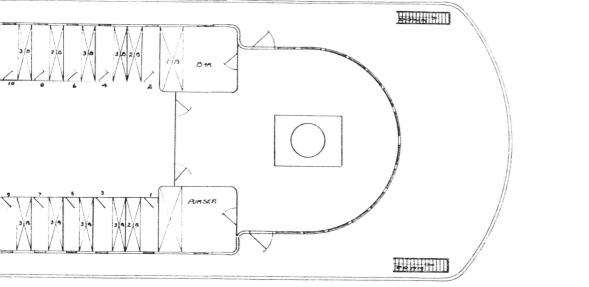

*Saloon deck plan of the **Columbian**.*

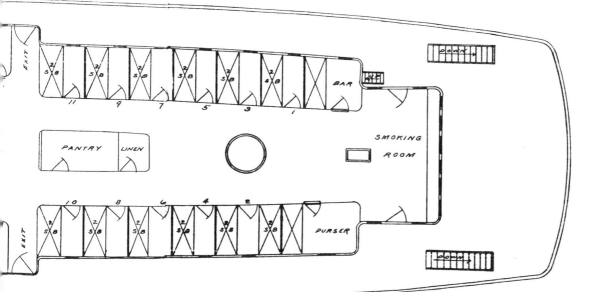

*Saloon deck plan of the **Selkirk**.*

A N.A.T. & T. Co. sternwheeler stopped along the shore and passengers and crew are walking on the beach.

YA
W & S Collection

Atlas of

American Diversity

Atlas of
American Diversity

Larry Hajime Shinagawa

Michael Jang

ALTAMIRA
PRESS

A Division of Sage Publications, Inc.
Walnut Creek ■ London ■ New Delhi

For information contact:

AltaMira Press
A Division of Sage Publications, Inc.
1630 North Main Street, Suite 367
Walnut Creek, California 94596 U.S.A.
explore@altamira.sagepub.com

Sage Publications Ltd.
6 Bonhill Street
London EC2A 4PU United Kingdom

Sage Publications India Pvt. Ltd.
M-32 Market
Greater Kailash 1
New Delhi 110 048 India

PRINTED IN THE UNITED STATES OF AMERICA

Library of Congress Cataloging-in-Publication Data

Shinagawa, Larry Hajime.
        Atlas of American diversity / by Larry Hajime Shinagawa and Michael Jang.
        p. cm.
        Includes bibliographical references and index.
        ISBN 0-7619-9127-1 (cloth : acid-free paper). — ISBN 0-7619-9128-X (pbk. : acid-free paper)
        1. Minorities—United States—Social conditions—Statistics. 2. United States—Ethnic relations—
        Statistics. I. Jang, Michael. II. Title.
E184.A1S575   1997
305.8'00973—dc21   97-4827

        1998   1999   2000   2001   2002   9 8 7 6 5 4 3 2 1

Table of Contents

List of Maps and Charts   9

About the Authors   15

Acknowledgments   16

Introduction   17

Chapter 1

African Americans   23

Introduction   23
Population Growth   23
Population Projections   23
Regional Dispersion   24
State Populations   24
Southern Regional Concentration   24
Metropolitan Concentration   25
Major City Concentrations   25
Moving   26
Age Distribution   26
Elderly   26
Educational Attainment   27
Labor Force Participation   28
Occupations   28
Income   29
    Family Income   29
    Individual Income   30
Marital Status   31
Family Composition   31
Poverty   32
Housing   33
Voter Turnout   34
Agriculture   34

Chapter 2

Asian Pacific Americans   41

Introduction   41
Laws Affecting Asian Immigration   41
Immigration   43
Population Growth   45
Regional Dispersion   45
Age Distribution   47
    Elderly   47
Educational Attainment   48
Labor Force Participation   48

Occupations   48
    Occupational Distribution of Recent Immigrants   49
Income   50
    Family Income   50
    Individual Earnings   50
    Per Capita Income   50
Market Power   51
Poverty   51
Housing   51
Family Composition   52
Voter Turnout   54
Agriculture   54
Pacific Islander Americans   54
    Introduction   54
    Population Growth   54
    Regional Dispersion   55
    Nativity   55
    Age Distribution   55
    Educational Attainment   55
    Labor Force Participation   55
    Income   56
    Poverty   56
    Family Composition   56
    Language   56

Chapter 3

Hispanic Americans   75

Introduction   75
General Demographics   75
Population Growth   76
Regional Dispersion   76
Ethnic and Cultural Backgrounds   76
Residential Dispersion   77
Nativity   78
Citizenship   79
Foreign-Born   79
Immigration   79
Age Distribution   79
    Elderly   79
    Educational Attainment   80
    Variations in Educational Attainment   80
Occupations   81
Income   82
    Family Income   82
Market Power   83
Poverty   83
Family Composition   84
Housing   84
Health   85
Language   85
Voter Turnout   85
Agriculture   85

C h a p t e r   4

Native Americans   97

Introduction	97
Population Growth	97
Regional Dispersion	97
Metropolitan Concentration	98
U.S. Population	98
State Populations	98
Reservation Populations	99
Age Distribution	99
Children	100
Elderly	100
Educational Attainment	100
Labor Force Participation	100
Occupations	100
Income	101
Poverty	101
Family Composition	101
Reservation Housing Characteristics	102
Structural Characteristics	102
Plumbing Facilities	102
Equipment and Fuels	103

C h a p t e r   5

Non-Hispanic Whites/European Americans   111

Introduction	111
Population Growth	111
Metropolitan Concentration	111
U.S. Population	111
Age Distribution	112
Children	112
Elderly	112
Educational Attainment	112
Labor Force Participation	113
Net Worth and Income	113
Per Capita Income	114
Family Income	114
Poverty	114
Family Composition	115
Health Care	115
Housing	115
Moving	115
Voter Turnout	115
Endnotes	116

C h a p t e r　6

A Comparison of American Race and Ethnic Social and Economic Status

A Comparison of American Race and Ethnic Social and Economic Status **135**

Introduction	135
Perception and Reality	136
Racial Classification	136
American Indian, Eskimo, and Aleut (Native American)	136
Asian and Pacific Islander (Asian Pacific American)	136
Black (African American)	136
Hispanic	136
White	136
Population Growth	136
Metropolitan and Nonmetropolitan Concentrations	138
Ancestry	138
Regional Concentrations by Ancestry	138
Educational Attainment	139
Educational Attainment of Mothers	139
Marital Status	139
Labor Force Participation	140
Family Income	140
Per Capita Income	141
Immigration	141
Earnings	142
Health Care	143
Poverty	143
Home Ownership	144
Family Composition	145
Elderly	145
Moving	145
Voter Turnout	146

For Further Reading	**155**
Index	**161**

List of Maps and Charts

Chapter 1

African Americans

Map 1.1	African Americans by State, 1990	35
Map 1.2	African Americans by County, 1990	35
Map 1.3	African Immigrant Americans by County, 1990	36
Map 1.4	West Indian Americans by County, 1990	36
Chart 1.1	African American Population, 1900–1994 (Millions)	37
Chart 1.2	States with an African American Population of One Million or More, 1990 (Thousands)	37
Chart 1.3	African American Population in Metropolitan Areas by Region, 1990 (Percent)	37
Chart 1.4	Ten Largest African American Metropolitan Statistical Areas, 1990 (Thousands)	37
Chart 1.5	Top Ten Cities with the Largest African American Population, 1990 (Thousands)	37
Chart 1.6	Resident African American Population by Age, 1990 (Percent)	37
Chart 1.7	Age and Sex of the African American Population, 1990 (Percent)	38
Chart 1.8	African American Population 65 Years and Over by Sex, 1990 (Percent)	38
Chart 1.9	African American and Non-Hispanic White Educational Attainment by Sex, 1990 (Percent, 25 years and older)	38
Chart 1.10	African American and Non-Hispanic White Labor Force Participation Rates by Sex, 1990 (Percent, 16 years and older)	38
Chart 1.11	African American Occupational Distribution by Sex, 1990 (Percent, 16 years and older)	38
Chart 1.12	Selected Occupational Groups of African Americans by Sex, 1990 (Thousands)	38
Chart 1.13	Median African American Income by Family Composition, 1979 and 1989 (Thousands)	39
Chart 1.14	Median Earnings for African Americans and Whites—Year-Round, Full-Time Workers by Sex, 1979 and 1989 (Thousands)	39
Chart 1.15	African American Marital Status by Sex, 1990 (Percent, 15 years and older)	39
Chart 1.16	African American and non-Hispanic White Family Composition, 1990 (Percent)	39
Chart 1.17	Changes in African American Family Composition, 1950–1991 (Percent)	39
Chart 1.18	Poverty Rates for African American Persons and Families, 1989 (Percent)	39
Chart 1.19	African Americans and Whites Below the Poverty Level, 1991 (Percent)	40
Chart 1.20	African American and White Housing Tenures, 1990 (Percent)	40
Chart 1.21	African American and White Home Ownership, 1990 (Percent)	40
Chart 1.22	African American and White Home Values, 1990 (Thousands)	40
Chart 1.23	Crowded Living Conditions for African Americans and Whites, 1990 (Percent of households with more than one person per room)	40

Chapter 2

Asian Pacific Americans

Map 2.1	Asian Pacific Americans by State, 1990	57
Map 2.2	Asian Pacific Americans by County, 1990	57
Map 2.3	Chinese Americans by State, 1990	58
Map 2.4	Chinese Americans by County, 1990	58
Map 2.5	Filipino Americans by State, 1990	59
Map 2.6	Filipino Americans by County, 1990	59
Map 2.7	Japanese Americans by State, 1990	60
Map 2.8	Japanese Americans by County, 1990	60
Map 2.9	Korean Americans by State, 1990	61
Map 2.10	Korean Americans by County, 1990	61
Map 2.11	Asian Indian Americans by State, 1990	62
Map 2.12	Asian Indian Americans by County, 1990	62
Map 2.13	Vietnamese Americans by State, 1990	63
Map 2.14	Vietnamese Americans by County, 1990	63
Map 2.15	Cambodian Americans by County, 1990	64
Map 2.16	Thai Americans by County, 1990	64
Map 2.17	Laotian Americans by County, 1990	65
Map 2.18	Hmong Americans by County, 1990	65
Map 2.19	Other Asian Americans by County, 1990	66
Map 2.20	Pacific Islander Americans by State, 1990	66
Map 2.21	Pacific Islander Americans by County, 1990	67
Map 2.22	Hawaiian Americans by County, 1990	67
Map 2.23	Samoan Americans by County, 1990	68
Map 2.24	Guamanian Americans by County, 1990	68
Map 2.25	Tongan Americans by County, 1990	69
Chart 2.1	Asian Pacific American Population by Place of Origin, 1990 (Percent)	70
Chart 2.2	Asian American Population by Place of Origin, 1990 (Percent)	70
Chart 2.3	Average Year-of-Entry Age for Asian American Immigrants, 1990 (Percent)	70
Chart 2.4	Resident Asian Pacific American Population by Age, 1990 (Percent)	70
Chart 2.5	Median Asian American Ages by Place of Origin, 1990	70
Chart 2.6	Asian American and Non-Hispanic White Educational Attainment, 1990	70
Chart 2.7	Asian American Employment Rates, 1990 (Percent, 16 years and older)	71
Chart 2.8	Asian American Families with Three or More Workers, 1990 (Percent)	71
Chart 2.9	Asian American and Total Population Occupational Distribution, 1990 (Percent, 16 years and older)	71
Chart 2.10	Asian American Wages by Place of Origin, 1990 (In 1989 dollars)	71
Chart 2.11	Median Asian American and White Family Incomes, 1994 (Thousands)	71
Chart 2.12	Asian American Poverty Rate by Place of Origin, 1990 (Percent)	71
Chart 2.13	Crowded Living Conditions for Asian Pacific Americans and Whites, 1990 (Percent of households with more than one person per room)	72
Chart 2.14	Asian Pacific American and White Home Values, 1990	72
Chart 2.15	Asian Pacific American and White Home Owners by Metropolitan Location, 1990 (Percent)	72
Chart 2.16	Asian American Family Size by Place of Origin, 1990	72
Chart 2.17	Comparison of Asian American and Non-Hispanic White Family Size, 1990 (Percent)	72
Chart 2.18	Pacific Islander American Ethnicities, 1990 (Percent)	72
Chart 2.19	Foreign Born Among Pacific Islanders, 1990 (Percent)	73
Chart 2.20	Median Pacific Islander American Age by Place of Origin, 1990	73

Chart 2.21   Major Occupations for Pacific Islander Americans and Asian Americans, 1990 (Percent, 16 years and older) 73
Chart 2.22   Pacific Islander American Labor Force Participation Rates, 1990 (Percent, 16 years and older) 73
Chart 2.23   Pacific Islander American Per Capita Income, 1990 (In 1989 dollars) 73
Chart 2.24   Pacific Islander American Families with Three or More Workers, 1990 (Percent) 73
Chart 2.25   Pacific Islander American Poverty Rates by Place of Origin, 1990 (Percent) 74
Chart 2.26   Pacific Islander American Family Size by Place of Origin, 1990 74

C h a p t e r 3

Hispanic Americans

Map 3.1   Hispanic Americans by State, 1990 86
Map 3.2   Hispanic Americans by County, 1990 86
Map 3.3   Mexican Americans by State, 1990 87
Map 3.4   Mexican Americans by County, 1990 87
Map 3.5   Puerto Rican Americans by State, 1990 88
Map 3.6   Puerto Rican Americans by County, 1990 88
Map 3.7   Cuban Americans by State, 1990 89
Map 3.8   Cuban Americans by County, 1990 89
Map 3.9   Dominican Americans by County, 1990 90
Map 3.10   El Salvadoran Americans by County, 1990 90
Map 3.11   Honduran Americans by County, 1990 91
Map 3.12   Guatemalan Americans by County, 1990 91
Map 3.13   Nicaraguan Americans by County, 1990 92
Map 3.14   Panamanian Americans by County, 1990 92

Chart 3.1   Projected Hispanic American Growth Rate, 1930–2050 (Millions) 93
Chart 3.2   Hispanic American Population Growth Rate, 1970–1990 (Percent) 93
Chart 3.3   Hispanic American Population by State, 1990 (Percent) 93
Chart 3.4   Nativity and Citizenship for Selected Hispanic American Origin Groups, 1990 (Percent) 93
Chart 3.5   Hispanic American Population by Place of Origin, 1990 (Percent) 94
Chart 3.6   Hispanic American Immigrants by Decade (Percent) 94
Chart 3.7   Resident Hispanic American Population by Age, 1990 (Percent) 94
Chart 3.8   Hispanic and Non-Hispanic White Age Distribution, 1990 (Percent) 95
Chart 3.9   Hispanic American and Non-Hispanic White American Educational Attainment, 1970–1990 (Percent) 95
Chart 3.10   Educational Attainment for Selected Hispanic American Origin Groups, 1990 (Percent, 25 years and older) 95
Chart 3.11   Hispanic American Occupational Distribution by Sex, 1994 (Percent, 16 years and older) 95
Chart 3.12   Major Occupations for Hispanic and Non-Hispanic White Americans by Sex, 1990 (Percent, 16 years and older) 95
Chart 3.13   Median Hispanic American Income by Family Composition, 1990 (Thousands, in 1989 dollars) 95
Chart 3.14   Hispanic American-Owned Firms, 1972–1988 (Thousands) 96
Chart 3.15   Hispanic American Composition by Place of Origin, 1990 (Percent) 96
Chart 3.16   Hispanic American and Non-Hispanic White American Home Ownership, 1990 (Percent) 96

Chart 3.17   Crowded Living Conditions for Hispanic and Non-Hispanic White
              Americans, 1990 (Percent of households with more than one person
              per room)   96
Chart 3.18   Hispanic and Non-Hispanic White Home Values, 1990 (Thousands)   96

Chapter   4

Native Americans

Map 4.1   Native Americans by State, 1990   104
Map 4.2   Native Americans by County, 1990   104
Map 4.3   American Indians by State, 1990   105
Map 4.4   American Indians by County, 1990   105
Map 4.5   Eskimo Americans by County, 1990   106
Map 4.6   Aleutian Americans by County, 1990   106

Chart 4.1   Native American Population, 1890–1990 (Thousands)   107
Chart 4.2   Native American Population Growth Rate, 1890–1990 (Thousands)   107
Chart 4.3   Native American Population by Type of Area, 1990 (Percent)   107
Chart 4.4   Ten Largest American Indian Tribes, 1990 (Thousands)   107
Chart 4.5   Top Ten States with the Largest Native American Populations, 1990
              (Thousands)   107
Chart 4.6   Reservations with the Largest Number of Native Americans, 1990
              (Thousands)   107
Chart 4.7   Resident Native American Population by Age, 1990 (Percent)   108
Chart 4.8   Native American Age Distribution, 1990 (Percent)   108
Chart 4.9   Native American Median Age, 1990   108
Chart 4.10   American Indian Median Age, 1990   108
Chart 4.11   Native American Educational Attainment, 1990 (Percent, 25 years and
              older)   108
Chart 4.12   American Indian Educational Attainment, 1990 (Percent, 25 years and
              older)   108
Chart 4.13   American Indian School Enrollment, 1990   109
Chart 4.14   Native American Labor Force Participation Rates by Sex, 1990 (Percent, 16
              years and older)   109
Chart 4.15   American Indian Employment Rates, 1990 (Percent, 16 years and older)   109
Chart 4.16   Native American Occupational Distribution, 1990 (Percent, 16 years and
              older)   109
Chart 4.17   Median Native American Income by Family Composition, 1990
              (Thousands, in 1989 dollars)   109
Chart 4.18   American Indian Per Capita Income, 1990   109
Chart 4.19   Native American and Total Population Poverty Rates by Family
              Composition, 1990 (Percent)   110
Chart 4.20   American Indian Poverty Rates, 1989 (Percent)   110
Chart 4.21   Native American and Total Population Family Composition, 1990 (Percent) 110
Chart 4.22   Percentage of American Indian Old and New Homes, 1990   110

Chapter   5

Non-Hispanic Whites/European Americans

Map 5.1   Non-Hispanic White Americans by State, 1990   117
Map 5.2   Non-Hispanic White Americans by County, 1990   117
Map 5.3   Northern European Americans by State, 1990   118
Map 5.4   Northern European Americans by County, 1990   118

Map 5.5	Irish Americans by State, 1990	119
Map 5.6	Irish Americans by County, 1990	119
Map 5.7	English Americans by State, 1990	120
Map 5.8	English Americans by County, 1990	120
Map 5.9	German Americans by State, 1990	121
Map 5.10	German Americans by County, 1990	121
Map 5.11	French Americans by State, 1990	122
Map 5.12	French Americans by County, 1990	122
Map 5.13	Scotch-Irish Americans by State, 1990	123
Map 5.14	Scotch-Irish Americans by County, 1990	123
Map 5.15	Scotch Americans by State, 1990	124
Map 5.16	Scotch Americans by County, 1990	124
Map 5.17	Scandinavian Americans by State, 1990	125
Map 5.18	Scandinavian Americans by County, 1990	125
Map 5.19	Welsh Americans by State, 1990	126
Map 5.20	Welsh Americans by County, 1990	126
Map 5.21	Southern, Central, and Eastern European Americans by State, 1990	127
Map 5.22	Southern, Central, and Eastern European Americans by County, 1990	127
Map 5.23	Italian Americans by State, 1990	128
Map 5.24	Italian Americans by County, 1990	128
Map 5.25	Polish Americans by State, 1990	129
Map 5.26	Polish Americans by County, 1990	129
Map 5.27	Greek Americans by State, 1990	130
Map 5.28	Greek Americans by County, 1990	130
Map 5.29	Russian Americans by State, 1990	131
Map 5.30	Russian Americans by County, 1990	131
Map 5.31	Hungarian Americans by State, 1990	132
Map 5.32	Hungarian Americans by County, 1990	132
Map 5.33	Portuguese Americans by State, 1990	133
Map 5.34	Portuguese Americans by County, 1990	133
Chart 5.1	Resident Non-Hispanic White Population by Age, 1990	134

Chapter 6

A Comparison of American Race and Ethnic Social and Economic Status

Map 6.1	"American" Americans by State, 1990	147
Map 6.2	"American" Americans by County, 1990	147
Map 6.3	Arab Americans by State, 1990	148
Map 6.4	Arab Americans by County, 1990	148
Map 6.5	Multiethnic Americans by State, 1990	149
Map 6.6	Multiethnic Americans by County, 1990	149
Chart 6.1	U.S. Population by Race, 1990 (Percent)	150
Chart 6.2	U.S. Population by Race, 1790–2050 (Thousands)	150
Chart 6.3	U.S. Population by Race, 1970–2050 (Percent)	150
Chart 6.4	Resident Population by Hispanic and Non-Hispanic Origin, 1995 and 2050 (Projected) (Percent)	150
Chart 6.5	U.S. Metropolitan and Non-Metropolitan Residence by Race, 1990 (Percent)	150
Chart 6.6	Selected Metropolitan Areas Minority Populations, 1990 (Percent)	150
Chart 6.7	Top Fifteen U.S. Ancestry Groups, 1990 (Millions)	151
Chart 6.8	U.S. Regional Population by Race, 1990 (Percent)	151

Chart 6.9   Regional U.S. Population by Race, 1990 (Thousands)   151
Chart 6.10   Educational Attainment by Race, 1990 (Percent)   151
Chart 6.11   Educational Attainment by Race and Sex, 1990 (Percent receiving
             bachelor's degree)   151
Chart 6.12   Educational Attainment by Race, 1940 and 1990 (Percent, 25 years and
             older)   151
Chart 6.13   College Completion Rates by Race and Sex (Percent, 25 years and older)   152
Chart 6.14   Associate's and Bachelor's Degrees Earned by Race, 1990 and 1992 (Percent)   152
Chart 6.15   Graduate Degrees Earned by Race, 1990 and 1992 (Percent)   152
Chart 6.16   Percentage of Children Living in Two-Parent Families, 1970, 1980, and
             1990   152
Chart 6.17   Occupational Distribution of the Civilian Labor Force by Race and Sex,
             1990 (Percent, 16 years and older)   152
Chart 6.18   Income Brackets by Race, 1990 (Thousands)   152
Chart 6.19   Legal Immigration by Area of Origin, 1952–1990 (Thousands)   153
Chart 6.20   Male Income by Race, 1990 (Percentage of Non-Hispanic White earnings,
             35–44 years old)   153
Chart 6.21   Female Income by Race, 1990 (Percentage of non-Hispanic White earnings,
             35–44 years old)   153
Chart 6.22   Minority Owned Firms, 1988 (Thousands)   153
Chart 6.23   AIDS Deaths by Race, 1982–1994   153
Chart 6.24   Victims of Child Abuse and Neglect by Race, 1993 (Percent)   153
Chart 6.25   Poverty Rates for Families, Persons, and Children by Race, 1990 (Percent)   154
Chart 6.26   AFDC Recipients by Race, 1990   154
Chart 6.27   U.S. Housing Tenures by Race, 1980 and 1990 (Percent)   154
Chart 6.28   Birth Rate by Race, 1992 (Per 1,000 population)   154
Chart 6.29   Family Composition by Race, 1970, 1980, and 1990 (Percent)   154

About the Authors

Larry Hajime Shinagawa received his doctorate from the University of California at Berkeley in sociology. He is the Chair of the Department of American Multi-Cultural Studies at Sonoma State University, California, and Coordinator of its Asian American Studies Program. He is an acknowledged authority on research and methodology in race relations and Asian American studies and is a former director of the California State University Census Information Center.

In the past six years, Shinagawa has worked on numerous federal and nonprofit research projects to study racial classification, intermarriage, health delivery systems, redistricting, and political behavior. He has authored numerous articles and publications on applied research and social policy topics regarding multi-cultural studies. He has been featured on the "Donahue Show," "All Things Considered," CNN, and other television and radio programs as well as in newspapers. He currently teaches in ethnic studies and American multi-cultural studies, develops curricula in such programs, serves on boards and projects among ethnic minority community organizations, works on a number of research projects involving race and ethnic issues, and serves as editorial consultant of a series of books on Asian Pacific Americans for AltaMira Press. Research areas of special interest to him are Asian American voting rights and electoral politics, race and ethnic demography, intermarriage, immigration, racial identity formation, and racial classification.

Michael Jang is the founder and Chief Executive Officer of Four Winds Research Corporation and the Research Director of the URSA Institute. He is responsible, in both research organizations, for project management, methodological design, and technical support. Over the past 20 years, he has been the principal investigator in dozens of applied research projects with such organizations as the Asian American Recovery Services, Bureau of Primary Health Care, Department of Public Health, National Institute for Justice, Bureau of Indian Affairs, City of Oakland, and National Firefighters Association.

Jang has researched such diverse topics as tobacco use among Filipino Americans, drug abuse among Asian Pacific Americans, correlates of fire and sociodemographics, needs assessments for various municipalities and organizations, evaluation research of numerous corporations and organizations, redistricting and planning studies for cities and municipalities, and sociocultural factors for the transmission of AIDS among drug users in inner-city neighborhoods. He is widely acknowledged for the combination of sociological imagination that he brings to research projects, his technical expertise, and his methodological rigor and training. He is also an affiliate of the Survey Research Center's Center for Computer Assisted Telephone Interviewing and is a board member of the American Red Cross.

Acknowledgments

We would like to acknowledge the assistance of the following companies and organizations that have helped make this book possible: U.S. Bureau of the Census; ESRI; Mapinfo Corporation; Geolytics Corporation; Wessex, Inc.; Four Winds Corporation; School of Arts and Humanities, Sonoma State University; and staff, colleagues, and students of the Department of American Multi-Cultural Studies at Sonoma State University.

We would like to thank the U.S. Bureau of the Census in particular for their great dedication to providing information for the nation and its citizens.

We would like to give special thanks both to Lyman Louie, who assisted in the preparation of the maps, and to the helpful editorial staff of AltaMira Press: Denise Santoro, our associate editor, and Mitch Allen, publisher of AltaMira Press. This book is dedicated to all those who are curious about the world around them and continue to ask "Why?"

Larry Hajime Shinagawa
Michael Jang

Introduction

Who am I? What is my place? What marks the boundaries of my life? Who belongs to my community? What issues that confront my family or community today seem to be the most pressing? How am I doing, compared to others? These are questions that we humans have been asking ourselves for centuries, and as we approach a new millennium we find concerned individuals, community leaders, and policy makers still asking them on our behalf.

Answering such questions, whether as an individual or a group leader, requires that we reference and orient ourselves—both figuratively on the map and literally in the life of our nation, state, and community. That is why this book was written: to help anchor us in the realities of life in America today and help us see how we relate to one another.

Probably the most effective and intuitive way that we absorb information and understand complex relations and issues is through a visual display, with the addition of data and analyses that are presented in summary fashion and are easy to follow. Because we are naturally inclined to view phenomena visually and spatially, such tools as charts, graphs, and especially maps give us handy information and references that can't be gathered easily from perusing dusty tomes of statistical tables or reading long, dry passages of text. The adage "a picture is worth a thousand words" rings true to all of us, especially to us contemporary Americans who are deluged by numbers, documents, and statistics and cannot readily find the time to identify and absorb all the information that relates to our lives.

As the eminent statistician Edward R. Tufte relates in his book *The Visual Display of Quantitative Information* (Graphics Press, 1983), "Graphics *reveal* data. Indeed graphics can be more precise and revealing than conventional statistical computations." Tufte goes on to illustrate what the visual display of data can do:

- Show the data
- Induce the viewer to think about the substance rather than about methodology, graphic design, the technology of graphic production, or something else
- Avoid distorting what the data have to say
- Present many numbers in a small space

- Make large data sets coherent
- Encourage the eye to compare different pieces of data
- Reveal the data at several levels of detail, from a broad overview to the fine structure
- Serve a reasonably clear purpose: description, exploration, tabulation, or decoration
- Be closely integrated with the statistical and verbal descriptions of a data set (Tufte, p. 13)

Building on Tufte's enumerations of the advantages of visually displayed data, this book presents readers with easily accessible and understood information about the diversity of experiences in the United States. Because the book minimizes the use of dense phraseology and replaces long descriptions with summary facts and figures and the creative use of graphs, charts, simplified tables, and particularly maps, the reader is allowed to concentrate on the substance, meaning, and relationships implied by our visual display of data.

The Focus on Race and Ethnicity

This book deals with the racial and ethnic diversity of America. Like Atlas, the mythical Titan who bore the heavens on his shoulders, it supports a world of statistics and analyses, in both graphical and textual form. This *Atlas of American Diversity* provides readers and policy makers with the most important baseline information, enabling them to assess the conditions of ethnic and racial groups in the United States. By using this book, they can empower communities by helping them target resources and programs to those in need: the most disadvantaged communities and racial or ethnic groups in our society.

Race continues to be one of the more vexing problems of American life today. The Glass Ceiling Commission continues to find that 94 percent of all executive positions are held by White males (1995). Massey reports that segregation in the United States is at an all-time high this past decade (1993). The California Civil Rights Initiative, the O.J. Simpson criminal and civil trials controversy, the 1992 riots in Los Angeles following the Rodney King verdict, California's Proposition 187 (restricting social services to immigrants), and similar laws and events show that there continues to be a racial divide in the consciences of Americans on issues of civil rights and affirmative action, crime and punishment, immigration, and perceptions of fairness and opportunity. With all the festering ethnic and racial tensions in America, policy makers and community leaders alike need to be able to apply concise information in summary format and in graphical chart and map display, to give their constituents a baseline to evaluate and assess their own perceptions and impressions.

Consider one concrete example of the usefulness of maps such as those found in this book (leaving aside that of charts and graphs, because most of us are familiar with their advantages). Typically, many governmental tables such as those issued by the U.S. Bureau of the Census can be long and extended. For example, one that depicts the population count of African Americans in the United States, county by county, can comprise over 29 pages of a census document (which is itself probably about 75 pages of a normal document). Although the information may be useful to some in this form, it's hard to detect patterns and relationships, such as where African Americans are concentrated or where they live in comparison to others. Let's imagine a likely scenario. Say a national civil rights policy advocate is interested in developing a national African American voter rights and civil rights research institute. He or she is seeking a location for the institute that would be strategically centered, near university and governmental/business resources, and with access to a ready pool of patrons and clients. Chances are that the site will be chosen after examining where African Americans live in heavy concentrations, since that usually implies greater need. Density and concentration maps can therefore provide an excellent guide to the appropriate location and can condense dozens of pages of statistical data into a single useful map.

To illustrate this, look at Map 2.2 showing the percent of African Americans by county for the United States in 1990. (In this book, maps and charts are presented at the end of each chapter.) Viewers of the map will find that African Americans are still heavily concentrated below the Mason-Dixon line, marking the southern boundary of Pennsylvania— that is, clustered in the historical areas where African Americans had been enslaved prior to the Civil War. We can also see where African Americans migrated to the northern and western urban centers during the two Great Migrations between the 1880s and the

1970s—to Chicago, New York, Detroit, Trenton, Oakland, and Los Angeles. The viewer will probably note how few African Americans live in the Northwest and in New England. A few readers or viewers would probably be thinking that the spatial distribution of African Americans might account for why so-called Neo-Nazis, "skinheads," and members of the Aryan Nation are attempting to establish a White Nation in the Pacific Northwest. The national civil rights policy maker would probably recommend, viewing this large-scale map, that the African American civil rights and advocacy research organization center its national headquarters and advocacy efforts in the South. In fact, this is exactly where the Center for Policy Studies (in Washington, D.C., and Richmond, Virginia) and the Southern Regional Council (Atlanta, Georgia)—both African American research/advocacy centers—eventually located their headquarters.

In designing Atlas of American Diversity, we have endeavored to keep the topics both ethnic/racial-specific and ethnic/racial-comparative. This book emphasizes the domestic experience of ethnic and racial groups in the United States. International statistics and experiences are brought in only as they relate to immigration. The book focuses on the social and economic characteristics of ethnic and racial groups in the United States and emphasizes both their commonalities and their differences. Showing factually the great diversity and inequality in American society, the book consciously uses nationally recognized federal and state sources of information (all in the public domain) as the basis for evaluating and assessing the conditions of the diverse peoples of the United States. Providing the baseline, we hope that this book empowers and informs the American people, enabling them to assess the conditions of their own and other Americans' ethnic and racial groups in a new light—a light that illuminates their common experiences as well as their unique qualities and cultural backgrounds.

In writing this book, we have chosen to recognize race and ethnicity as two broadly framed social constructs. By race, we mean a group of individuals who at birth are given a set of characteristics and behaviors (stereotypes) based upon their average, visible phenotype. Thus race is a social construct, subject to the political and social whims at play in our society. Historically, this view of race has been the American experience of how we designate "Whites." In the nation's early days, state and federal governments defined being White to include only Anglo-Americans. Later, this was expanded to include Northern Europeans, and, after World War II, to include South, Central, and Eastern Europeans (Steinberg, 1989). According to Andrew Hacker, based on research on the large-scale nature of intermarriage, the concept of "White-ness" may soon encompass historically non-Anglo populations such as Hispanic Americans, Asian Americans, and persons from North Africa and the Middle East (Hacker, 1992). In essence, race is a fluid concept, yet it has a strong social reality in that people designated as a member of a specific race are treated partly by the terms of unwritten social rules applied to "their" race. As sociologist W. I. Thomas (Thomas and Znaniecki, 1918) stated, "if men [sic] define situations as real they are real in their consequences."

According to the Office of Management and Budget (OMB) Directive 15 (1984), by law and policy the United States recognizes only four racial groups and one cultural group. The four racial groups are African Americans, Asian Pacific Americans, Native Americans, and Whites. The sole cultural group recognized, based on language and heritage, is Hispanic Americans. In practice, Hispanic Americans can actually identify with any race, including the "Other Race" category included in the census, which is taken every ten years. For purposes of this book, however, and partly because of their growing numbers, we treat Hispanic Americans as a separate "racial" group.

In contrast to race, by *ethnicity* we refer in this book to a group of individuals who share a common history and culture, and sometimes also a language or a slang/idiom, who at one time in their collective experience came to the United States from some other part of the globe. If groups remain relatively near where they were situated originally and are given political and boundary status of some sort, then they are also considered as nationalities. Some examples of ethnic groups are West Indian American, Chinese American, and Irish American. Examples of "ethnic" groups who are also nationalities (politically recognized and in many cases indigenous to their region) are Cherokee Americans, Eskimo Americans, and Hawaiian Americans.

Most ethnic groups, by American custom and behavior, fit within socially predefined racial categories. For example, Chinese Americans are usually considered submembers of the Asian Pacific American racial category. Irish Americans are typically considered White. Honduran Americans are associ-ated with Latino Americans. Hawaiian Americans, as Pacific Islanders, are included in the Asian Pacific American category. Cherokee tribal members are Native Americans.

Hence, the book presents discrete chapters on African Americans, Asian Pacific Americans, Hispanic Americans, Native Americans, and Non-Hispanic White/European Americans, plus a chapter that treats comparative progress on social and economic fronts. These broad "racial" categories encompass diverse ethnic groups and experiences. In several of the chapters, considerable attention is given to unique ethnic experiences. In others, the focus has been given more to the "racial" background of group members. Part of the reason is the availability of data; for instance, information on African Americans is much more readily available by race than by ethnicity.

At times, language to describe race and ethnic groups can be quite confusing—because various government documents may not use the same descriptions, and also because race and ethnic identification changes with time and locale. For the sake of simplicity and regularity, we have chosen to follow the U.S. Census definition of White as anyone who self-identifies himself or herself as White; in some statistics, this may include Whites of Hispanic origin. A subgroup of Whites, Non-Hispanic Whites are those who self identified themselves as White but who are *not* of Hispanic origin. Hispanic-origin Whites, along with others who have marked themselves as being of Hispanic-origin, are discussed in this book in the chapter on Hispanic Americans.

We have also chosen to use the concept of "White" with great caution. We recognize that this concept has been given legal recognition since 1790 and is officially the standard category usually associated with persons of European ancestry. Yet the present concept of White also includes persons originally from North Africa and the Middle East (west of Pakistan). Here, we encounter a dissociation between the "common sense" understanding of "White-ness" and the governmental version of the term. Because of a lack of consensus, and to discuss both Whites and non-Hispanic Whites in the same chapter, we have chosen to title that chapter, "Non-Hispanic Whites/European Americans."

Our personal inclination, though, is to describe "racial" groups by identifying broad pan-ethnic categories formed both by perceived "race" and by proactively formed history and culture. The "politically correct" version would have required chapters on African Americans, Asian Americans, Pacific Islander Americans, Latino Americans[1], Native Americans, Middle Eastern Americans, and European Americans; but the reader would undoubtedly be confused by this multiplicity of terms. Given this dilemma, and somewhat bound by the categories of information provided by the census and by other government programs and agencies, we have chosen to report the characteristics of groups based on the "racial" and "ethnic" categories that have been applied by various government agencies since the passage of OMB Directive 15.

Data Sources

Atlas of American Diversity uses primarily public-domain information drawn from various federal and state agencies as well as from a variety of research organizations. Here is a sample of the sources of information:

- Bureau of the Census
- Department of Commerce
- Department of Agriculture
- Bureau of Economic Analysis
- National Center for Health Statistics
- National Center for Education Statistics
- Energy Information Administration
- Environmental Protection Agency
- Equal Employment Opportunity Commission
- Department of Housing and Urban Development
- Immigration and Naturalization Service
- Internal Revenue Service
- Bureau of Justice Statistics
- Bureau of Labor Statistics
- National Technical Information Service
- Social Security Administration
- Department of Veterans Affairs
- California Registrar's Office
- Election Data Services, Inc.
- U.S. Commission on Civil Rights
- U.S. Small Business Administration

Most of the information comes from the 1980 and 1990 Decennial Censuses of the U.S. Bureau of the Census. The term *census* refers to everyone who

is counted; in actual practice, undocumented immigrants, racial minorities, the homeless, and migrants are undercounted, sometimes substantially. Overall, the U.S. government believes that it missed a mere 1.5 percent of the total population in 1990. Yet follow-up work done by some groups has indicated that undercoverage can be as high as 9.5 percent (among African Americans).

The primary sources of information are Summary Tape Files 1A, 3A, and 4B; various publications of the census data; the 5 percent Public Use Microdata Sample (PUMS); and the annual Current Population Survey. All these data sources are from the U.S. Bureau of the Census, Department of Commerce. PUMS data is derived from questions that were asked in 1980 and 1990 of 17 percent of the population. A subset of the 17 percent questioned is further used to create the public use 5 percent data set. Examples of data that come from these sources are detailed questions about ancestry and income sources.

Applications of the Atlas

The main audience of *Atlas of American Diversity* consists of college-level students, scholars, academicians, government researchers and policy analysts, and community leaders who need information thematically focused and available in an attractive layout with clear and concise information.

In terms of fields covered, this book runs a gamut, from social sciences and business to public policy and related areas. Social science fields such as American studies, American multicultural studies, anthropology, archeology, economics, ethnic studies, history, law, linguistics, sociology, political science, and religious studies would also benefit from much of the sociodemographic information provided herein. Business areas such as marketing, business administration, strategic planning and forecasting, and economic analysis could similarly use the volume to identify and describe demographic factors as well as labor and consumer markets. Fields of public administration, social welfare, and public policy could use the information for courses and research on land-use planning, crime analysis, philanthropy, regional planning, urban transit planning, risk analysis, redistricting, and environmental studies.

---

1   "Latino American" refers to persons who have been acculturated within the Americas yet with a common experience of Iberian heritage (that of the peoples of the peninsula comprising Spain and Portugal). Because of this definition, the term "Latino American" (or simply "Latino") usually *excludes* Spanish Americans and Portuguese Americans (that is, those born in Spain or Portugal). Currently, "Hispanic American," as the term is used by the federal government, *includes* such ethnic groups as these, along with Mexican Americans, Puerto Rican Americans, Cuban Americans, and Peruvian Americans, among others.

Libraries, nonprofit organizations, community organizations, philanthropic funds, businesses, and the educated layperson would also be interested in reading this book. Libraries seeking reference works like this one can serve their many patrons who need accessible information. Nonprofit and community organizations can use the book for planning and needs assessment. Philanthropic organizations can find this book useful for strategic planning. Businesses constantly need up-to-date demographic, social, and economic information of this type, to help in marketing, planning, and decision-making. Educated laypersons fascinated by the subject matter may find their curiosity piqued and their cultural awareness enhanced by reading these pages.

Whatever your affiliation or background, we hope that you find this book serves your needs. We offer it with the wish that it can help all of us realize and appreciate the great diversity that is America, and we trust that it will aid us in understanding the many obstacles, challenges, and opportunities we face as we forge a new America in the next millennium.

Chapter 1

African Americans

Introduction

African Americans are people whose ancestry stems from the continent of Africa south of the Sahara desert. The first members of what would come to be known as that group arrived in the New World at the Jamestown Colony, initially as indentured servants and later, for many, as slaves of White plantation owners and masters. Most African Americans today consider their origin to be the former tribal kingdoms (now nations) of western Africa, because that area was the primary source of indentured servants and slaves during the slave trade of the 1500s through the 1800s. More recently, African Americans have immigrated to the United States from all regions of the continent of Africa, as well as from Central America, the Caribbean, and South America.

Population Growth *(See Chart 1.1)*

In 1790, when the first census was taken, African Americans numbered about three-quarters of a million individuals (760,000). By 1860, at the beginning of the Civil War, the African American population had increased to 4.4 million, though the percentage had dropped from 19 percent to 14 percent of the total U.S. population. Most African Americans at that time were slaves, with only 488,000 counted as "freemen" and "free-women."

By the turn of the 20th century, African Americans had doubled their population to 8.8 million. Regionally, the vast majority (90 percent) of the African American population lived in the South. Around this time, however, large numbers of African Americans started migrating north (and west) looking for better job opportunities and living conditions and, not incidentally, to escape Jim Crow laws facing them in the South. Many found jobs in the major cities of the Midwest and Northeast.

In another 40 years, the African American population nearly doubled in size, amounting to 15 million in 1950. By 1980, there were 27 million African Americans. Ten years later, in 1990, African Americans numbered 30 million, having doubled their numbers since the beginning of the Civil Rights movement in the early 1950s.

Two years later, the African American population in the United States numbered 31.4 million. According to the U.S. Census Bureau, the African American population increased an average of 1.4 percent per year between 1980 and 1992, more than twice the annual growth rate of the non-Hispanic White population (0.6 percent).

Population Projections

From 1980 to 1990, the African American population increased by 3.5 million. In 1994, the number of African Americans was estimated at 33 million people, or 13 percent (just over one in ten), of the total U.S. population. The African American population has grown faster than either the total or the non-Hispanic White population since the 1980 decennial census. Eighty-four percent of the growth in the African American population since 1980 was a result of natural increase (births over deaths), while immigration accounted for the remaining 16 percent. Compared to 1990 figures, it is estimated that by the year 2000 the African American population will increase by 5 million people; by 2010 by some 10 million; and by the year 2030 by perhaps 20 million. *By that time, it is projected that the African American population will have doubled its 1990 population to 62 million.*

Regional Dispersion

In all regions except the West, the African American population is projected to be the second fastest growing among the four racial groups, and to make the second largest gain in absolute population between 1990 and 2020. Between 1980 and 1990, the African American population growth rate was highest in the western states (west of Colorado) and lowest in the Midwest. African Americans continued to move from urban areas to suburban areas. The African American suburban population grew by a third between 1980 and 1990, reaching about 7 percent of the nation's suburban population.

State Populations *(See Chart 1.2)*

African Americans were represented in every one of the 50 states in 1990, from about 2,000 in sparsely populated Vermont to 2.9 million in New York;16 states had 1 million or more African Americans in 1990. *The 16 states with an African American population of 1 million or more accounted for over 80 percent of the African American population.* New York and California (the nation's most populous state) contain the largest shares of the nation's African American population. California and Texas joined New York during the 1980s as the only states with African American populations exceeding 2 million.

Three states had African American populations exceeding 2 million in 1990: New York, California, and Texas. Together these three states contained nearly one-fourth (24 percent) of the nation's African American population. During the decade between 1980 and 1990, the four states of Alabama, Maryland, New Jersey, and South Carolina surpassed the 1 million mark in African Americans.

In 1990, the African American population continued to be heavily concentrated in the South. Slightly over half (53 percent) of all African Americans lived in the South in 1990, roughly the same percentage as in 1980 and 1970. Six of the ten states with the largest African American populations were in the South.

The region containing the smallest proportion of the African American population in 1990 continued to be the West, with 9 percent of the nation's African Americans. The West, however, had the largest percentage gain in African Americans of any region during the 1980s—25 percent—almost double the rate of increase for the African American population nationally and in the South (13 percent each). By contrast, the Northeast and Midwest regions each contained about 19 percent of the U.S. African American population.

The largest numerical gain in the African American population during the 1980–1990 period occurred in New York (457,000), while the highest percentage gain was recorded in New Hampshire (80 percent). Only West Virginia and the District of Columbia lost African American population, while the number of African Americans in Arkansas remained about the same over the decade.

By the year 2020, Florida may have the biggest net gain in the African American population, rising 1.5 million to over 3 million. Texas and Georgia will have roughly 3 million African Americans each, and thus would comprise the top three states with the largest African American population in 2020. According to the U.S. Census Bureau, more than half the 13 million African Americans added to the nation over the projected period will likely be living in the South.

Southern Regional Concentration

The southern region of the U.S. currently is home to 93 percent of rural African Americans. According to the 1990 U.S. Census, 18.5 percent of the population in southern states is African American (compared with 11 percent in the Northeast, 9.6 in the Midwest, and 5.3 percent in the West). Of the entire African American population in the U.S. in 1990, 52.8 percent resides in the South. Two years later, according to the 1992 Current Population Survey, more than one-half of African Americans, but less than one-third of non-Hispanic Whites, lived there.

During the period between 1980 and 1985, the rural southern African American population increased by approximately 87,000 people. The most recent analysis of rural population trends in the late 1980s suggests that the largest portion of out-migration is now over. The introduction of industry to rural southern areas has caused an influx of African Americans from other regions. This in-migration has been attributed partially to the economic reawakening of the South and to the poor living conditions of the African American underclass in northern cities.

In the South, African Americans are less concentrated in metropolitan areas than in any other regions of the United States. While 95 percent of the African American population lived in metropolitan areas outside the South in 1990, less than 75 percent of African Americans in the South resided in such areas.

Metropolitan Concentration *(See Charts 1.3 and 1.4)*

African Americans form a largely urban population, they live mostly in cities and in large metropolitan areas (MAs). In 1990, 84 percent of the nation's African American population lived in metropolitan areas, with 57 percent in the central cities (a central city is the urban core of a city, excluding its suburbs) and 27 percent in the suburbs. The majority of African Americans live in the 20 largest metropolitan areas of the nation. According to the 1992 Current Population Survey, African Americans were twice as likely as Whites to live in central cities (56 percent compared to 26 percent) but far less likely to live in the suburbs (29 percent versus 51 percent). Nonetheless, African Americans are increasingly more likely to buy their own homes than in the past, especially in the suburbs.

In 1990, about 40 percent of the African American population resided in just 10 consolidated metropolitan statistical areas (CMSAs) and metropolitan statistical areas (MSAs)—nearly the same proportion as in 1980.

Seven of these ten metropolitan areas were also among the ten most populous in the nation.

New York (763,309), Chicago (439,938), Washington, D.C. (371,387), Los Angeles (352,679), and Detroit (329,319) had more African American households than any other metropolitan areas. Combined, these five metropolitan areas accounted for about one in four metropolitan African American households. Three in four lived in one of the top 50 MAs that had more than 40,000 African American households. Twenty-six of these MAs were located in the South; seven were found in either Georgia or the Carolinas.

African Americans represented 20 percent or more of the total population in 4 of these 10 MAs. For example, African Americans represented 27 percent of all persons residing in the Washington, D.C., MSA. Although the ten metropolitan areas are scattered across the country, five are in the South.

In the Jackson, Mississippi, MA, 37 percent of householders were African American—the highest percentage of any of the top 50 MAs. The Memphis, Tennessee–Arkansas–Mississippi MA (36 percent) and the New Orleans, Louisiana, MA (31 percent) followed closely. All in all, there were 10 MAs in the top 50 where African Americans counted for at least one-quarter of all householders. All ten were in the South.

Major City Concentrations *(See Chart 1.5)*

The ten cities with the largest African American populations in 1990 were the same as in 1980, as were the rankings for the top five cities. There were a couple of changes in the rankings for the sixth through tenth positions. Washington, D.C., slipped from sixth to eighth place, while the cities occupying the nineth and tenth positions in 1980 (New Orleans and Memphis, respectively) exchanged places in 1990. Of the ten cities with the largest African American population, five gained population and five lost population during the 1980s. New York City had the largest numerical and percentage increase, while Chicago decreased by about 9 percent and Washington,

D.C., lost about 11 percent between 1980 and 1990. In five of these ten cities, African Americans represented more than 50 percent of the total population. They were Detroit, Washington, D.C., New Orleans, Baltimore, and Memphis. In all but one of the ten cities (Los Angeles), African Americans accounted for at least 25 percent of the city's total population in 1990. Five of these cities had a majority African American population: Detroit (76 percent), Washington, D.C. (66 percent), New Orleans (62 percent), Baltimore (59 percent), and Memphis (55 percent). New York City (the borough of Manhattan) had the largest African American population of any city in

1990, with 2.1 million African American residents. The only other city with more than a million African American residents was Chicago. The cities with the most populous African American population in both 1980 and 1990 were New York, Chicago, Detroit, and Philadelphia. Among the 100 cities with the largest African American populations, the city with the highest proportion of African Americans in both 1980 and 1990 was East St. Louis, Illinois, where 98 percent of its residents were African American.

Moving

Historically, because of poor economic conditions and a lack of employment opportunities for minorities, many African Americans, especially in the rural areas, chose to move out of the South around the turn of the century. Out-migration of the southern African American rural population took place on a large scale beginning in the 1910s. During the 1920s, more than three-quarters of a million African Americans left the South and headed to other areas of the country such as the West Coast, the Midwest, and the Northeast. Much of this population moved to northern cities seeking greater opportunities for advancement, but found access to equal opportunities in housing and employment difficult to come by. As a result of discrimination and segregation, the Midwest and Northeast saw the rise of African American ghettos from the 1940s to the present.

Recently, African Americans are returning to the South. Out-migration from the South to other areas has slowed considerably or has ceased. The current trends show that there is a marked influx of African Americans returning to the South, as the South experiences economic growth and offers greater political opportunities for African Americans.

In 1994, both the South and the West had higher mobility rates than the national average: 18.1 percent of southerners and 20.2 percent of westerners had moved in the previous year. When people do move, they tend to head for the suburbs. Between 1993 and 1994, central cities lost 2,936,000 persons due to migration while the suburbs gained 2,850,000 movers. African Americans have a 19 percent chance of moving in general, and a 13.8 percent rate of moving within the same county. In the year 1993, just less than one in five African Americans moved.

Age Distribution *(See Charts 1.6 and 1.7)*

The average life expectancy for a newborn African American baby in 1980 was 68 years, compared with 74 years for a non-Hispanic White baby. By 1990, life expectancy for African Americans averaged 69 years, still about 6 years less than that for non-Hispanic Whites. In 1990, about one-third of the African American population was under 18 years old. Also in 1990, about 47 percent of the African American population was male, and 53 percent female.

The median age of African Americans in 1990 was 28 years, up from 25 years in 1980, and 6 years younger than that of the non-Hispanic White population. African American males had a lower median age than African American females. A smaller proportion of African American males than African American females were 65 years old and over. These figures represent, in part, the higher mortality rate of African American males. Each group's age structure in 1990 reflects this: 33 percent of African Americans were under 18; 8 percent were age 65 or over. For non-Hispanic Whites, the comparable figures were 25 and 13 percent, respectively.

Elderly *(See Chart 1.8)*

Between 1980 and 1990, the number of African American persons 65 years old and over increased from 2.1 to 2.5 million. From 1990 to 2050, the percentage of elderly in the African American population could nearly double from 8 percent to 15 percent.

The proportion of African Americans who were elderly grew from 7.9 percent in 1980 to 8.4 percent in 1990. In contrast, the elderly constituted a higher proportion among non-Hispanic Whites; they were 14 percent in 1990, up from 12 percent in 1980.

African American elderly persons are located in all 50 of the states. The regional distribution of African American elderly persons was similar to the distribution of all African Americans in the United States—55 percent of the African American elderly were in the South. In 1990, across the country, of the 31 million elderly people of all races, 2.5 million (12.4 percent) were African American.

There were many more African American women than African American men in the older age groups. In 1990, 62 percent of African American elderly persons were women, while only 38 percent were men.

Poverty rates among African American elderly were high. In fact, poverty rates were higher among elderly African Americans (33 percent) than for non-Hispanic Whites (11 percent) in 1994. Elderly African American women had less than half the income in 1992 of elderly non-Hispanic White men ($6,220 versus $15,276).

In 2050, there could well be 79 million elderly Americans (over 65 years). While the number of elderly non-Hispanic Whites could more than double to 62 million in 2050, the number of elderly African Americans could nearly *quadruple* to over 9 million.

Educational Attainment *(See Chart 1.9)*

Arican Americans are experiencing higher levels of educational attainment than ever before. In 1940 only 7.7 percent of African Americans 25 years old and over had completed high school. In 1965, the corresponding figure was 27.2, almost four times as many graduates. By 1993, 70.4 percent of African Americans 25 years and older had completed high school. Only 10.6 percent of African American and Other Race men between the ages of 25 and 29 in 1940 had completed four years of high school. In 1993 this figure was 85 percent for African American men.

Fewer African Americans are dropping out of high school. The annual dropout rate for African Americans enrolled in grades 10 through 12 declined from 11 percent in 1970 to 5 percent in 1993. (In the middle of that period, 1980 to 1990, the high school dropout rate for African Americans declined from 16 percent to 14 percent.) The corresponding dropout rates for non-Hispanic Whites changed only slightly, from 5 percent in 1970 to 4 percent in 1993. In 1993, there was no statistical difference in the annual high school dropout rate of African Americans and and non-Hispanic Whites and of males and females. African Americans have thus closed the historical differential between their annual high school dropout rates and those of non-Hispanic Whites. Consistent with a lower dropout rate is the growing proportion of African Americans with at least a high school education. In 1994, 73 percent of African Americans 25 years and over were at minimum high school graduates, while 13 percent had attained a bachelor's degree or an advanced degree. The corresponding educational attainment rates were 34 and 4 percent in 1970 and 51 and 8 percent in 1980.

The proportion aged 25 to 34 who were college graduates remained unchanged for both African Americans and non-Hispanic Whites, at 12 and 25 percent, respectively. The proportion of African American male high school graduates who were attending college did not change significantly between 1973 and 1993. However, the comparable percentage for women rose significantly, so much so that the 1973 difference in enrollment rates between African American women and men disappeared by 1993.

In 1990, there were one and a half times as many African Americans enrolled in college (2 million) as there were in 1980. Between 1980 and 1990, African Americans made significant gains in both educational attainment and college enrollment. More African American women than African American men have completed college. Twelve percent of African American females and 11 percent of African American males 25 years old and over had at least a bachelor's degree in 1990.

Eleven percent of African Americans, compared with 22 percent of non-Hispanic Whites, had earned at least a bachelor's degree in 1990. The corresponding figures for 1980 were 8 percent and 17 percent, respectively.

In 1994, 13 percent of African American adults (25 years and over) had a bachelor's degree compared with 8 percent in 1980. Corresponding percentages for non-Hispanic Whites were 23 percent and 18 percent respectively. One-third of African Americans 18 to 24 years old and 42 percent of comparable non-Hispanic Whites were enrolled in college in 1993.

In 1993, differences in field of study by race and ethnicity were not large. Compared with non-Hispanic White degree holders, African American degree holders were more likely to have earned their highest degrees in business/management (24 percent for African Americans and 19 percent for non-Hispanic Whites). Yet for African Americans, a much larger proportion of those business/management degrees were at the associate/vocational level than for non-Hispanic Whites: 46 percent compared with 28 percent. Conversely, a significantly smaller proportion of African American business degree holders than non-Hispanic White business degree holders held master's degrees (5 percent and 16 percent, respectively). African Americans were more likely than non-Hispanic Whites to have earned their highest degrees in the social sciences and less likely to have earned that degree in engineering or the liberal arts/humanities.

According to the 1993 Survey of Income and Program Participation (SIPP), a college education does appear to pay off. The median earnings of 1991 year-round, full-time African American workers aged 25 and over who were only high school graduates was $18,400. But those with at least a bachelor's degree earned $32,360. In that year, about 58 percent of African American college students received financial aid toward their education and brightening future earnings prospects, receiving on average $2,527.

Labor Force Participation *(See Chart 1.10)*

Currently, a higher proportion of African American women than African American men are in the labor force; and there are now more African American females than African American males in the civilian labor force (apart from the military). Further, the number of African Americans employed in professional jobs, such as lawyers, doctors, and engineers, has increased.

More African American women (6 million) than men (5.4 million) were employed at the time of the 1990 census, and thus represented a larger percentage (53) of African American workers than did comparable males (47 percent). The Current Population Survey showed a smaller differential among African American workers in 1993, when 51 percent (6.2 million) were women and 49 percent (6.0 million) were men. The 1990 differential may thus in part reflect the higher undercount of African American men than women in the 1990 decennial census.

African Americans were less likely than non-Hispanic Whites to participate in the labor force in 1989. Of the 21 million African Americans 16 years old and over, 63 percent were in the labor force in 1989, 2 percentage points below the 65 percent rate for both the non-Hispanic White and total populations. Sixty-seven percent of African American males 16 years old and over were in the labor force in 1989 compared with 75 percent of non-Hispanic White males. The proportion of African American women in the labor force increased from 53 percent in 1979 to 60 percent in 1989. Their participation rate was higher than that for non-Hispanic White women.

The proportion of African American male adults aged 25 to 54 years who worked year-round, full-time, dropped from 62.1 percent in 1979 to 56.6 percent in 1992. Among comparable African American female adults aged 25 to 54, there was an increase of 8.3 percent between 1979 and 1992. In 1979, the figure was 39.9 percent; by 1992, the figure had risen to 48.2 percent.

In 1979, the African American unemployment rate was about twice that of non-Hispanic Whites. Ten years later, the 1989 unemployment rate among African Americans was more than twice that of non-Hispanic Whites, 13 percent and 5 percent, respectively.

In 1994, a higher proportion of non-Hispanic Whites (67 percent) than African Americans (63 percent) 16 years and over were in the civilian labor force. However, African Americans were more likely than non-Hispanic Whites to be unemployed. The civilian unemployment rate for African Americans was more than twice that of non-Hispanic Whites in both 1994 and 1980 (11 versus 5 percent and 14 versus 6 percent respectively). The unemployment rate for African Americans grew from 14 percent in 1980 to a high of 20 percent in 1983 (just after the end of the 1981–82 recession). It then dropped to 11 percent in 1989, increased to 13 percent in 1993, and dropped again to 11 percent in 1994. The unemployment rate for non-Hispanic Whites also fluctuated from a high of 9 percent in 1982 to a low of 4 percent in 1989. In 1994, 5 percent of all non-Hispanic White civilians in the labor force were unemployed.

Occupations *(See Charts 1.11 and 1.12)*

In 1990, proportionately fewer African American than non-Hispanic White men worked in manage-

rial and professional specialty jobs (14 percent versus 27 percent); relatively more African American men were operators, fabricators, and laborers (31 percent versus 19 percent) and held service jobs (19 percent compared with 9 percent). It was more common for African American women than for non-Hispanic White women to work in service jobs (28 percent versus 17 percent), but less likely for them to work either in managerial and professional specialty jobs (20 percent versus 29 percent) or in technical, sales, and administrative support jobs (38 percent versus 45 percent).

A smaller proportion of African American men than African American women were managers and professionals. Larger percentages of African American women also worked in technical, sales, and administrative support and in service occupations than did African American men.

However, a larger proportion of African American men than African American women were employed as operators, fabricators, and laborers; in precision production, craft, and repair jobs; and in farming, forestry, and fishing occupations.

In 1990, 22 percent of all African American managers and professionals were teachers. The majority of both African American male and African American female teachers taught in elementary schools.

Nearly three out of every ten African American females employed in technical, sales, and administrative support jobs were cashiers, secretaries, and typists. Half of African American females employed in service occupations were nursing aides, orderlies and attendants, cooks, janitors, and cleaners.

Thirty-one percent of African American males were operators, fabricators, and laborers. Of these males, 30

percent were truck drivers, assemblers, and stock handlers and baggers. Within service occupations, 45 percent of African American males were employed as janitors and cleaners or as cooks; and 12 percent as guards and police, except in public service.

Between 1987 and 1992, African American–owned businesses increased by 46 percent (from 424,165 to 620,912), and receipts grew from $19.8 billion to $32.2 billion, representing a 63 percent increase. In comparison to the national averages, all businesses showed an increase of 26 percent, from 13.7 million to 17.3 million businesses, with a receipt increase of 67 percent ($1.995 trillion to $3.324 trillion). That means that while African American–owned businesses grew at almost double the rate of the national average, the proceeds were equal to or just less than the average.

Fifty-four percent of all African American–owned businesses in 1992 were in the service industry; 47 percent of those were in business and personal services, and 14 percent in retail trade, the two accounting for 57 percent of all the service industry receipts.

Eleven percent of all African American–owned businesses (and 17 percent of the receipts) were based in California. New York was close behind with 8 percent of the businesses and 7 percent of the receipts. Texas, while it ranks just below New York with numbers of businesses (8 percent, but about 1,300 fewer actual storefronts), outranks New York in terms of total receipts—both come in at 7 percent of the total, though Texas claims $2.3 billion compared to New York's $2.2 billion.

Income *(See Charts 1.13 and 1.14)*

Family Income

*G*enerally, the median family incomes of African Americans have not grown significantly in recent decades. Part of this is attributable to the large number of African American families maintained by women with no husbands present, with the low incomes of these families contributing to the lower average. Between 1979 and 1989, the median family income for African Americans changed very little.

Among all African American families, the 1979 median family income was about $21,110, compared to the 1989 median income of $22,430. For those families that were maintained by women alone, the 1979 median income stood at $12,520, more than one-third less than the median income for African American married-couple families.

Several factors are reflected in the family median incomes, including family composition, the number of workers within a family, their educational attainments, and the jobs available. In 1989, one-third of African American families had only one worker, just over a third had two workers, and only a little more than one-eighth had three or more workers.

Between 1967 and 1990, African American families saw their median income rise 12 percent in real terms (constant 1990 dollars), from $19,080 to $21,420. Non-Hispanic White families experienced a similar real increase—$32,220 to $36,920, a 15 percent rise.

In 1990, African American median family income was 58 percent that of non-Hispanic White median family income, a gap statistically unchanged from 1967. Income gains, however, varied considerably among African Americans by family type.

African American married-couple families saw their real median income rise 47 percent over the period, from $22,910 to $33,780; in 1990 their income stood at 84 percent of comparable non-Hispanic White families, up from 68 percent in 1967. This reflects gains made by African American families with working wives and also the fact that those families comprise an increasing share of all African American married-couple families: 66 percent in 1990, up from 50 percent 23 years earlier.

Real median income of African American families maintained by women with no husband present remained (in 1990 dollars) virtually unchanged over the period: $11,800, in 1967, and $12,130 in 1990. They earned 62 percent of comparable non-Hispanic White families in 1990, no change from 1967.

By 1993, African American married-couple families with children had a median income of $36,670, about 12 percent higher than that of African American married-couple families without children ($32,810). Non-Hispanic White married-couple families with children had a median income of $48,630—33 percent higher than that of comparable African American families and 17 percent higher than that of non-Hispanic White married-couple families without children ($41,440). African American families maintained by women with children had a median income of only $10,380—a mere 28 percent of that for African American married-couple families with children ($36,670). Non-Hispanic White families had a median income almost twice that for all African American families in 1993 ($41,110 versus $21,550).

The 1993 median income for African American householders was $19,532, a drop from the figure of $23,430 in 1990. In comparison, non-Hispanic Whites had incomes of $32,960, Asian Pacific Americans $38,347, and Hispanic Americans $22,886. The real median income for all these groups was lower in 1993 than in 1989.

Wages or salary (including self-employment) constituted the only source of income in 22 percent of all African American families in 1993. Six percent received public assistance only, and an additional 1 percent received a combination that included public assistance. In contrast, wages or salary made up the only source of income in only 10 percent of non-Hispanic White

families in 1993. One percent received public assistance only, and an additional 0.2 percent received a combination including public assistance. Eighty-eight percent of non-Hispanic White and 65 percent of African American families had incomes from earnings combined with other sources (including, for example, Social Security, public assistance, retirement and survivor's benefits, interest, and dividends). Two percent of non-Hispanic White and 6 percent of African American families either had incomes not related to earnings or no income at all.

Individual Income

The median earnings of year-round, full-time workers rose in terms of dollars between 1979 and 1989, though in ratios of race and sex there was not a significant change. In 1991, African American men were still earning less than three-fourths that of their non-Hispanic White male counterparts ($22,080 compared to $30,270), and while African American women fared better, they were still only earning 90 cents to the dollar of non-Hispanic White females ($18,720 compared to $20,790).

The value of more education is most evident in the substantial earning differences between year-round, full-time workers with only a high school diploma and those with a bachelor's degree or greater. In 1993, the median earnings of African Americans 25 years old and over, who worked year-round, full-time, and had only a high school diploma, was $18,460, compared with $32,360 for those with at least a bachelor's degree. Only 15 percent of African American college graduates earned less than $20,000 compared with 55 percent of those with just a high school diploma. African American women with only a high school diploma who worked year-round, full-time had median earnings of $16,460, about 80 percent of the salaries earned by comparable African American men and 83 percent of the salaries earned by comparable non-Hispanic White women. Among college graduates, African American women earned 87 percent of the salaries earned by comparable African American men and 95 percent of comparable non-Hispanic White women. Among those with just a high school diploma, African American men earned 73 percent of what non-Hispanic White men earned; the ratio remained unchanged at 73 percent among the college graduates.

Marital Status *(See Chart 1.15)*

Today, both African American and non-Hispanic White families are less likely to contain a married couple. Such families comprised 56 percent of all African American families in 1980, but just 47 percent in 1992. The corresponding decline for non-Hispanic Whites was smaller, from 86 percent to 82 percent (1980 compared to 1992). Greater proportions of African Americans are postponing marriage or not marrying at all. Forty-four percent of African American men were never married in 1990, compared with 41 percent in 1980. For African American women, the figures were 38 percent and 34 percent, respectively. Since 1980, there has been a 27 percent increase in the number of young African American adults 15 years old and over who have never married. In 1990, a higher proportion of African American men (nearly 4 of every 10) than African American women (about 3 of every 10) were married. A larger proportion of African American women than African American men were separated. The proportion of divorced African American men increased from 6 percent in 1980 to 8 percent in 1990, while the proportion of divorced African American women increased from 9 percent to 11 percent. In addition, four times as many African American women as African American men were widowed.

Family Composition *(See Charts 1.16 and 1.17)*

Eighty-three percent of the seven million African American families in 1990 had at least one worker; one-half had two or more workers, 13 percent had three or more workers, and 17 percent had no workers. *Contrary to stereotypes, about three-fourths (77 percent) of single-parent families had at least one worker, while 30 percent had two or more.*

The number of African American households, especially female-headed African American households, has increased since 1980, in part because of the increase in divorce and separation rates. As a result, fewer African American children are being reared in two-parent households. Also, consistent with national trends, more African American men and women are choosing not to marry or electing to live alone. Also, African American families are not as large as they used to be. The average number of persons per family dropped from 3.7 persons in 1980 to 3.5 persons in 1990.

By 1990, children who were non-Hispanic African American (i.e., those African Americans who do not identify themseles as Hispanic) were the largest non-White group of children (14.7 percent). Among their characteristics were:

- Non-Hispanic African American children (3 percent) in two-parent families were about equally likely to live with a grandparent; 80 percent of non-Hispanic African American preschoolers lived in small families.
- The proportion of non-Hispanic African American adolescents in families with one to three children was 64 percent.

- Non-Hispanic African American children were one-half as likely as non-Hispanic White children to have a mother with a bachelor's degree.
- One in 20 non-Hispanic African American children had mothers with less than 9 years of education.
- Four in 10 non-Hispanic African American children living with their fathers had fathers who worked part-time or not at all.
- The proportion of children living with mothers whose mothers were full-time workers was 30 percent for non-Hispanic African Americans.
- The proportion of children living with mothers who were part-time workers was 41 percent for non-Hispanic African Americans.

The percentage of African American families maintained by women with no husband present more than doubled between 1970 and 1990. Much of this growth occurred between 1970 and 1980, when the proportion of such families climbed from 28 to 40 percent. High rates of marital separation and divorce, as well as a larger proportion of never-married women with children maintaining families, are factors for this rise.

Married-couple families have declined from 78 percent of all African American families in 1950 to 48 percent by 1991—a 30 percent drop. While declines also occurred among non-Hispanic Whites during the same period, the rate of decline was much less: from 88 percent to 83 percent, reflecting only a 5 percent drop in those 41 years.

As a consequence, fewer African American children under 18 years old lived with two parents. In

1960, about 2 in 3 (67 percent) lived with two parents; a little over one in three (36 percent) did in 1991. The respective figures for non-Hispanic White children are 91 and 79 percent.

Families maintained by women with no spouse present rose from 40 percent to 46 percent of African American families; the proportion maintained by men with no spouse rose from 4 percent to 7 percent (1980 compared to 1992).

The percent of custodial fathers for children of divorced families was 12 percent, smaller than that of African American custodial mothers, which was 27 percent in 1992.

By 1993, African American children in single-parent families were nearly three times as likely as non-Hispanic White children (46 percent versus 17 percent) to live in poverty. Among the 19.7 million African American children in 1993, 36 percent of them lived with both parents and 54 percent with their mothers only. In comparison, 70 percent of non-Hispanic White children lived in two-parent families, and 16 percent lived with their mother only.

Unmarried African American women in 1994 were also three times more likely to bear children than unmarried non-Hispanic White. Of all African American babies born in 1994, 66 percent were born to unmarried women, compared with 19 percent for non-Hispanic White women (women never married, widowed, or divorced at the survey date). About one in two never-married African American women had a baby present in their household in 1994.

More families were also being maintained by women without a husband among African Americans. The pro-

portion rose from 11 percent of all families in 1970 to 18 percent in 1994. They constituted 48 percent of African American families and 14 percent non-Hispanic White families in the latter year. Single parents accounted for almost two-thirds (65 percent) of all African American family groups with children present in 1994.

Also, single parents accounted for almost two-thirds (65 percent) of all African American family groups with children present, compared with 35 percent among Hispanic Americans and 25 percent among non-Hispanic Whites. In 1994, single fathers were twice as common among non-Hispanic Whites (16 percent of all non-Hispanic White single parents) as among African Americans (8 percent of all African American single parents). By 1994, over half of all African American children were living in female-headed households. This can be attributed to the rapid growth in the proportion of parents who have separated, who get divorced, or who were never married.

By 1994, less than one-half (47 percent) of all African American families were married couples, compared with 68 percent in 1970 and 56 percent in 1980. The increase in the proportion of African American families maintained by either a male or female with no spouse present was greater between 1970 and 1980 than it was between 1980 and 1994 (32 to 44 percent and 44 to 54 percent respectively). In 1970, 4 percent of all African American families were male-householder families with no spouse present, compared with 6 percent in 1994. This trend is occurring in both African American and non-Hispanic White families.

Poverty *(See Charts 1.18 and 1.19)*

More than one-quarter (27 percent) of African American families were living in poverty in 1989. (Families and unrelated individuals are classified as above or below the poverty level by comparing their total 1989 income to an income cutoff or "poverty threshold." The income cutoffs vary by family size, number of children, and age of the household or unrelated individuals.) In families where the householder worked, the rate declined to 16 percent and, if the householder worked full-time (that is, 35 hours or more per week), it declined to 12 percent, and was even lower—6 percent—when the householder worked full-time, year-round.

In 1990, the median duration of "poverty" was considerably longer for African Americans (5.8 months) than for Whites (4.1 months).

In 1992, 13 percent of African Americans worked their way out of poverty. Notably, however, exit rates have worsened for African Americans: 17 percent of those who were poor in 1990 escaped poverty in 1991. *In 1991, 16 percent of African Americans were chronically poor, much higher than the 3 percent for Whites. Of the chronically poor, 40 percent were African American.*

About 1 in 4 African American mothers of childbearing age (1.5 million) were AFDC (Aid to Families with Dependent Children) recipients, higher than the 1 in 14 corresponding White mothers (2.1 million). However, African American AFDC mothers did *not* have significantly more children than their White counterparts.

In 1990, African Americans were three times as likely as Whites to be poor in an average month. Twenty-nine percent of African American families were poor in 1990, down from 34 percent in 1967. For White families, the rate dropped from 9 percent to 8 percent over the period. Among African American families maintained by a woman with no husband present, 48 percent were poor in 1990, compared with 27 percent of comparable White families. African American–related children under 18 in families had a poverty rate of 44 percent; African Americans 65 and over had a rate of 34 percent. Overall, African American poverty rates improved only slightly between 1979 and 1989: from 29.5 percent to 29.2 percent.

Between 1990 and 1992, while one in four Americans as a whole experienced a lapse in health insurance coverage, more than one in three African Americans experienced such hardships.

By 1993, the percent of African Americans experiencing poverty had risen to 33.1 percent, close to three times higher than that for Whites (12.2). Nearly half (46 percent) of all poor African American persons were children under 18 years old. Among poor persons 15 years old and over, 35 percent of all African Americans and 42 percent of all non-Hispanic Whites worked. A similar proportion of poor African American men and women worked (35 percent), while among non-Hispanic Whites a larger proportion of men than women were working

poor (51 percent versus 36 percent). ("Working poor" are families and unrelated individuals who remain below the poverty level even though a member of the family or household is working.) However, there were more African American women (1.5 million) than African American men (0.8 million) among the working poor.

In 1993, about one in four African American mothers of childbearing age (1.5 million) were AFDC recipients, higher than the 7 percent of corresponding non-Hispanic White mothers (2.1 million). Despite these differences in recipiency rates, African American AFDC mothers did *not* have significantly more children than their non-Hispanic White counterparts.

In 1993, about 1 in 16, or 1.7 million, non-Hispanic White mothers of childbearing age received benefits from the Women, Infants, and Children (WIC) supplemental food program. This compares to 1 in 10, or 600,000, African American mothers receiving WIC. Despite the different WIC recipiency rates, African American and non-Hispanic White WIC mothers had about the same number of children.

In 1994, about one in three African American mothers of childbearing age were food stamp recipients (1.9 million) compared with one in nine for non-Hispanic White mothers (3.2 million).

Housing *(See Charts 1.20–1.23)*

In 1990, ten million of the nation's homes and rental units contained an African American householder. More than half (59 percent) of the nation's African American households lived in the central cities of metropolitan areas; another quarter (25 percent) resided in the suburbs. Nearly one in eight metro area householders (12 percent) were African American. This proportion was much higher in central cities (20 percent) than in suburbs (6 percent).

Most of them (8.5 million, or 85 percent) lived in a metropolitan area. New York City had the highest number of African American households (762,309) among metro areas in 1990, but Jackson, Mississippi, had the highest percentage of African American householders (37 percent).

Nationally, metro African American households contained a median of 2.50 persons, higher than the 2.23 in metro White households. African American households in central cities were smaller than those in the suburbs (2.42 versus 2.71 persons.) The corresponding medians for White households were lower (2.03 in central cities, 2.34 in the suburbs). Of the top 50 MAs, Nassau–Suffolk, New York (3.30), and Fort

Lauderdale–Hollywood–Pompano Beach, Florida (2.95), had the largest African American households.

In metro areas, African American–owned homes had a median value of $55,500, nearly 40 percent lower than that of homes owned by Whites ($91,700). The gap was largest in the Philadelphia–New Jersey metropolitan area, where the African American median home value was 68 percent lower than that of Whites. Among the top 50 African American metro areas, the most expensive African American–owned homes were in San Francisco, where the median value was $223,200.

Only four in ten African American "householders" were homeowners, much lower than the two in three metro White householders. In 1991, about three out of five African American householders were central city residents. About 43 percent were owners, with a median home value of $55,400. Seventy-two percent of African Americans residing in rural areas owned their own homes compared with 40 percent of urban African Americans. Inside metropolitan areas, 41 percent of African American householders were homeowners, compared with 59 percent of those outside metropolitan areas. Half of African American low-income renters lived in public or subsidized housing.

African American households were more than three times more likely than Whites to be living in crowded quarters. Households with more than one person per room are considered "crowded." Within MAs, African American households were more likely than White households to face this problem (10 percent versus 3 percent). Miami and Fort Lauderdale, where more than one in five African American households were crowded, led the top 50 MAs in congested living quarters.

In 1993, White households had a net worth of $45,740, about 10 times that of African American households, which had a net worth of $4,418.

Voter Turnout

African Americans throughout their history have experienced harsh discrimination and restrictions of their civil rights. After the Civil War, during the period of Reconstruction, the Fourteenth and Fifteenth Amendments were added to the U.S. Constitution to protect the voting rights of all male citizens, which for the first time included African Americans. For a period, African Americans actively participated in the political process, becoming appointed to such offices as state treasurer, state supreme court justice, superintendent of public instruction, secretary of state, lieutenant governor, mayor, Congressman, and other public offices. However, after the Compromise of 1877 and the demise of Reconstruction, the civil rights of African Americans were again severely abrogated. To bypass the constitutional protections, Whites in the South implemented such practices as the "grandfather clause," poll taxes, Jim Crow laws, reading comprehension tests, and property eligibility requirements. The grandfather clause, introduced during the 1880s, stated that only persons whose grandparents had voted could vote. This deliberately excluded the majority of African Americans. Because of these and other discriminatory and racist laws, African Americans were denied the same rights and protections as other citizens of the United States. The U.S. Supreme Court finally declared the grandfather clause to be unconstitutional in 1915. It was not until the 1960s, with the Voting Rights Act of 1965, that Congress made a concerted effort to protect the voting rights of African Americans and to enhance their participation in the political process as well.

Today, the legacy of discrimination remains. Voter turnout for Whites in 1994 congressional elections was 47 percent, compared with 37 percent for African Americans. Overall turnout was 45 percent. In the November 1994 election, 58.3 percent of all African Americans of voting age were registered, with 37 percent reporting that they had voted. Sixty-three percent did not vote. Among those not voting, 33.9 were registered but did not vote. Less than one in ten (7.9 percent) of those not voting were not U.S. citizens.

On the positive side, since the 1980s, more African Americans are coming of age and both becoming eligible to vote and registering their political affiliation. The African American voting-age population increased by 3.3 million people between 1980 (17.1 million) and 1990 (20.4 million). Today, major voter participation organizations and many African American civil rights organizations are making concerted efforts to enhance the participation of African Americans in the political process and other aspects of civic life.

Agriculture

Just 1.5 percent of all farm owners are African American, according to the 1992 Census of Agriculture. Ninety-five percent of the entire nation's African American–owned farms are located in the South. The majority of these farms are dedicated to producing grain, raising livestock, and growing tobacco.

Map 1.1 African Americans by State, 1990

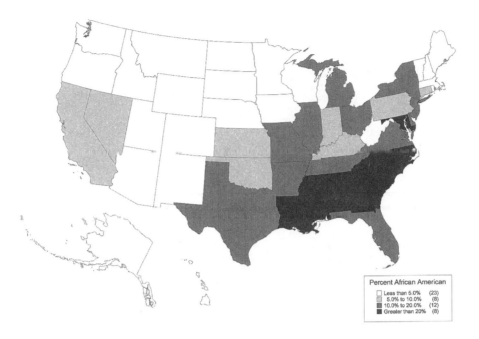

Percent African American
- Less than 5.0%   (23)
- 5.0% to 10.0%   (8)
- 10.0% to 20.0%   (12)
- Greater than 20%   (8)

Map 1.2 African Americans by County, 1990

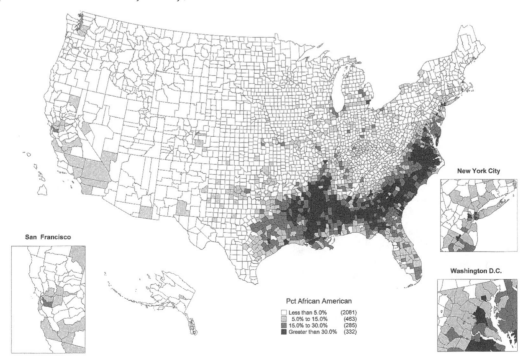

New York City

San Francisco

Washington D.C.

Pct African American
- Less than 5.0%   (2061)
- 5.0% to 15.0%   (463)
- 15.0% to 30.0%   (285)
- Greater than 30.0%   (332)

Map 1.3 African Immigrant Americans by County, 1990

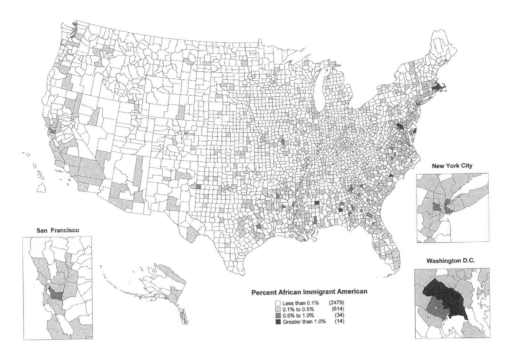

Map 1.4 West Indian Americans by County, 1990

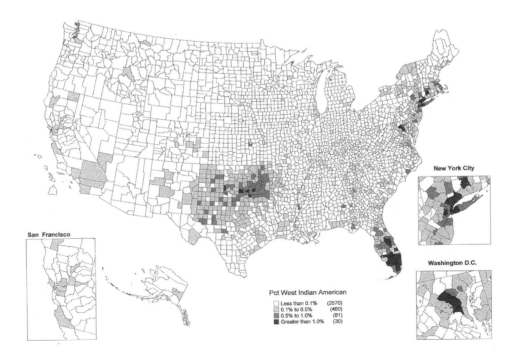

Chart 1.1 African American Population, 1900–1994 (Millions)

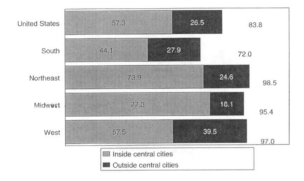

Note: Numbers in bars represent African Americans as a percent of the total population.

Chart 1.2 States with an African American Population of One Million or More, 1990 (Thousands)

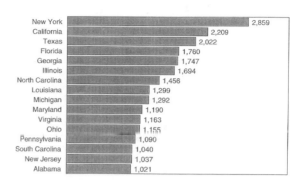

Chart 1.3 African American Population in Metropolitan Areas by Region, 1990 (Percent)

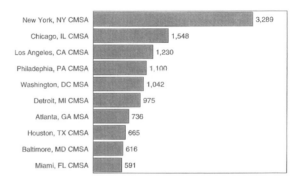

Chart 1.4 Ten Largest African American Metropolitan Statistical Areas, 1990 (Thousands)

Chart 1.5 Top Ten Cities with the Largest African American Population, 1990 (Thousands)

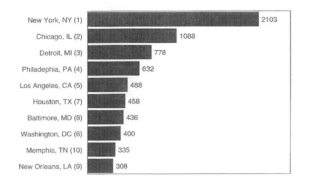

Chart 1.6 Resident African American Population by Age, 1990 (Percent)

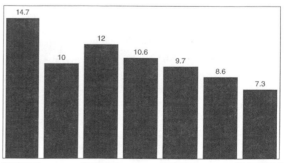

Chart 1.7 Age and Sex of the African American Population, 1990 (Percent)

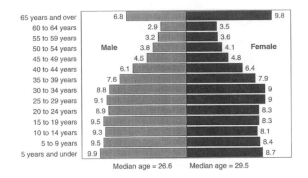

Chart 1.8 African American Population 65 Years and Over by Sex, 1990 (Percent)

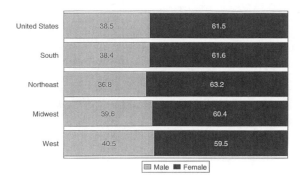

Chart 1.9 African American and Non-Hispanic White Educational Attainment by Sex, 1990 (Percent, 25 years and older)

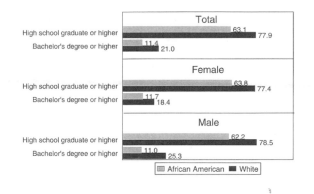

Chart 1.10 African American and Non-Hispanic White Labor Force Participation Rates by Sex, 1990 (Percent, 16 years and older)

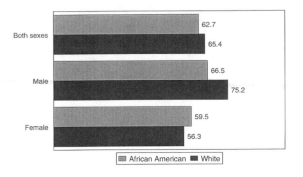

Chart 1.11 African American Occupational Distribution by Sex, 1990 (Percent, 16 years and older)

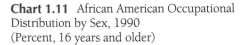
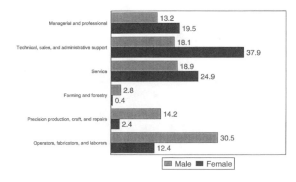

Chart 1.12 Selected Occupational Groups of African Americans by Sex, 1990 (Thousands)

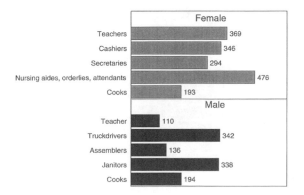

Chart 1.13 Median African American Income by Family Composition, 1979 and 1989 (Thousands)

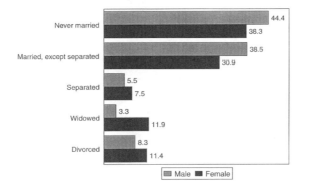

Chart 1.14 Median Earnings for African Americans and Whites—Year-Round, Full-Time Workers by Sex, 1979 and 1989 (Thousands)

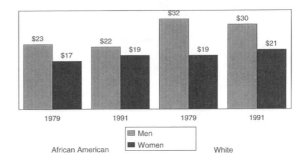

Chart 1.15 African American Marital Status by Sex, 1990 (Percent, 15 years and older)

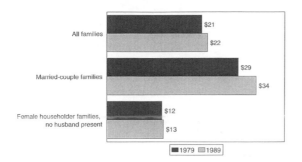

Chart 1.16 African American and non-Hispanic White Family Composition, 1990 (Percent)

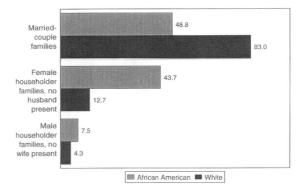

Chart 1.17 Changes in African American Family Composition, 1950–1991 (Percent)

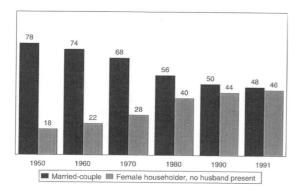

Chart 1.18 Poverty Rates for African American Persons and Families, 1989 (Percent)

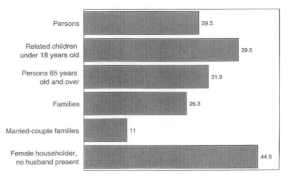

Chart 1.19 African Americans and Whites Below the
Poverty Level, 1991 (Percent)

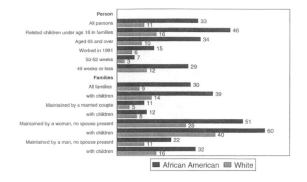

Chart 1.20 African American and White Housing
Tenures, 1990 (Percent)

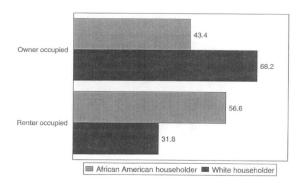

Chart 1.21 African American and White Home
Ownership, 1990 (Percent)

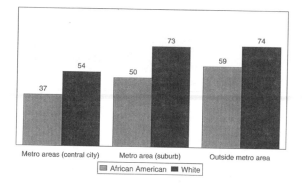

Chart 1.22 African American and White Home
Values, 1990 (Thousands)

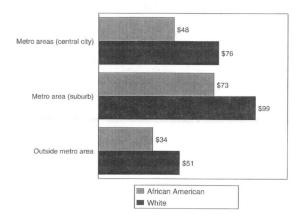

Chart 1.23 Crowded Living Conditions for African
Americans and Whites, 1990 (Percent of households
with more than one person per room)

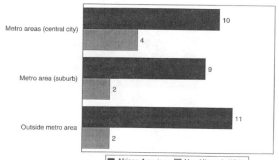

Chapter 2

Asian Pacific Americans

Introduction (See Chart 2.1)

More than any current "racial" group in the United States, Asian Pacific Americans are affected by immigration. Historically, the ebbs and flows of Asian Pacific American immigration have been chiefly responsible for the size and diversity of the Asian Pacific American populations. While immigration between 1850 and 1965 came in spurts and stops, the majority of Asian Pacific American immigration occurred after the passage of the Immigration and Nationality Act Amendments of 1965. This law and its successors caused an amazing growth of the Asian Pacific American population. Between 1960 and 1990 the Asian Pacific American population increased 700 percent; between 1970 and 1990 the population more than tripled, and between 1980 and 1990 it doubled.

By 1994, the Asian Pacific American population had increased 880 percent since 1960. In 1990, there were 7,273,662 Asian Pacific American individuals, represented by 31 diverse groups, constituting nearly 3 percent of all Americans. *Asian Americans include, but are not limited to, Chinese, Filipinos, Koreans, Asian Indians, Japanese, Vietnamese, Cambodians, Laotians, Hmong, and Thai. Pacific Islanders include Hawaiians, Samoans, Guamanians, and Tongans, among others.*

The dramatic increase in population in part is the result of increased immigration from China, India, Korea, the Philippines, and other Asian and Pacific Island areas following the adoption of the Immigration Act of 1965. In addition to immigration and natural increase, part of the growth during the 1970s reflects changes in the census race definition to include more groups, as well as improvements in review and verification procedures in the 1990 census.

Laws Affecting Asian Immigration

In comparison to the record high percentages of immigration during the 1980s, Asian Pacific Americans never reached more than one-quarter of 1 percent of the total U.S. population before 1940, despite several waves of immigration from Asian and Pacific countries. Racist legislation, which effectively minimized Asian immigration, was repeatedly passed and amended so as to bar Asians of various nationalities and classes from entering the United States because it was feared that they would compete with "native" non-Hispanic White workers for jobs and resources.

Chinese Americans were the first Asian immigrants to be affected by these discriminatory laws. In 1853, shortly after 20,000 Chinese immigrants arrived (upon hearing news about the California Gold Rush), they were slapped with a Foreign Miners' Tax. That year, Chinese immigration would drop to less than 5,000.

Although by 1870 Congress amended the 1790 Naturalization Act that had limited citizenship through naturalization to "free white persons" (so as to extend the rights of citizenship to aliens of African ancestry, following the Emancipation Proclamation), foreign-born Asian Americans would be defined from 1870 on as "aliens ineligible for citizenship." They would repeatedly be barred from entering the United States in substantial numbers, on the basis of this interpretation of the 1790 Naturalization Act.

By 1882, alarmed by the number of Chinese in California, Congress passed the Chinese Exclusion Act of 1882 (repealed only in 1943), which excluded most Chinese from entering the United States. The law suspended Chinese labor immigration for ten years. In 1892 the Geary Act extended these exclusion laws another decade. In 1902, exclusion of Chinese immigrants was extended indefinitely. The Exclusion Act would be the first immigration law directed against a specific ethnic group on the basis of nationality.

The exclusion of Chinese immigrants, however, did not end Asian immigration altogether. Shortly after the passage of the Chinese Exclusion Act, Japanese immigrants began arriving in the United States. In time, they would make up the major labor force of both Hawaii's agricultural plantation economy and California's agricultural fields. By 1908, there were 55,000 Japanese Americans on the mainland, primarily in California, and about 150,000 on the Hawaiian islands. Between 1908 and 1924, despite a gentleman's agreement between the United States and Japan that limited the greater majority of Japanese American laborers from emigrating to the United States, another 168,000 Japanese immigrants arrived there. Many of these were students studying abroad and "picture brides" (ordered by mail) of Japanese immigrants.

In 1917, Congress created a "barred zone," whereby natives of China, South and Southeast Asia, the Asian part of Russia, Afghanistan, Iran, part of Arabia, and those Pacific and Southeast Asian Islands not owned by the United States were declared inadmissible simply because they were members of groups deemed "ineligible for citizenship." Japan, for diplomatic reasons, was not included in the barred zone. Filipinos and some Samoans, because they were U.S. nationals, were allowed admission in limited numbers, although they could not be naturalized.

The Johnson-Reed Act of 1924 codified racial discrimination and exclusion. It set a yearly limit of 150,000 on immigrants from outside the Western Hemisphere and then divided the 150,000 into quotas based on a country's share of the total U.S. population as of 1920 (later this was pushed back to 1890, so as to exclude more Eastern and Southern Europeans). Immigration was limited for each nationality group to only 2 percent of the U.S. residents of that nationality living in the United States in 1890. For all intents and purposes, the 1924 act restricted legal immigration to peoples from the Western Hemisphere. Since aliens from the Western Hemisphere were exempted from the quota and classified as nonquota immigrants, many more immigrants from Western Europe could arrive legally in the United States. The national origins system favored the descendants of those who had been here the longest—primarily the British and Northern Europeans. The act also contained a section of the law that excluded immigrants who were ineligible to become citizens, which effectively barred people of color. Japanese were added to the barred list of 1917. A token annual quota of 100 was allowed for each country in Asia. These slots were in fact reserved for Whites born in Asia.

By 1934, the Tydings-McDuffie Act would close the small door of immigration available to Filipino nationals of the United States. By guaranteeing future Philippine independence, the act repealed Filipino status as nationals to persons coming from an inde-

pendent nation, thereby placing Filipino immigrants under the same laws as other groups from Asia. Only a token 50 persons per year would be allowed to enter the United States after the passage of the act. Filipino "deportation" was also encouraged by the passage of laws that paid, with public funds, for the permanent return of Filipino immigrants to the Philippines.

Beginning with World War II, immigration policy directed toward Asian Pacific Americans changed markedly. In 1943, Congress repealed the Chinese Exclusion Act of 1882. And in 1946, Congress extended the privilege of naturalization to Filipinos and "persons of races indigenous to India." President Truman raised the Filipino quota to a token 100 by proclamation. In the same year, Congress approved a law that allowed Chinese wives of American citizens to enter on a nonquota basis. In 1950, the law was liberalized and extended to give the same rights to spouses and minor children of members of the armed forces. By 1952, these rights were extended to Japanese Americans and to other Asian Americans as well.

The McCarran-Walter Immigration and Nationality Act of 1952 eliminated racial barriers to naturalization and thereby to immigration. Specifically, the law overturned the Naturalization Act of 1790 and its amendment in 1870. The new law, however, still retained most of the quota preferences of the 1924 law. While it abolished the 1917 act's Asiatic barred zone, the law created a new restrictive zone called "the Asia-Pacific triangle." The triangle consisted of countries from India to Japan, and embraced all the Pacific islands north of Australia and New Zealand. A maximum of 2,000 were allowed to immigrate yearly. For the 19 nations within the triangle, each was allotted a percentage of the 2,000. Asians were now eligible to enter the United States as immigrants, though their numbers, like those of Southern Europeans, were kept low.

The Immigration and Nationality Act Amendments of 1965 undid this pattern. Passed during a period of optimism and amid the civil rights revolution, the law went far toward undoing many of the racial biases of the 1924 Immigration Act. For the first time the new amendment applied a limit of immigration on peoples of the Western Hemisphere. Of the 290,000 immigrants who came under the law's quota restriction, only 120,000 could be from the Western Hemisphere. The new bill abandoned all race-based immigration restrictions. The dominating principle was family reunification. Eighty percent of numerically limited visas were reserved for close relatives of American citizens or residents. In addition, a substantial number of immediate relatives of

U.S. citizens, refugees, and special immigrants were no longer subject to the numerical cap.

Senator Robert F. Kennedy said about the 1965 law that the number of Asian Pacific American immigrants "to be expected from the Asia-Pacific triangle would be approximately five thousand." The 1965 amendments, however, had a major loophole. With a goal of "family reunification," parents, spouses, and minor children of any adult U.S. citizen—in other words, the immediate relatives of U.S. citizens—could enter without being subject to numerical restrictions.

As a result of this legal opportunity, many immigrants subsequently arrived in the United States without being subject to the numerical limitations under the first through sixth preferences, which are the system of preferences that determine primarily eligibility for admission as an immigrant under the numerical limitations set by federal immigration laws. In the 1990s, immediate relatives remained a substantial proportion of immigration. For example, in 1993, among the 708,394 immigrants who were admitted into the United States, 251,647 of these were immediate relatives of U.S. citizens (amounting to 35 percent of the total immigrants).

The 1986 Immigration Reform and Control Act (IRCA) was a law passed to halt illegal immigration. Any undocumented immigrant who entered the United States before 1982 and had lived here continuously since then was granted amnesty. In turn, employers who hired undocumented aliens were now subject to fines, and, if a pattern of hiring undocumented aliens could be found, the employers were given jail sentences as well. IRCA offered amnesty to an estimated 3.7 million undocumented immigrants (2.6 million of whom accepted amnesty). Few Asian Pacific American immigrants were affected directly by the act.

The Immigration Act of 1990 increased legal immigration even further and had a profound effect on Asian immigration. Designed to overcome the 1965 law's emphasis on family reunification, the 1990 law was drafted with the idea of supplying skilled workers and needed capital (there were 10,000 visas for those willing to invest $1 million in a new business that employed at least ten workers). The law raised to 140,000 the number of immigrants who could be admitted on the basis of their job skills or the special contributions they offered. The law increased the average, previous immigration levels by 35 percent each year. Skilled workers and their families got roughly 120,000 visas; the unskilled, 10,000. The final 10,000 visas were reserved for people willing to invest $1 million in the United States. The law also had a "lottery" that allows about 40,000 winners to emigrate each year, from a pool of about 1.4 million applicants.

Since the 1940s, refugees from Asia have been able to take advantage of the passage of refugee laws shaped mainly by Cold War policy, as well as the 1965 amendments. In 1948 the first of two Displaced Persons Acts was passed. Under its provisions, *displaced persons* were defined as: those who had been victims of fascist and totalitarian regimes; who were considered refugees, persecuted for reasons of race, religion, nationality, or political opinion; or who were deported or obliged to leave their country of nationality or place of former habitual residence. Persons from China, Korea, and other nations came to the U.S. through this provision. In 1980, the Refugee Act of 1980 changed this Cold War bias. A refugee was now more broadly defined as someone who was unable or unwilling to return to his country because of a well-founded fear of persecution on account of race, religion, nationality, membership in a particular social group, or political opinion. As a result of the liberalization of refugee laws, and because of the 1965 amendment, in addition to the impact of events in Southeast Asia during the 1970s and 1980s and the recent crackdown on mainland Chinese students, many refugees have come to the United States from Southeast Asia and from China. Between 1980 and 1991, 327,183 Vietnamese came as refugees to the United States, while more recently, after the passage of the Chinese Student Protection Act of 1992, 48,212 students became legal immigrants between 1992 and 1993.

As a result of changes brought about by immigration laws, we have seen an overall dramatic rise in the number of immigrants from Asia and a general downward trend of immigration from Europe. In the 1950s, 53 percent of immigrants came from Europe and just 6 percent from Asia. By contrast, in the 1980s, only 11 percent came from Europe; most of the rest were evenly split between Asians and Hispanics. Asians settled mainly in California and New York; Hispanics settled throughout the United States.

Immigration *(See Charts 2.2 and 2.3)*

In 1820, precisely six Asian immigrants to the United States were recorded. With the news of the discovery of gold in California, immigration increased substantially between 1851 and 1860.

During those years, 41,397 Chinese immigrants arrived. Even with this substantial number, Asian immigrants only constituted a small percentage of the overall immigration during that decade (1.6 percent). Prior to the growth experienced after World War II, the period between 1871 and 1880 evidenced the greatest flow of Chinese immigrants (123,201), a flow halted by the 1882 Chinese Exclusion Act. The period between 1901 and 1910 saw the peak years of Japanese immigration (129,797), restricted by the Gentleman's Agreement of 1907; Asian Indian immigration (4,713); and Korean immigration (7,697), stemmed by the 1917 Law and the 1924 Immigration Act. Filipino immigrants, arriving as nationals, peaked in their immigration in the period between 1921 and 1930 (54,747), effectively barred by the Tydings-McDuffie Act of 1934.

Between 1930 and 1960, few Asian immigrants entered the United States. Even with the passage of the 1965 law, many of its enactments did not go into effect until 1968 and 1969, thereby in effect producing a demographic impact only after the late 1960s.

By the 1970s, though, substantial Asian immigration began. In that decade Asian immigration totaled 1,586,140; it was followed in the 1980s with 2,817,391, and, more recently (between 1991 and 1994), with 1,356,447 individuals. During the 1980s, Chinese, Asian Indian, Korean, Filipino, and Vietnamese immigrants all numbered over a quarter million.

Since 1988, the number of Chinese immigrants has substantially increased in the United States, with a peak of 65,552 in 1993. Japanese immigrants between 1960 and 1992 numbered below 6,000 each year, but more recently (1992 through 1994), they have grown in number. In 1992, a record 10,975 Japanese immigrants arrived in the United States. Among Filipinos, there has been a gradual and substantial rise each year in the number of immigrants to the United States. In 1960, only 2,954 Filipino immigrants were admitted. By 1990, Filipino immigrants reached an all-time yearly high of 64,756 individuals. Since then, there has been a small decline in their numbers. For Korean immigrants, large-scale immigration began in the late 1970s, peaking in 1987 (35,849), and declining to 15,985 in 1994. Since the Los Angeles Riots, yearly immigration has declined by over 10,000 per year. Asian Indian immigration gradually rose from 1970 to 1990. In 1991, Asian Indian immigration rose dramatically to 45,064. Since that time, immigration has declined somewhat (34,873 in 1994). Among Viet-

namese immigrants, peaks in immigration flows coincide with forced departures from Vietnam during or after the Vietnam War. In 1978, 88,543 Vietnamese immigrants, primarily refugee "boat people," fleeing on flimsy and overcrowded small boats, arrived in the United States. Subsequently, in 1982, with further crackdowns on ethnic Chinese Vietnamese, another 72,553 arrived. Since that time, another peak occurred in 1992 (77,726). The 1992 peak was due partly to the wholesale immigration from Vietnam of Amerasian children (children fathered on Vietnamese mothers by American service members). Since then, Vietnamese immigration has declined somewhat (41,344 in 1994).

Immigration has contributed heavily to the growth of the Asian American population in the past two decades, though the percentages who are foreign-born differ considerably among groups. By 1990, foreign-born Asian Pacific Americans constituted 68.2 percent of all Asian Pacific Americans. Because only 6.2 percent of the overall American population was foreign-born in 1990, *Asian Pacific Americans were 11 times more likely to be foreign-born than the general population.* In descending order, the population rankings of the foreign-born among Asian Pacific American ethnic groups were: Laotian American (93.9 percent), Cambodian American (93.7 percent), Vietnamese American (90.4 percent), Thai American (82.1 percent), Korean American (81.9 percent), Tongan American (74.7 percent), Asian Indian American (70.4 percent), Filipino American (64.7 percent), Chinese American (63.3 percent), Samoan American (35.5 percent), and Japanese American (28.4 percent).

The 1990 U.S. census counted 6,908,638 Asian Americans, not including Pacific Islanders— a 99 percent increase over the 1980 census count of 3,455,847. The largest proportions of Asian Americans were Chinese (24 percent) and Filipino (20 percent), followed by Japanese (12 percent). Newer immigrant groups, such as Laotian, Cambodian, Thai, and Hmong, each accounted for 2 percent or less of the Asian Americans in the United States.

The IndoChina Migration and Refugee Assistance Act of 1975 established a program of resettlement for refugees who fled Cambodia and Vietnam. One year later, the Immigration Act of 1976 made Laotians eligible for the same refugee resettlement programs. Seventy-five percent or more of the Vietnamese-born, Cambodian-born, and Laotian-born entered the country since 1975.

Population Growth *(See Charts 2.4 and 2.5)*

In March 1994, the Asian Pacific American population in the United States was estimated at 8.8 million, up from 7.3 million in 1990. In both 1994 and 1990, this population accounted for about 3 percent of America's population. In March 1991, the Asian Pacific American population in the United States was just over 7 million—still about 3 percent of the nation's total. Since 1990, the Asian Pacific American population has grown by an average of 4.5 percent per year. Eighty-six percent of the growth is attributable to immigration; the remainder was due to natural increase (births over deaths).

The Asian Pacific American population is rather heterogeneous, with differences in language, culture, and recency of immigration. The 1990 census provided population totals for 30 Asian groups and 21 Pacific Islander groups. Ninety-five percent were Asian Americans, including (but not limited to) Chinese, Filipino, Japanese, Korean, and Vietnamese, while the remaining 5 percent were Pacific Islanders, including Hawaiians, Samoans, Guamanians, and Tongans. The socioeconomic characteristics of the groups are quite varied; so too is the length of their presence in the United States. Several of the Asian American groups, such as Chinese and Japanese, have been in this country for generations, while

relatively few of the Pacific Islanders are foreign-born. Hawaiians, of course, are native to the United States (the Hawaiian Kingdom was annexed by the United States in 1898, and the islands became a state in 1959).

By the year 2000, Asian Pacific Americans are projected to reach 12.1 million and to represent 4.3 percent of America's population. Until the year 2000, 75 percent of the Asian Pacific American population growth will be attributable to immigration. By the year 2050, the Asian Pacific American population will likely have increased five times its size from 1995. By then, it will comprise 10 percent of the total U.S. population.

Regionally, the western states, and California in particular, will continue to be the favorite locations of Asian Pacific Americans. Between 1993 and 2020, there will be an increase in the western Asian Pacific American population by 8 million persons. By the year 2000, 40.5 percent of all Asian Pacific Americans will live in California, as compared to 40 percent in 1995 and 39.1 percent in 1990. By the year 2000, California is projected to have almost ten million Asian Pacific Americans. By 2020, Texas and New York will each have more than one million Asian Pacific Americans.

Regional Dispersion

In 1990, Asian Pacific Americans were more likely than non-Hispanic Whites to reside in metropolitan areas (95 percent compared to 75 percent). Similar proportions (about 53 percent) resided in the suburbs of metropolitan areas. The proportion of Asian Pacific Americans living in central cities was almost twice that of non-Hispanic Whites.

In 1990, about one-half (49 percent) of the nation's Asian Pacific American households lived in central cities of metropolitan areas; another 45 percent resided in the suburbs. Nationally, 3 percent of metro households were Asian Pacific American.

Regionally, as of 1994, Asian Pacific Americans were most likely to live in the West. According to the March 1994 Current Population Survey, six out of every ten Asian Pacific Americans lived in the West, accounting for 8 percent of the total population in the West (in comparison, 54 percent of the Asian Pacific American population lived in the West in 1990).

Asian Pacific Americans are, by and large, heavily concentrated on the western and eastern seaboards of

the United States. More than half the nation's Asian Pacific Americans live in the West, where their share of the population, 7.7 percent, is now higher than the percentage of African Americans. They also live in metropolitan areas, with disproportionately more living in central cities as compared to non-Hispanic Whites.

Map 2-1 shows the percent distribution of Asian Pacific Americans by *state* in 1990. The ten states with the largest 1990 Asian Pacific American populations, in descending order, were: California, New York, Hawaii, Texas, Illinois, New Jersey, Washington, Virginia, Florida, and Massachusetts. These states were home to 5,769,651 Asian Pacific Americans, and accounted for close to 80 percent of the total Asian Pacific American population. With the exception of Illinois and Washington, Asian Pacific American populations in most of these states more than doubled between 1980 and 1990. Most of this increase was attributable to immigration. Among the top ten states, immigration accounted for 79.2 percent of the total Asian Pacific American population.

Approximately 66 percent of Asian Pacific Americans lived in just five states—California, New York, Hawaii, Texas, and Illinois. The Asian Pacific American population was highly concentrated in California, New York, and Hawaii. Thirteen states had Asian Pacific American populations surpassing 100,000 in 1990 (Washington, California, Hawaii, Texas, Illinois, Michigan, New York, Massachusetts, Pennsylvania, New Jersey, Maryland, Virginia, and Florida). California ranked first with 2.8 million Asian Pacific American persons, followed by New York (694,000) and Hawaii (685,000). About 58 percent of the total Asian Pacific American population lived in these three states. In one state—Hawaii—the Asian Pacific American population was the largest racial group in the state.

By contrast with the state map, Map 2-2 illustrates the percent concentration by *county* for Asian Pacific Americans in the United States in 1990. The map clearly shows that most Asian Pacific Americans reside in the western region or the northeast region of the United States. The map also shows that Asian Pacific Americans are heavily concentrated in the major metropolitan areas throughout the United States. The western region, including Hawaii, accounted for 58.5 percent of all Asian Pacific Americans, while the northeast region accounted for 17.3 percent. Only 10.3 percent and 13.8 percent of Asian Pacific Americans settled in the Midwest and South respectively.

In each state, Asian Pacific Americans were distributed differentially by ethnic group. In California, Filipino Americans were the most numerous (731,685), followed closely by Chinese Americans (704,850). In New York, Chinese Americans were first in size (284,144), followed by Asian Indian Americans (140,985). In Hawaii, a state with tremendous Asian Pacific American ethnic diversity, Japanese Americans numbered 247,486, constituting 22.3 percent of the state population. Second in population size were Filipino Americans, with 168,682, making them 15.2 percent of the state population. In Texas, Vietnamese Americans were the largest group (69,634), followed by Chinese Americans with 63,232. In Illinois, the largest Asian Pacific American group is Filipino Americans, with 64,224, closely followed by Asian Indian Americans with 64,200. In New Jersey, Asian Indian Americans were the largest group (79,440), representing 1 percent of the state's population; second were Chinese Americans (59,084). In Washington, Virginia, and Florida, Filipino Americans were the largest group, with Japanese Americans being the second largest in Washington,

Korean Americans in Virginia, and Asian Indian Americans in Florida. In Massachusetts, Chinese Americans were the largest population with 53,792, followed by Asian Indian Americans with 19,719.

The distribution of Asian Pacific Americans in the top ten cities with the largest Asian Pacific American populations showed the typical bicoastal pattern and the regional concentration in Chicago and in Houston. According to the 1990 Summary Tape File 1C (STF1C), Asian Pacific Americans represented 28 percent of San Francisco's population, 19 percent of San Jose (California), 11 percent of San Diego, 9 percent of Los Angeles, 7 percent of New York City, and 5 percent of Boston. These cities were among the 20 largest in the United States. The top ten cities with the largest Asian Pacific American population were, by descending order: New York City, Los Angeles, Honolulu, San Francisco, San Jose, San Diego, Chicago, Houston, Seattle, and Long Beach, California.

Among counties in the United States, Los Angeles County had the largest Asian Pacific American population (954,485), followed by Honolulu County; Queens County, New York; Santa Clara County, California; Orange County, California; San Francisco County; San Diego County; Alameda County, California; Cook County, Illinois; and Kings County, New York. Among these counties, the three with the largest Asian Pacific American percentage concentration were Honolulu (63 percent); San Francisco (29.1 percent); and Santa Clara, California (17.5 percent). Among the top ten counties, six of these counties were in California, while seven out of ten were in the West.

According to the Summary Tape File 3C, the *counties* and *cities* with the largest population of a specific Asian Pacific American ethnic group were as follows: Chinese American (Los Angeles County; New York City); Filipino American (Los Angeles County and City); Japanese American (Honolulu County and City); Asian Indian American (Queens County, New York; New York City); Korean American (Los Angeles County and City); Vietnamese American (Orange County, California; San Jose City, California); Hawaiian American (Honolulu County and City); Laotian American (Fresno County and City, California); Cambodian American (Los Angeles County; Long Beach City); Thai American (Los Angeles County and City); Hmong American (Fresno County and City); Guamanian American (Los Angeles County; San Diego City); Samoan American (Honolulu County and City); Tongan American (Salt Lake County and City).

Age Distribution

The Asian Pacific American populations had a median age of 32.4 years in 1994, younger than the national median of 34 years. In 1992, 30 percent of the Asian Pacific American population was under 18 years of age, compared to the national average of 25 percent, and only 6 percent of Asian Americans were 65 years old and older compared with 13 percent for the total population.

Japanese Americans were the eldest of the Asian American populations with a median age of 36 years, in part because fewer Japanese Americans were foreign-born. Hmong Americans and Cambodian Americans, with their large proportions of recent immigrants (many forced out of their homelands by political strife), were the youngest Asian Americans, with a median age of 13 years and 19 years, respectively. Immigrant populations tend to have much higher birth rates than native populations (often for cultural or practical reasons, such as high infant mortality in their homelands).

According to the 1992 March Current Population Survey, Asian Pacific Americans had the highest proportion of persons of working age. Sixty-five percent of Asian Pacific Americans were between the ages of 18 and 64, as compared to 61 percent among non-Hispanic Whites, 60 percent among Hispanic Americans, 59 percent among African Americans, and 58 percent among Native Americans (who often have a shorter life span).

Asian Pacific American females had a median age of 31.1 years while males had a median age of 29 years. Just over half (51.2 percent) of Asian Pacific Americans were female, while 48.8 percent were male.

Disparities in the median age appear when comparing the U.S.-born general population and the U.S.-born Asian Pacific American population. While the general population in 1990 had a median age of 32.5 among U.S.-born, Asian Pacific Americans had a median age of only 15.8 among the U.S.-born. With the exception of Japanese Americans, the median ages of the selected Asian Pacific American groups among the U.S.-born are markedly lower than among the general population. These lower figures reflect the youthful population structure of immigrant Asian Pacific Americans. For example, among the U.S.-born Asian Indian Americans, the median was 8.8 years. Among Korean Americans, the median age was

nine. The lowest median age among U.S.-born Asian Pacific Americans was among Cambodian Americans, with a median age of 4.7 years.

Most Asian Pacific Americans, even among the foreign-born, are youthful, with the general age being lower than that of the general population. Many of the Asian Pacific American immigrants have arrived since 1980, and among that population, they tend to be more youthful than their cohorts who arrived prior to 1980. Also, most of the foreign-born remain non-naturalized (59 percent). Those who are not naturalized tend to be older than those who are, though only slightly (35.7 as compared to 35 years). The Hmong American population has the highest proportion of persons not naturalized (90 percent).

The elderly constituted 6 percent of the Asian Pacific American population in 1990 and could reach 16 percent of this group in 2050.

Sex ratio imbalances among Asian Pacific American groups were highest among Pakistani Americans, Thai Americans, Korean Americans, and Japanese Americans. Among Thai Americans and Pakistani Americans, there were more males than females, while among Korean Americans and Japanese Americans, there were more females than males. For Pakistani Americans, this may result from the large influx of professionals from Pakistan, while for Korean Americans and for Japanese Americans, much of the sex imbalance is attributable to the longer life expectancy of females as compared to males, together with more elderly immigrant females arriving among Korean Americans, and the presence of wives of U.S. service members among Filipino Americans, Korean Americans, and Japanese Americans.

Elderly

The elderly (65 years of age and older) constituted 6 percent of the Asian Pacific American population in 1990 and could reach 16 percent of this group in 2050.

In 1990, of the 31 million elderly people of all races, 454,000 were Asian Pacific American. By the year 2050, the number of Asian Pacific Americans will grow 14 times larger than the size of the Asian Pacific American elderly population in 1990. By 2050, they will approach seven million.

Educational Attainment *(See Chart 2.6)*

In 1994, among Asian Pacific American men 25 years and older, nine out of ten had at least a high school diploma. Among Asian Pacific American women of the same age range, eight out of ten had at minimum a high school diploma. Two-fifths of Asian Pacific Americans 25 years of age or older had a bachelor's degree or greater (46 percent of men, 37 percent of women, as opposed to non-Hispanic Whites of the same age: 28 percent of men, 21 percent of women).

According to William O'Hare (1992), based on his analysis of the March 1991 Current Population Survey, 49 percent of Asian Pacific Americans between the ages of 16 and 24 were attending school only, 19 percent were attending school and working, 21 percent were working only, and 11 percent were neither working nor going to school. In comparison, 26 percent of non-Hispanic Whites were attending school only, 26 percent were going to school and working, 40 percent were working only, and 8 percent were neither working nor going to school.

Among the specific Asian American groups in the 1990 census, Asian Indians had the highest proportion earning at least a bachelor's degree (58 percent), while Tongans, Cambodians, Laotians, and Hmongs had the lowest (6 percent or less each). Educational attainment continues to be high for the Asian Pacific American population as a whole. According the U.S. National Science Foundation, in 1993, 7 percent of all doctorates were awarded to Asian Pacific Americans (though Asian Pacific Americans make up only about 3 percent of the total U.S. population).

In 1994, high school graduation rates varied widely among Asian Pacific American groups. The 1990 census, the latest in which subgroup information was available, showed that among Asian Americans the rates varied from 31 percent for Hmong Americans, who are the most recent Asians to immigrate, to 88 percent for Japanese Americans, who have been in the country for several generations (some since the 1800s). Within the Pacific Islander American group, the proportion with at least a high school diploma ranged from 64 percent for Tongan Americans to 80 percent for Hawaiian Americans.

In general, Asian American men had higher rates of high school or higher graduation than Asian American women—82 percent versus 74 percent in 1990. Among Asian American women, Japanese American women had a high school or higher completion rate of 86 percent, compared with 19 percent for Hmong American women.

At the college level, 38 percent of Asian Americans had graduated with a bachelor's degree or higher by 1990, compared with 20 percent of the total population. In comparison, the proportion of college graduates among Pacific Islander Americans was much lower, at 11 percent.

Labor Force Participation *(See Charts 2.7 and 2.8)*

In 1990, 67 percent of Asian American Americans, compared with 65 percent of all Americans, were in the labor force. Filipino Americans, Asian Indian Americans, Thai Americans, and Chinese Americans had labor participation rates higher than the national average—75 percent, 72 percent, 71 percent, and 66 percent, respectively.

Asian American women had higher participation rates than all women. Sixty percent of Asian American women were in the labor force compared with 57 percent of all women in the United States. Asian American men had about the same participation rate as all men, 75 percent and 74 percent, respectively, and Asian Indian American men had the largest participation rate of 84 percent.

The proportion of Asian American families with three or more workers was 20 percent compared with the national proportion of 13 percent. Among Asian American families, Filipino Americans (30 percent) and Vietnamese Americans (21 percent) had the highest proportions of families with three or more workers. Hmong American families had the lowest proportion with three or more workers (8.4 percent).

Occupations *(See Chart 2.9)*

In 1993, 16 percent of Asian Pacific American men 25 or older worked in executive occupations; 21 percent of them worked in professional occupations. Of women the same age, 18 percent worked in executive occupations, 20 percent worked in professional occupations, and 23 percent worked in administrative support (such as clerical) occupations.

College-educated Asian Pacific American men were twice as likely as comparable non-Hispanic White men to work in technical (7 and 3 percent, respectively) and administrative support occupations (10 and 4 percent, respectively).

Similar proportions of college-educated Asian Pacific American and non-Hispanic White women 25 years old and over were employed in executive, technical, and sales occupations. A higher percentage of college-educated non-Hispanic White women (49 percent) than of comparable Asian Pacific American women (36 percent) worked in professional occupations.

The proportion of college-educated Asian Pacific American women who worked in administrative and clerical jobs (20 percent) was about twice that of comparable non-Hispanic White women (11 percent), and the proportion who worked in service occupations was three times higher (6 and 2 percent, respectively).

When comparing the occupational characteristics of Asian Pacific American men and women with non-Hispanic White men and women, noticeable patterns emerge. Asian Pacific American men were less likely to be in executive positions than non-Hispanic White men (16.3 percent compared to 18.5 percent), and Asian Pacific American women were also less likely to be in such positions in comparison to non-Hispanic White women (17.5 percent compared to 18.9 percent).

The largest differences between the two groups occurred in service occupations, where the percentage of Asian Pacific American men was three times that of non-Hispanic White men (10 and 3 percent, respectively), and in precision production, craft, and repair jobs (12 and 19 percent, respectively).

The proportions of Asian Pacific American men and women in most occupations were similar, except in administrative support, farming, precision production, and transportation. Asian Americans were more likely to be in technical, sales, and administrative support, as well as in managerial and professional specialty jobs (33 percent and 31 percent, respectively), than the total population—32 percent and 26 percent, respectively.

The proportion in technical, sales, and administrative support occupations varies from 37 percent for Korean American workers to 5 percent for Laotian American workers.

Asian Americans are less likely than the total population to work in precision production, craft, and repair occupations or to work as operators, fabricators, and laborers.

Occupational Distribution of Recent Immigrants

Recent immigrants from Asia vary widely in their occupational distribution. Overall, among immigrants who came to the United States between 1991 and 1993, of those reporting occupations, 11.2 percent were managerial, 13.3 percent professional, 16.9 percent technical, 17.1 percent service, 14.5 percent craft, and 27.1 percent were laborers or unspecified. Among Asian immigrant groups, Vietnamese Americans had the highest percentage of laborers (42.6 percent), followed by Chinese Americans (21.6 percent) and Korean Americans (20 percent). Among the combined managerial and professional occupations, Asian Indian Americans had the highest percentage (51.2 percent), followed by Japanese Americans with 41.1 percent and Chinese Americans with 38 percent. Vietnamese Americans were the least likely to be within the managerial and professional ranks; only 2.6 percent were in these occupations.

Disparities by ethnicity and gender were also apparent when occupations were standardized using the National Opinion Research Center standardized occupational scores representing socioeconomic prestige. Using a scale from 0 to 100, occupations were given rank scores by the level of prestige associated with them. Thus, managerial and professional occupations were given high scores, while jobs as laborers were given low scores. Immigrants from Asia were shown to have roughly the same socioeconomic prestige as immigrants from Europe. Among immigrants from China, Japan, Korea, and India, their mean SES (socioeconomic scores) were higher than those of European immigrants. The lowest scores were among Vietnamese immigrants, with a mean score of 50.4. The highest scores were among Asian Indian immigrants, with a mean score of 66.9. In most instances, males had higher occupational prestige than females. The exceptions were among Filipino and Vietnamese immigrants.

Income *(See Charts 2.10 and 2.11)*

Family Income

In 1993, the median family income of Asian Pacific Americans was $44,640, as compared to $41,110 for non-Hispanic Whites (married-couple families without children).

A higher proportion of Asians and Pacific Islander family householders worked year-round, full-time (62 percent) than did comparable non-Hispanic White family householders (58 percent). In 1990, census data showed that 30 percent of Asian Pacific American families, compared with 13 percent of non-Hispanic White families, had three or more wage or salary earners.

Asian Pacific American married-couple families had a higher median income than comparable non-Hispanic White families ($49,510 compared with $45,240). Both the husband and wife worked in about 60 percent of both Asian Pacific American and non-Hispanic White married-couple families in 1993. However, the husband was the only earner in 18 percent of Asian Pacific American and 15 percent of non-Hispanic White married-couple families.

In 1993, the median income of Asian Pacific American families maintained by women with no spouse present ($28,920) was higher than that for comparable non-Hispanic White families ($21,650). Among male householder families with no spouse present, non-Hispanic Whites made considerably more than Asian Pacific Americans, though the figure was not statistically verifiable ($30,170 and $23,130, respectively).

Despite their higher median family incomes, Asian Pacific Americans had lower per capita income in 1993 than non-Hispanic Whites ($13,420 versus $15,260). The fact that Asian Pacific American families contained more income earners—20 percent had three or more earners, compared with 14 percent of non-Hispanic White families—likely contributed to the higher family income.

Individual Earnings

In 1993, Asian Pacific American males 25 years and older who worked year-round, full-time had median earnings ($31,560) higher than comparable females ($25,430).

Asian Pacific American and non-Hispanic White females with at least a bachelor's degree had similar earnings ($31,780 versus $32,920), while comparably educated Asian Pacific American males ($41,220) earned about $87 for every $100 of non-Hispanic White males' earnings ($47,180).

Among high school graduates, however, the median earnings of both Asian Pacific American women ($17,330) and men ($23,490) were less than non-Hispanic White women ($19,850) and men ($28,370).

Across the major occupations in 1993, college-educated Asian Pacific American men had higher median earnings than comparable non-Hispanic White men only in technical and related support and occupations. Non-Hispanic White men had higher median earnings in executive, sales, and administrative support jobs.

The 1993 median earnings ratio of college-educated Asian Pacific American men to comparable non-Hispanic White men in administrative support jobs was 0.83 (although the proportion of Asian Pacific American men in these jobs was twice that of non-Hispanic White men).

Asian Pacific American and non-Hispanic White women 25 years old and over with at least a bachelor's degree had similar earnings in most occupations. Two exceptions occurred: Asian Pacific American women had significantly higher median earnings than non-Hispanic White women in professional jobs ($41,130 compared to $34,440), but considerably lower earnings in sales positions ($24,680 compared to $33,100).

Per Capita Income

Per capita income among Asian Pacific Americans in 1990 was $13,420, as compared to $15,265 for non-Hispanic Whites. In the West, per capita income among Asian Pacific Americans was $13,774, as compared to $15,444 for non-Hispanic Whites. In California, per capita income among Asian Pacific Americans in 1990 was an even lower ratio, $13,733 as compared to $19,028 for non-Hispanic Whites. Thus, in California, Asian Pacific American per capita income was 27.8 percent below the non-Hispanic White population.

The 1994 national median per capita income for *all* races was $16,555; for non-Hispanic Whites, $17,611; for Asian Pacific Americans, $16,902; for African Americans, $10,650; and for Hispanic Americans, $9,435.

Market Power

According to the Asian Pacific American Center for Census Information and Services (ACCIS), in 1993 Asian Pacific Americans represented a $94 billion consumer market—5 percent of the total consumer market. In 1987, businesses owned by Asian Pacific Americans had gross receipts of over $33 billion. Asian Pacific Americans earned a total of $79 billion in wage and salary income in 1990.

Poverty (See Chart 2.12)

In 1994, 14.5 percent of the U.S. population was living below the poverty level. Among non-Hispanic Whites, only 9.4 percent were below poverty; among Hispanic Americans, the figure was 30.7 percent; among African Americans it was 30.6 percent; and among Asian Pacific Americans the proportion experiencing poverty was 14.6 percent. In 1991, Asian Pacific Americans who immigrated between 1980 and 1990 had a poverty rate three times that of those who immigrated prior to 1980 (21 percent versus 7 percent).

Asian Pacific American families who immigrated to the United States during the 1980s had a median income that was just 59 percent of that for the families who arrived in the United States prior to 1980. One reason for the higher median incomes was that earlier immigrants had more workers per family compared with later immigrants.

Despite higher educational attainment and a similar median family income, the poverty rate for Asian Pacific American families (14 percent) was higher than that for non-Hispanic White families (8 percent) in 1993. Only 16 percent of poor families in both groups had a householder who worked year-round, full-time.

Among families with high-school-educated householders, the poverty rate of Asian Pacific American families (13 percent) was higher than that of non-Hispanic White families (8 percent); among college-educated householders, the poverty rate of Asian Pacific American families was more than three times that of non-Hispanic White families (7 percent versus 2 percent).

In 1993, 12 percent of Asian Pacific American and 5 percent of non-Hispanic White married-couple families lived in poverty. In 1993, about 15 percent of Asian Pacific Americans were poor compared with 10 percent of non-Hispanic White persons.

Asian Pacific American families and Asian Pacific American individuals are, on average, more likely to be in poverty. Between 1990 and 1994, poverty among Asian Pacific American families rose from 11.9 in 1990 to 13.5 percent in 1994. Among individuals, it rose from 14.1 percent in 1990 to 15.3 percent in 1994.

According to 1990 figures, Hmong American and Cambodian American families had the highest family poverty rates: 62 percent and 42 percent, respectively. The lowest poverty rates were among Filipino American (5 percent) and Japanese American (3 percent) families.

Housing (See Charts 2.13–2.15)

In 1990, about 52 percent of Asian Pacific American householders around the nation owned their homes; a similar proportion (47 percent) were renters. In contrast, about 70 percent of non-Hispanic White householders were homeowners.

Asian Pacific Americans residing in central cities were less likely to be owners (41 percent) than renters (57 percent). In contrast, Asian Pacific Americans living outside central cities had a higher proportion of home owners (61 percent) than renters (38 percent). Non-Hispanic White householders tend to have more owners than renters regardless of whether they lived inside or outside central cities.

Asian Pacific Americans were *nine* times more likely to be crowded than non-Hispanic White households. Households with more than one person per room are considered "crowded." Within metropolitan areas (MAs), Asian Pacific American households were *eight* times more likely than non-Hispanic White households to be crowded (24 percent compared with 3 percent). In central cities, these rates were even higher. In the top 25 MAs, crowding most frequently occurred in the Stockton, California, MA, where 4 in 10 Asian Pacific American households had to live in this condition. The lack of elbow room was also a problem for many Asian Pacific American households in the Minneapolis–St. Paul, Minnesota–Wisconsin MAs; the San Diego MA; the Los Angeles–Long Beach MA; and the New York MA. In each of these four metropolitan areas, more than three in ten Asian Pacific American homes were termed crowded.

In 16 of the 25 metro areas with the highest Asian Pacific American populations, home values were higher for Asian Pacific Americans than for non-Hispanic Whites. The Detroit MA (with an average $111,000 home value for Asian Pacific Americans, $74,200 for non-Hispanic Whites) had the largest differential. Value is the owner's estimate of how much their property would sell for if it were on the market. (The value data in this section apply to single-family homes on less than ten acres without a commercial establishment or medical office on the property.) Within metropolitan areas, the median value of homes owned by Asian Pacific Americans was $184,000, double that of non-Hispanic White-owned homes ($91,700). This wide variation at the national level is largely a consequence of the fact that Asian Pacific American owners are heavily concentrated in California and Hawaii, where median home values are well above the U.S. median. In the top 25 MAs, the most expensive Asian Pacific American–owned homes were in the San Francisco MA; the San Jose, California, MA; the Honolulu MA; and the Anaheim–Santa Ana, California, MA, where their median value topped $250,000. Despite the high value in Honolulu, Asian Pacific Americans living there have considerably lower home value than non-Hispanic Whites ($274,000 and $324,900, respectively).

Of the top 25 MAs with heavy Asian Pacific American concentration, the Nassau-Suffolk, New York, MA ($827) and the Bergen-Passaic, New Jersey, MA ($816) were the most expensive places for Asian Pacific Americans to rent homes. The Houston MA and the Minneapolis–St. Paul, Minnesota–Wisconsin MAs (each under $350) were at the other extreme.

In 1990, more than five out of ten Japanese American, Chinese American, Filipino American, and Asian Indian American householders in the United States were home owners, compared with about two in five Korean American, Vietnamese American, and Pacific Islander American householders.

The median home values of all Asian Pacific Americans were well above the national median in 1990. Among Asian Pacific Americans, the Chinese and Japanese owned the most expensive homes, with half valued above $200,000 in 1990. The median value of homes owned by Vietnamese households was the lowest, approximately $126,000.

In 1990, two million of our nation's households had an Asian Pacific American householder. An overwhelming majority of them (1.9 million, or 94 percent) lived in metropolitan Asian Pacific American households.

- Los Angeles–Long Beach MA   276,886
- New York MA   167,261
- Honolulu MA   155,189
- San Francisco MA   96,493
- Oakland, California, MA   77,154

The above five metropolitan areas had more Asian Pacific American households than any others. Combined, these five MAs accounted for two of every five metro Asian Pacific American household. Three in every four lived in one of the 25 MAs that had more than 13,800 Asian Pacific American households. Eleven of the top 25 MAs were in the West; nine of them were in California alone. In fact, 7 percent of the Golden State's households were maintained by an Asian Pacific American—the highest rate in the continental United States.

Nearly three in every five householders in the island metropolis of Honolulu were Asian Pacific Americans—by far the most sizable percentage of any MA in the nation. (Native Hawaiians are classified as Pacific Islanders.) Among the top 25 MAs, the 6 with the next largest percentages (between 6 and 15 percent) were all in California.

Asian Pacific American metro households paid the highest contract rent for housing ($495 a month), followed by non-Hispanic Whites ($414), Hispanic-origin persons ($405), and African Americans ($329). Within metro areas, Asian Pacific American renters paid a median of $495 in contract rent, 20 percent more than their non-Hispanic White counterparts ($414). In the suburbs, the difference was even greater ($579 versus $443).

Family Composition (See Charts 2.16 and 2.17)

In 1994, the average number of persons per Asian Pacific American family was 3.8; for non-Hispanic White families, the average was 3.1. Seventy-three percent of Asian Pacific American families had three or more persons in 1994, compared with 55 percent of non-Hispanic White families. Twenty-two percent

of all Asian Pacific American families had five or more persons, compared with 12 percent of non-Hispanic White families.

Sixty-one percent of Asian Pacific American families had related children under 18 years old, compared with almost half (49 percent) of non-Hispanic White families. In each group, about 80 percent of related children under 18 years old lived with two parents.

Seventy-eight percent of Asian Pacific American households contained families. Married-couple families accounted for 80 percent of all Asian Pacific American families, slightly less than the 83 percent of non-Hispanic White families. Seventy-four percent of Asian Pacific American families consisted of three or more persons. Asian Pacific American children under 18 years were more likely to be living with two parents than those in non-Hispanic White families (84 versus 80 percent). In 1990, 3.1 percent of American children belonged to Asian Pacific American groups.

Among specifically Asian American groups, Hmong Americans had the largest family size with an average of 6.6 persons, and Japanese Americans the smallest with 3.1 persons. Other groups with more than four persons per average family were Filipino Americans, Vietnamese Americans, Cambodian Americans, and Laotian Americans.

According to the 1991 Current Population Survey, Asian Pacific Americans' marital status for persons 15 years and older was as follows: 31.1 percent never married, 56.4 percent married with spouse present, 3.4 percent married with spouse absent, 5.1 percent widowed, and 4 percent divorced. Comparable statistics for non-Hispanic Whites are 22 percent never married, 58.1 percent married with spouse present, 2.6 percent married with spouse absent, 7 percent widowed, and 8 percent divorced. Asian Pacific Americans also had the smallest percentage of families headed by women (11.4 percent) of all racial groups.

In 1990, the proportion of specifically Asian American families maintained by a husband and wife was 82 percent, slightly higher than the national figure of 79 percent. The proportion of Asian American female-headed families with no husband present was significantly less than the national average, 12 percent versus 17 percent. However, two groups had proportions higher than the national average: Cambodian Americans at 26 percent, and Thai Americans at 20 percent.

In 1990, 31.2 percent of all Asian Pacific American husbands and 40.4 percent of all Asian Pacific American wives were intermarried (that is, married to someone of either a different race or a different ethnic group). Slightly less than 2 in 10 (18.9 percent) of Asian Pacific American husbands were interethnically married, and slightly more than one in ten (12.3 percent) were interracially married.

Among the interracially married, 9.9 percent of these husbands married non-Hispanic Whites. Among Asian Pacific American wives, 16.2 percent were interethnically married, and 24.2 percent were interracially married. Among the interracially married, 20.8 percent of Asian Pacific American wives had married non-Hispanic Whites. Japanese American wives and Filipino American wives had the highest proportion of intermarriages (51.9 percent and 40.2 percent, respectively). The high proportions of intermarriages among Japanese Americans was attributable to the large proportion of wives of U.S. servicemen.

In California in 1990, according to Summary Tape File 3A, of those who are native speakers of an Asian Pacific American language, 18.2 percent of those 5 to 17 years, 24 percent of those 18 to 64 years, and 51.3 percent of those 65 years and over responded that they speak English "not well" or "not at all." Slightly more than 4 in 10 (43.3 percent) of persons age 5 to 17 speak an Asian Pacific American language in a household where there is no one who speaks English "well" or "very well." Forty-one percent of persons age 65 and over are in a household where there is no one who speaks English "well" or "very well."

In California in 1990, there were 665,605 households where an Asian Pacific American language was spoken; among these, 32.8 percent were classified as linguistically isolated, that is, there were no persons in the household over the age of 13 who responded that he or she spoke English "well" or "very well."

Of the 4.1 million Asian Pacific Americans five years old and over, 56 percent did not speak English "very well," and 35 percent were linguistically isolated. Hmong Americans, Laotian Americans, and Cambodian Americans had the highest proportions of persons five years old and over speaking an Asian Pacific American language at home. Asian Indian Americans, at 15 percent, had the lowest proportion (many were raised bilingual).

Hmong Americans and Cambodian Americans who spoke an Asian Pacific American language at home had the highest proportion of linguistically isolated, 61 percent and 56 percent, respectively.

Over half of all foreign-born Asian Pacific Americans reported that they do not speak English "very well" and almost one-third were in linguistically isolated households. These figures were 60 percent and 41 percent, respectively, for Asian Pacific American immigrants arriving in this country between 1980 and 1990.

Voter Turnout

In 1994, voter turnout among non-Hispanic Whites in congressional elections was 47 percent of registered voters, compared with Asian Pacific Americans, who voted at levels similar to Hispanics: about 18 percent of those registered. Sixty-three percent of Asian Pacific Americans were registered to vote in 1994, compared with 74 percent of non-Hispanic Whites. Overall turnout was 45 percent.

Estimating turnout rates for the citizen population 18 years and over significantly increased turnout levels for Hispanics (34 percent) and more than doubled the rate for the Asian Pacific American population to 41 percent. Overall, computing voter turnout rates for citizens only, instead of all residents, increased the level of voter turnout for the nation as a whole from 45 to 48 percent.

Agriculture

In the 1992 Survey of Agriculture, Asian Pacific Americans constituted less than 0.5 percent of all farm owners.

Pacific Islander Americans

Introduction *(See Chart 2.18)*

The members of the Pacific Islander American group constitute a small but distinct and important component of the Asian Pacific American population. The 1990 census counted 365,024 Pacific Islanders, a 41 percent increase over the 1980 count of 259,566, making up about 5 percent of all Asian Pacific Americans in the later census. Pacific Islander Americans include diverse populations who differ in language and culture. They are of Polynesian, Micronesian, and Melanesian backgrounds. The Polynesian group is the largest of the three and includes Hawaiian Americans, Samoan Americans, Tongan Americans, and Tahitian Americans. The Micronesian group, the second largest, is primarily Guamanian American (or Chamorro), but also includes Mariana Islander Americans, Marshall Islander Americans, Palauan Americans, and several other groups. The Fijian American population is the largest Melanesian group.

Immigration was a major factor in the growth of the Asian Pacific American population as a whole, with large numbers coming to the United States from Asia and the Pacific Islands following the adoption of the Immigration Act of 1965.

Immigration played a much more varied role, however, in the growth of the Pacific Islander population in the United States. Only 13 percent of Pacific Islander Americans in 1990 were foreign-born. Hawaiian Americans are, of course, native to this land. Persons born in American Samoa are United States nationals with the right of free entry into the

United States, and since 1950 inhabitants of Guam have been U.S. citizens.

In addition to immigration and natural increase, part of Pacific Islander American growth between 1970 and 1990 reflects changes in the race question on the census form to include more groups, as well as improvements in collection and processing procedures in the 1990 census.

Although some groups are small, all Pacific Islander groups are important and make continuing contributions to the diversity of the United States.

Population Growth

The Pacific Islander American population grew at a tremendous rate—41 percent—between 1980 and 1990, from 259,566 to 365,024.

Hawaiian Americans, the largest Pacific Islander group, made up 58 percent of the total Pacific Islander population. Samoan Americans and Guamanian Americans were the next largest groups, representing 17 percent and 14 percent, respectively, followed by Tongan Americans and Fijian Americans who were 5 percent and 2 percent, respectively, of all Pacific Islander Americans.

Other Pacific Islander Americans include Palauan Americans, Northern Mariana Islander Americans, and Tahitian Americans, who each constituted less than 0.5 percent of Pacific Islander Americans.

The Tongan American population grew more rapidly (146 percent) during the 1980s than any of the top three groups.

Regional Dispersion

Eighty-six percent of the Pacific Islander American population lived in the American West in 1990, compared with 56 percent of the Asian Pacific American group as a whole and 21 percent of the total population.

Approximately 75 percent of Pacific Islander Americans lived in just two states—California and Hawaii. These two states had more than 100,000 Pacific Islanders. Washington was the only other state that had 15,000 or more Pacific Islander Americans.

Between 1980 and 1990, Oregon, Texas, and Utah joined the number of states with 5,000 or more Pacific Islander Americans. In each state, the Pacific Islander American population had more than doubled.

Nativity *(See Chart 2.19)*

Only 13 percent of Pacific Islanders living in the United States were foreign-born, much lower than the 63 percent for the Asian Pacific American population as a whole.

Among the Pacific Islander groups, Tongan Americans had the highest proportion of foreign-born at 61 percent. Samoan Americans and Guamanian Americans had much lower proportions of foreign-born: 23 percent and 11 percent, respectively. Only 1 percent of Hawaiian Americans, indigenous to the United States, were foreign-born.

Age Distribution *(See Chart 2.20)*

Pacific Islander Americans had a median age of 25 years in 1990. The median age was about 30 years for Asian Pacific Americans.

Only 4 percent of Pacific Islander Americans were 65 years old and over, compared with 6 percent of all Asian Pacific Americans and 13 percent of the total U.S. population.

In 1990, Hawaiian Americans had the oldest median age among Pacific Islander Americans, 26 years, followed by Guamanian Americans with a median age of 25. Samoan Americans, at 22 years, had the youngest median age among Pacific Islanders.

Educational Attainment

In 1990, 76 percent of all Pacific Islander Americans 25 years old and over were at least high school graduates. The rate for all Asian Pacific Americans was 78 percent while the national rate was 75 percent. Within the Pacific Islander American group, the proportion who received a high school diploma or

higher ranged from 80 percent for Hawaiian Americans to 64 percent for Tongan Americans.

In general, Pacific Islander American men had higher rates of high school completion than women, 77 percent versus 75 percent. Tongan American women, however, had a higher rate of high school completion than Tongan American men.

At the college level, 11 percent of Pacific Islander Americans were graduates compared with 37 percent of all Asian Pacific Americans and 20 percent of the total population. Hawaiian Americans had the highest college completion rate among Pacific Islander Americans at 12 percent, followed by Guamanian Americans at 10 percent, Samoan Americans at 8 percent, and Tongan Americans at 6 percent.

Labor Force Participation *(See Charts 2.21–2.22)*

A larger proportion of Pacific Islander Americans participated in the labor force than did the Asian Pacific American population as a whole. Only Samoan Americans and Tongan Americans were below the Pacific Islander average. Guamanian Americans had the highest labor force participation rate at 72 percent.

Sixty-three percent of Pacific Islander American women were in the labor force compared with 60 percent of all Asian Pacific American women and 57 percent of all women in the United States. The percent of Pacific Islander American women in the labor force ranged from 55 percent for Samoan Americans to 63 percent for Guamanian Americans.

Nearly one-third of Pacific Islander Americans were employed in technical, sales, and administrative support jobs. Pacific Islander Americans were more likely to be in service occupations than the total Asian Pacific American population, but less likely to be in managerial or professional occupations.

Tongan Americans were more likely than all other Pacific Islander Americans to work in service occupations but less likely to be managers or professionals.

Pacific Islander Americans were also more likely than all Asian Pacific Americans to work in precision production, craft, and repair occupations or as operators, fabricators, and laborers.

Although farming, forestry, and fishing are common in many Pacific Island areas, less than 3 percent of Pacific Islander Americans worked in farming, forestry, and fishing in the United States.

About 20 percent of both Pacific Islander American families and Asian Pacific Americans families had three or more workers, compared with 13 percent of the nation's families as a whole.

Pacific Islander American families were also less likely than all families to have no workers (9 percent compared with 13 percent). Only 3 percent of Tongan American families had no workers. Samoan Americans were somewhat more likely than other Pacific Islander Americans to have one-worker families (30 percent compared with 26 percent) and less likely to have two-worker families (40 percent compared with 46 percent).

Income *(See Chart 2.23)*

Pacific Islander American per capita income was below the national average in 1990. In 1989, the Pacific Islander per capita income was $10,342, lower than the $13,638 for Asian Pacific Americans and $14,143 for the United States generally.

The lower per capita income of Pacific Islander Americans in part reflects the larger average size of Pacific Islander American families (4.08), compared to all families nationally (3.16).

The median income of Pacific Islander American families ($33,955) is slightly lower than that for all families ($35,225). Pacific Islander American median household income in 1989 ($31,980) was slightly higher than that for all households ($30,056).

Hawaiian Americans had the highest per capita income ($11,446) of all Pacific Islander groups, followed by Guamanian Americans ($10,834). Tongan American and Samoan American per capita income was about half the national per capita income, $6,144 and $7,690, respectively.

Poverty *(See Chart 2.24)*

About 58,000, or 17 percent, of Pacific Islander Americans lived below the poverty level in 1989, higher than the 14 percent poverty rate for all Asian Pacific Americans.

Among Pacific Islander Americans that same year, Samoan Americans had the highest poverty rate at 26 percent, Tongan Americans the next highest at 23 percent. About one of every four Samoan American families and one of every five Tongan American families were below the poverty level in 1989.

Family Composition *(See Charts 2.25 and 2.26)*

The average Pacific Islander American family had 4.1 persons in 1990, larger than the average number of persons per family both for Asian Pacific Americans (3.8 percent) and for all American families as a whole.

Pacific Islander Americans were more likely to have a female householder with no spouse present (19 percent) than all Asian Pacific Americans (12 percent).

Language

Of the 78,000 Pacific Islander Americans five years old and over speaking a language other than English at home, 25 percent spoke an Asian Pacific American language. Thirty-three percent of these did not speak English "very well," while 11 percent were "linguistically isolated."

Among Pacific Islander Americans, Tongan Americans and Samoan Americans had the highest proportion of persons five years old and over speaking an Asian Pacific American language at home. Hawaiian Americans had the lowest proportion (though in recent years there has been a resurgence of interest in the native Hawaiian tongue). Tongan Americans had the highest proportion of persons who were linguistically isolated among Pacific Islander groups.

Map 2.1   Asian Pacific Americans by State, 1990

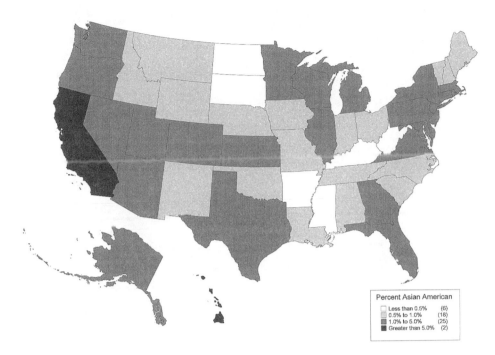

Map 2.2   Asian Pacific Americans by County, 1990

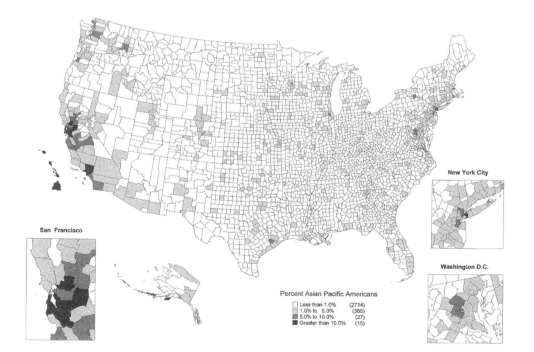

Map 2.3   Chinese Americans by State, 1990

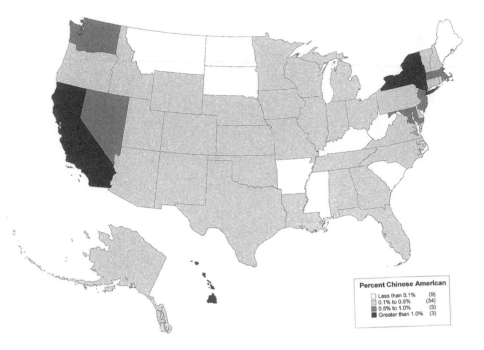

Map 2.4   Chinese Americans by County, 1990

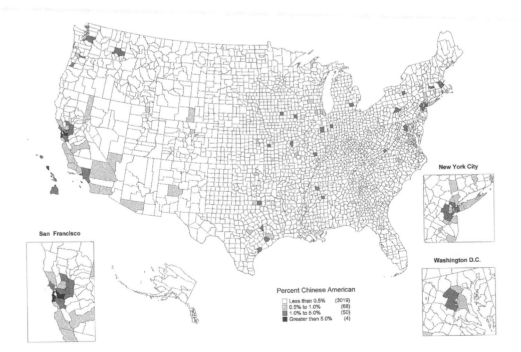

Map 2.5 Filipino Americans by State, 1990

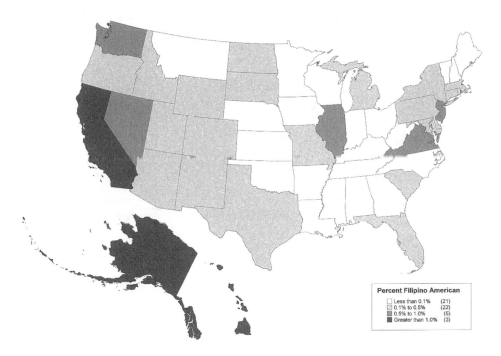

Percent Filipino American

☐ Less than 0.1%   (21)
☐ 0.1% to 0.5%   (22)
▨ 0.5% to 1.0%   (5)
■ Greater than 1.0% (3)

Map 2.6 Filipino Americans by County, 1990

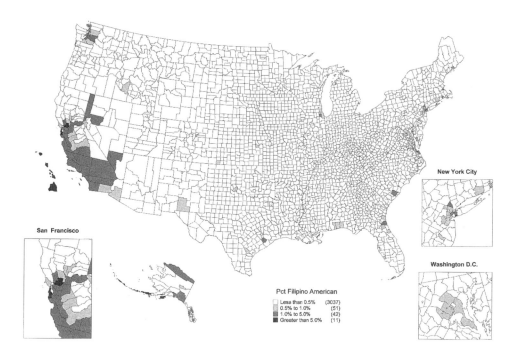

New York City

Washington D.C.

San Francisco

Pct Filipino American

☐ Less than 0.5%   (3037)
☐ 0.5% to 1.0%   (51)
▨ 1.0% to 5.0%   (42)
■ Greater than 5.0% (11)

Map 2.7 Japanese Americans by State, 1990

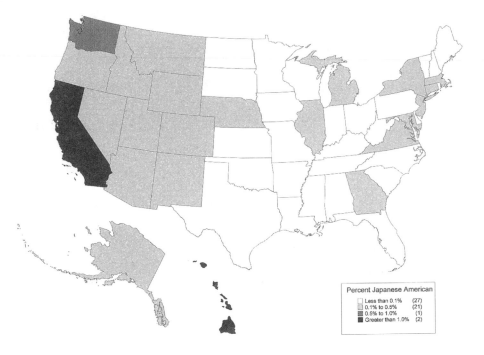

Percent Japanese American
☐ Less than 0.1%	(27)
▨ 0.1% to 0.5%	(21)
▦ 0.5% to 1.0%	(1)
■ Greater than 1.0%	(2)

Map 2.8 Japanese Americans by County, 1990

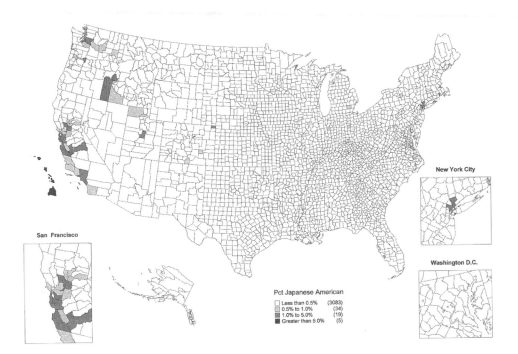

New York City

San Francisco

Washington D.C.

Pct Japanese American
☐ Less than 0.5%	(3083)
▨ 0.5% to 1.0%	(34)
▦ 1.0% to 5.0%	(19)
■ Greater than 5.0%	(5)

Map 2.9 Korean Americans by State, 1990

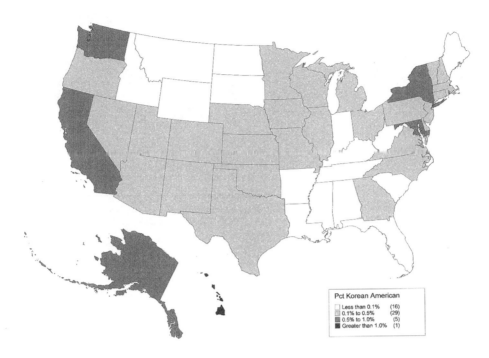

Map 2.10 Korean Americans by County, 1990

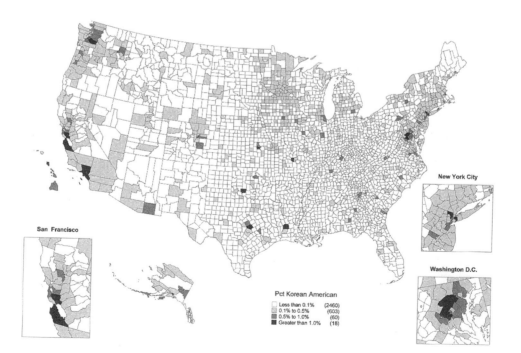

Map 2.11   Asian Indian Americans by State, 1990

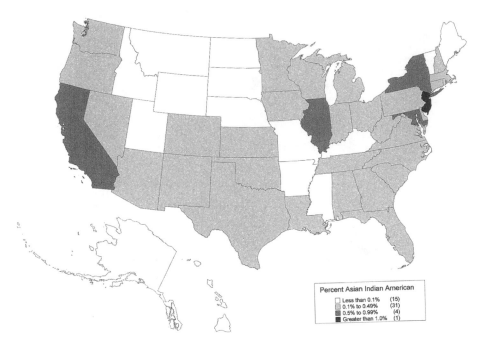

Map 2.12   Asian Indian Americans by County, 1990

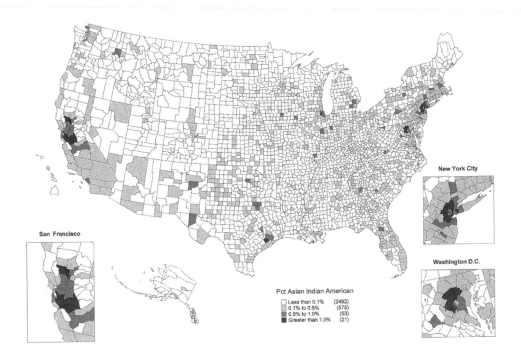

Map 2.13 Vietnamese Americans by State, 1990

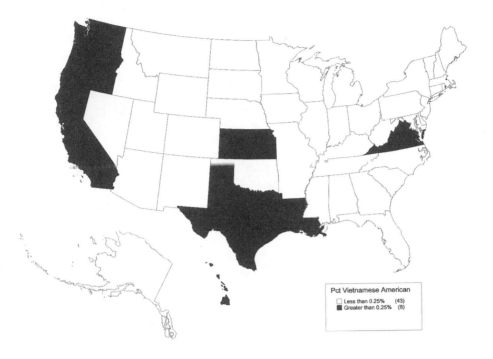

Map 2.14 Vietnamese Americans by County, 1990

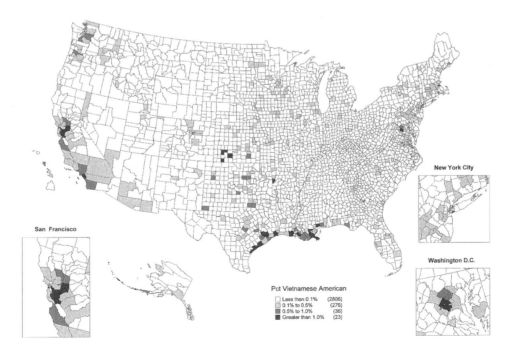

Map 2.15   Cambodian Americans by County, 1990

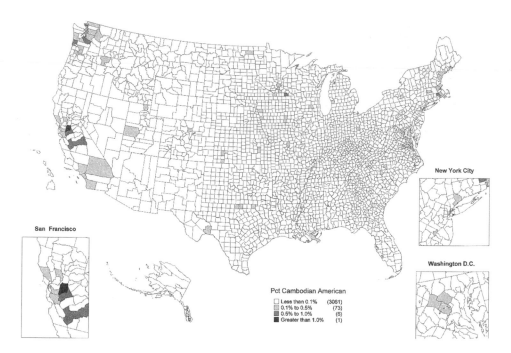

Map 2.16   Thai Americans by County, 1990

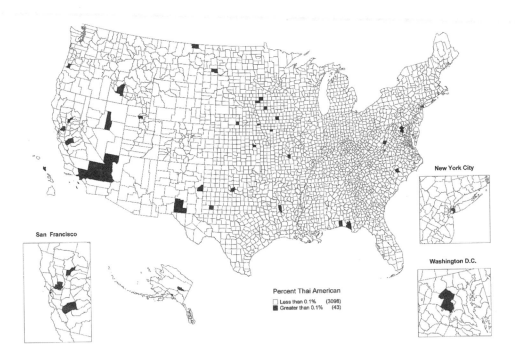

Map 2.17 Laotian Americans by County, 1990

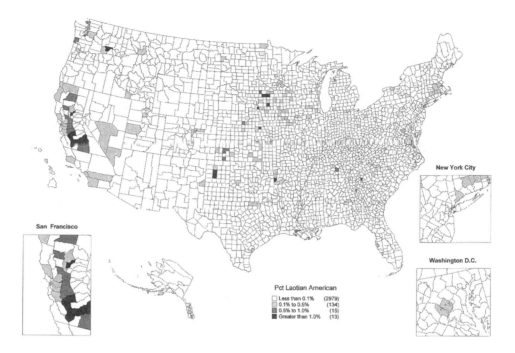

San Francisco

New York City

Washington D.C.

Pct Laotian American
Less than 0.1% (2979)
0.1% to 0.5% (134)
0.5% to 1.0% (15)
Greater than 1.0% (13)

Map 2.18 Hmong Americans by County, 1990

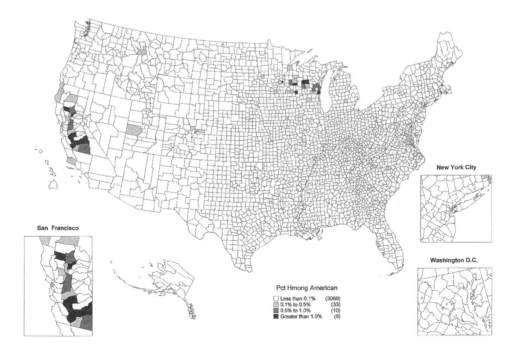

San Francisco

New York City

Washington D.C.

Pct Hmong American
Less than 0.1% (3069)
0.1% to 0.5% (33)
0.5% to 1.0% (10)
Greater than 1.0% (9)

Map 2.19   Other Asian Americans by County, 1990

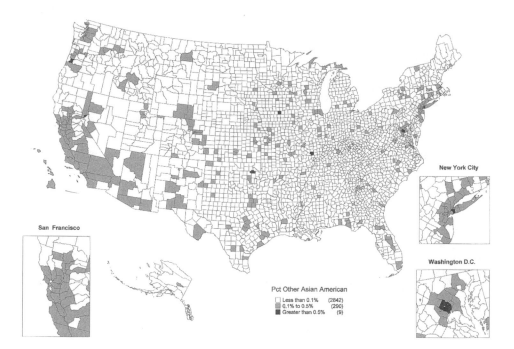

Map 2.20   Pacific Islander Americans by State, 1990

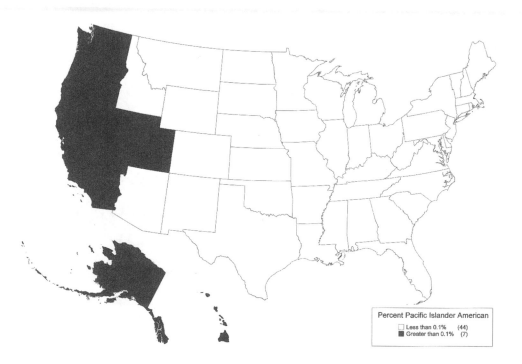

Map 2.21 Pacific Islander Americans by County, 1990

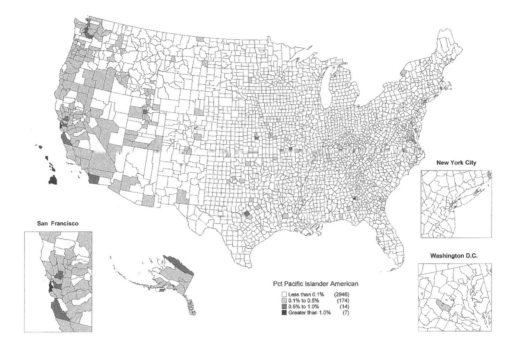

San Francisco

New York City

Washington D.C.

Pct Pacific Islander American

Less than 0.1% (2946)
0.1% to 0.5% (174)
0.5% to 1.0% (14)
Greater than 1.0% (7)

Map 2.22 Hawaiian Americans by County, 1990

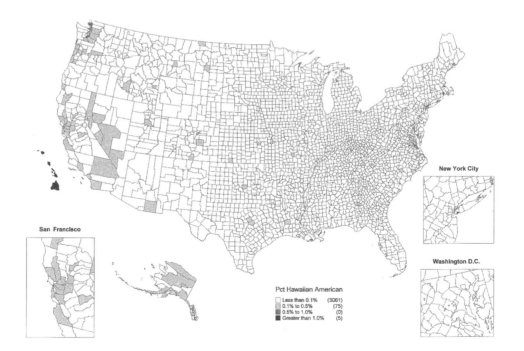

San Francisco

New York City

Washington D.C.

Pct Hawaiian American

Less than 0.1% (3061)
0.1% to 0.5% (75)
0.5% to 1.0% (0)
Greater than 1.0% (5)

Map 2.23 Samoan Americans by County, 1990

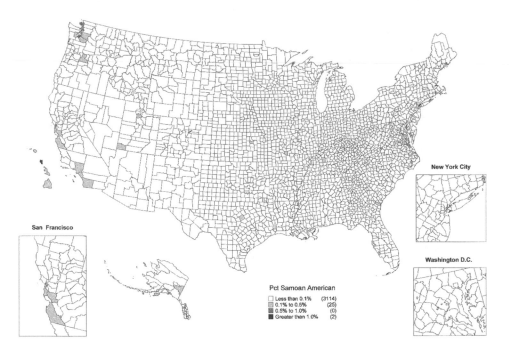

Pct Samoan American

- ☐ Less than 0.1%   (3114)
- ▨ 0.1% to 0.5%   (25)
- ▦ 0.5% to 1.0%   (0)
- ■ Greater than 1.0%   (2)

Map 2.24 Guamanian Americans by County, 1990

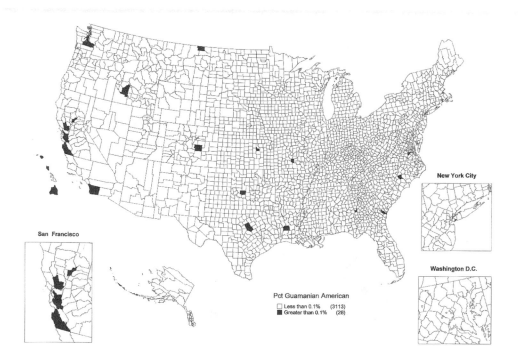

Pct Guamanian American

- ☐ Less than 0.1%   (3113)
- ■ Greater than 0.1%   (28)

Map 2.25 Tongan Americans by County, 1990

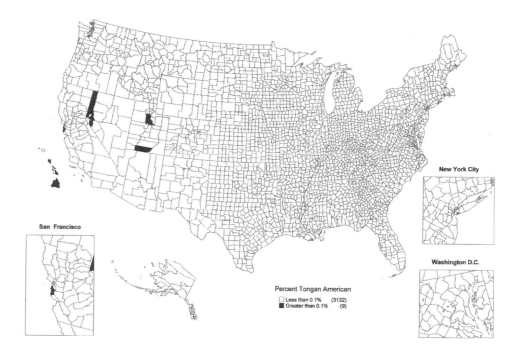

San Francisco

New York City

Washington D.C.

Percent Tongan American

☐ Less than 0.1%   (3132)
■ Greater than 0.1%   (9)

Chart 2.1 Asian Pacific American Population by Place of Origin, 1990 (Percent)

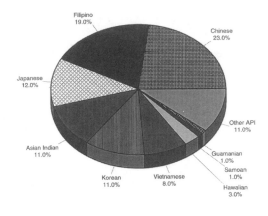

Chart 2.2 Asian American Population by Place of Origin, 1990 (Percent)

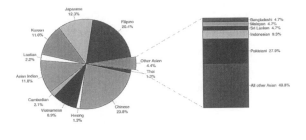

Chart 2.3 Average Year-of-Entry Age for Asian American Immigrants, 1990 (Percent)

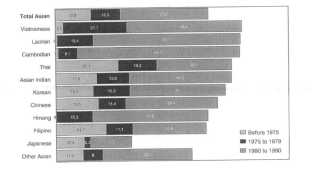

Chart 2.4 Resident Asian Pacific American Population by Age, 1990 (Percent)

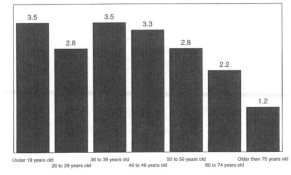

Chart 2.5 Median Asian American Ages by Place of Origin, 1990

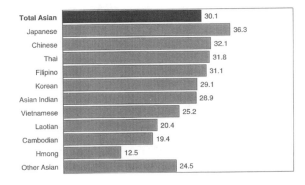

Chart 2.6 Asian American and Non-Hispanic White Educational Attainment, 1990

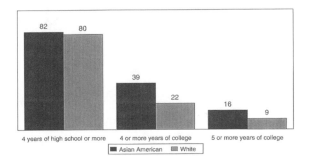

Chart 2.7 Asian American Employment Rates, 1990 (Percent, 16 years and older)

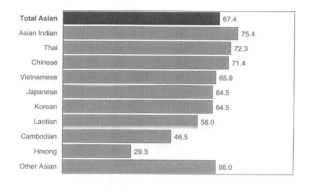

Total Asian	67.4
Asian Indian	75.4
Thai	72.3
Chinese	71.4
Vietnamese	65.9
Japanese	64.5
Korean	64.5
Laotian	58.0
Cambodian	46.5
Hmong	29.3
Other Asian	66.0

Chart 2.8 Asian American Families with Three or More Workers, 1990 (Percent)

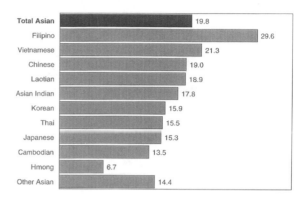

Total Asian	19.8
Filipino	29.6
Vietnamese	21.3
Chinese	19.0
Laotian	18.9
Asian Indian	17.8
Korean	15.9
Thai	15.5
Japanese	15.3
Cambodian	13.5
Hmong	6.7
Other Asian	14.4

Chart 2.9 Asian American and Total Population Occupational Distribution, 1990 (Percent, 16 years and older)

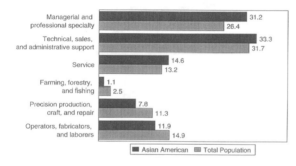
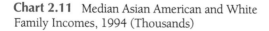

	Asian American	Total Population
Managerial and professional specialty	31.2	26.4
Technical, sales, and administrative support	33.3	31.7
Service	14.6	13.2
Farming, forestry, and fishing	1.1	2.5
Precision production, craft, and repair	7.8	11.3
Operators, fabricators, and laborers	11.9	14.9

Chart 2.10 Asian American Wages by Place of Origin, 1990 (In 1989 dollars)

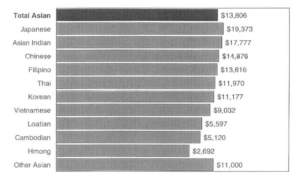
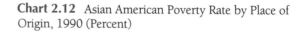

Total Asian	$13,806
Japanese	$19,373
Asian Indian	$17,777
Chinese	$14,876
Filipino	$13,616
Thai	$11,970
Korean	$11,177
Vietnamese	$9,032
Loatian	$5,597
Cambodian	$5,120
Hmong	$2,692
Other Asian	$11,000

Chart 2.11 Median Asian American and White Family Incomes, 1994 (Thousands)

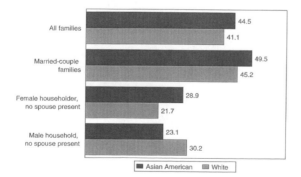

	Asian American	White
All families	44.5	41.1
Married-couple families	49.5	45.2
Female householder, no spouse present	28.9	21.7
Male household, no spouse present	23.1	30.2

Chart 2.12 Asian American Poverty Rate by Place of Origin, 1990 (Percent)

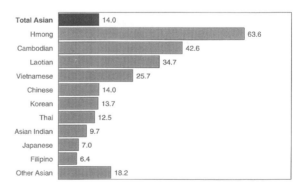

Total Asian	14.0
Hmong	63.6
Cambodian	42.6
Laotian	34.7
Vietnamese	25.7
Chinese	14.0
Korean	13.7
Thai	12.5
Asian Indian	9.7
Japanese	7.0
Filipino	6.4
Other Asian	18.2

Chart 2.13 Crowded Living Conditions for Asian Pacific Americans and Whites, 1990 (Percent of households with more than one person per room)

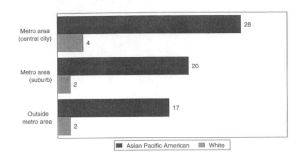

■ Asian Pacific American   ▨ White

Chart 2.14 Asian Pacific American and White Home Values, 1990

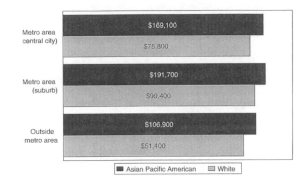

■ Asian Pacific American   ▨ White

Chart 2.15 Asian Pacific American and White Home Owners by Metropolitan Location, 1990 (Percent)

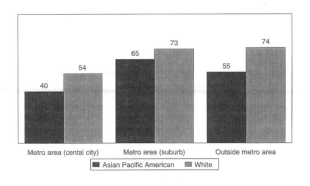

■ Asian Pacific American   ▨ White

Chart 2.16 Asian American Family Size by Place of Origin, 1990

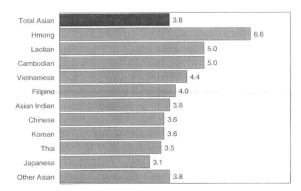

Chart 2.17 Comparison of Asian American and Non-Hispanic White Family Size, 1990 (Percent)

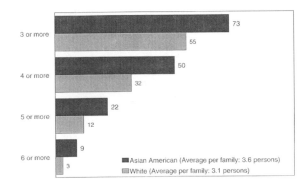

■ Asian American (Average per family: 3.6 persons)
▨ White (Average per family: 3.1 persons)

Chart 2.18 Pacific Islander American Ethnicities, 1990 (Percent)

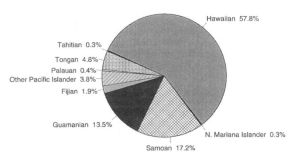

Chart 2.19 Foreign Born Among Pacific Islanders, 1990 (Percent)

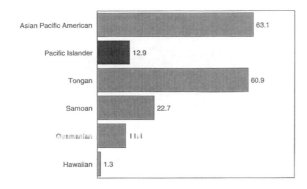

Chart 2.20 Median Pacific Islander American Age by Place of Origin, 1990

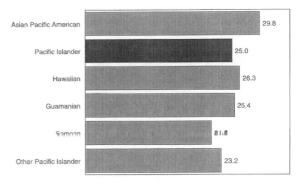

Chart 2.21 Major Occupations for Pacific Islander Americans and Asian Americans, 1990 (Percent, 16 years and older)

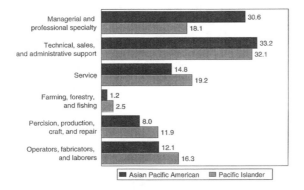

Chart 2.22 Pacific Islander American Labor Force Participation Rates, 1990 (Percent, 16 years and older)

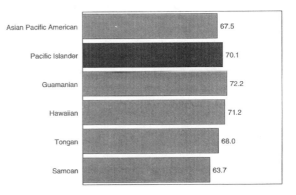

Chart 2.23 Pacific Islander American Per Capita Income, 1990 (In 1989 dollars)

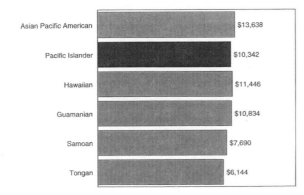

Chart 2.24 Pacific Islander American Families with Three or More Workers, 1990 (Percent)

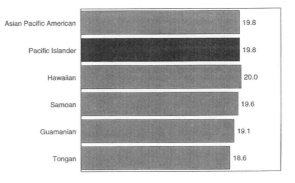

Chart 2.25 Pacific Islander American Poverty Rates by Place of Origin, 1990 (Percent)

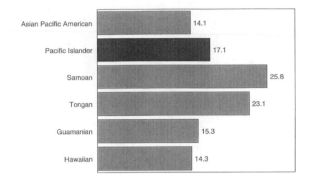

Chart 2.26 Pacific Islander American Family Size by Place of Origin, 1990

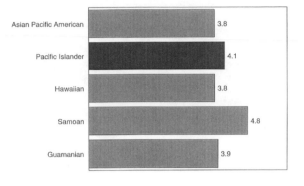

Chapter 3

Hispanic Americans

Introduction

Hispanic Americans trace their origin or descent either to the Iberian peninsula of Europe or to Mexico, Puerto Rico, Cuba, or many other Spanish-speaking countries of Latin America (a collective term that embraces all of the Americas south of the United States). Their ancestors were among the early explorers and settlers of the New World. In 1609, a decade before the Pilgrims landed at Plymouth Rock, their Mestizo (Indian and Spanish) ancestors settled in what is now Santa Fe, New Mexico.

A number of historical events also shaped Hispanic presence in the U.S. in recent centuries: the Louisiana Purchase; the Gadsden Purchase (in which Mexico sold what became part of Arizona and New Mexico to the United States); the admission of Florida and Texas into the Union; the Treaty of Guadalupe Hidalgo (which ended the Mexican-American War); the Spanish-American War; the Mexican Revolution; labor shortages dur-

ing World War I and World War II; the Cuban Revolution; and, in recent decades, political instability in certain countries in Central and South America. Although Hispanic Americans share a common ancestry and language, in their lives and cultural activities they are actually quite diverse.

On the U.S. Census, Hispanic Americans are usually designated solely as "Hispanic." In 1930, "Mexicans" were counted and in 1940 "persons of Spanish mother tongue" were reported. In 1950 and 1960, "persons of Spanish surname" were reported. The 1970 census asked persons about their "origin," and respondents could choose among several Hispanic origins listed on the questionnaire. In 1980 and 1990, persons of "Spanish/Hispanic" origin were tallied as Mexican, Puerto Rican American, Cuban, or "other Hispanic." In a recent burst of specificity, the 1990 census tabulated information for about 30 additional Hispanic origin groups.

General Demographics *(See Chart 3.1)*

Hispanic Americans comprise a large and rapidly growing part of this nation's population. Among the immigrants to the United States in 1990, almost one in five Hispanic Americans were naturalized citizens, while just over four out of five were not citizens; one in seven Mexican Americans were naturalized; about seven out of ten (two-thirds) of the entering Puerto Rican Americans were naturalized; just over one in six Central and South Americans were naturalized; and nearly half of the entering non-Hispanic White Americans gained citizenship status through naturalization.

In 1994, just under one-half of all non-Hispanic Whites were males; the figure was almost exactly the opposite among Hispanic Americans. Just over one-half of all Hispanic Americans were males in 1994.

It has only been since 1930 that portions of the Hispanic American population have been counted in the census; for example in that year, 1.3 million "Mexicans" were counted. Twenty years later, the Census Bureau counted 2.3 million persons with a "Spanish surname," and 20 years after that it reported 9.1 million persons of "Spanish origin."

By 1990, almost 9 percent of the nation's total population was Hispanic American; at 22.4 million people, that was just slightly less than the 1850 total United States population. If growth continues at a steady pace, the Census Bureau has predicted there will be approximately 31 million Hispanic Americans by the year 2000, and an astonishing 81 million by 2050. By 2050, one out of every four Americans would be Hispanic Americans.

Population Growth *(See Chart 3.2)*

In the four years between 1990 and 1994, the nation's average growth rate was a moderate 6 percent; the Hispanic American population, however, grew by 28 percent during that four-year period (a rough continuation of the trend for the past 20 years). Thus, nearly one in ten Americans today are of Hispanic origin.

Two of the reasons the Hispanic American population is growing so fast are the high birth rate and the large number of annual immigrants. Between 1990 and 1994, nearly 2 million Hispanic immigrants came to the United States.

In the decade between 1980 and 1990, the Hispanic American population grew more than seven times as fast as the rest of the nation. A major factor of the tremendous increase was the substantial immi-gration during that decade from Mexico, Central America, the Caribbean, and South America.

In the ten years between 1970 and 1980, the Mexican American population nearly doubled. In the following decade, it virtually doubled again. Also growing at a huge rate were both the Cuban American and Puerto Rican American populations (about four times as fast as the national average). The large influx of Central and South American immigrants between 1980 and 1990 was principally responsible for the dramatic growth of the Hispanic American population.

For the first time since the 18th century, non-Hispanic Whites are trailing another group in immigration. The number of Hispanic Americans added to the United States population during the 1993–94 fiscal year exceeded the number of non-Hispanic Whites.

Regional Dispersion *(See Chart 3.3)*

In 1990, almost nine out of ten Hispanic Americans lived in just ten states; the four states with proportionally the largest number of Hispanic Americans were California, Texas, New York, and Florida. Approximately 26 percent of the total population in both the first two states are Hispanic American; for the third and fourth states, the number is more than 10 percent. The remaining six most populous states were Illinois, New Jersey, Arizona (almost 20 percent Hispanic American), New Mexico (40 percent Hispanic American), Colorado (more than 10 percent), and Massachusetts. From this list it is easy to see that most Hispanic Americans lived in the Southwestern portion of the United States (chiefly in New Mexico, Texas, Arizona, and California).

In 1992, the ten cities with the highest number of Hispanic American people were: New York City, with 1.8 million people; Los Angeles, with 1.4 million; Chicago, with 546,000; San Antonio, with 520,000; Houston, with 450,000; El Paso, Texas, with 356,000; San Diego, with 230,000; Miami, with 224,000; Dallas, with 210,000; and San Jose, California, with 208,000.

In 1992, the ten cities with the highest percentage of Hispanic Americans per capita were: El Paso, Texas (356,000 Hispanic Americans, 69.0 percent of the city's total population); Santa Ana, California (191,000, 65.2 percent); Miami (224,000, 62.5 percent); San Antonio (520,000, 55.6 percent); Corpus Christi, Texas (130,000, 50.4 percent); Los Angeles (1.4 million, 39.9 percent); Albuquerque (133,000, 34.5 percent); Anaheim, California (84,000, 31.4 percent); Fresno, California (106,000, 29.9 percent); and Tucson (119,000, 29.3 percent). In 1970, Santa Fe would have been listed among these cities, with 65 percent of the town's total population being Hispanic American. However, in the last 20 years the town has become so popular (with a subsequent rise in property values) that by 1994 only 48 percent of the population remained Hispanic American. For the first time in the history of the town, Hispanic Americans are a minority.

During the 1980s, so many Salvadorans were fleeing the civil war in their country that the Hispanic American population in Washington, D.C., has more than doubled.

Ethnic and Cultural Backgrounds *(See Chart 3.4)*

In 1990, of the 22.3 million Hispanic Americans living in the United States, Mexican Americans made up by far the largest group, representing about 61 percent of the total. Puerto Rican Americans were the second largest group, comprising roughly one out of eight Hispanic Americans, while Cuban Americans were third, at only 1 in 20. Central Americans in general represented about 1 in 16 of all Hispanic Americans, and among the Central Americans about two-fifths of those were Salvadoran American, one-fifth Guatemalan American; only 15 percent (or 2 in 13) were Nicaraguan American. South Americans in general represented about 1 in every 20 Hispanic Americans. Specifically, of that 5 percent, one in three were Colombian American, just under one in five were Ecuadorian American, and a few more than one in six were Peruvian American. Dominican Americans, Spanish Americans, and other Hispanic American groups each constituted over 2 percent of the total Hispanic American population.

Residential Dispersion

In 1990, roughly two out of three non-Hispanic White metropolitan dwellers owned their own home; however, only two out of five metropolitan Hispanic Americans were home owners. In addition, in metropolitan areas, the median value of homes owned by Hispanic Americans was considerably lower than that of homes owned by non-Hispanic Whites ($85,000 compared to $92,000). The median value of a home is the owner's estimate of how much their property would sell for if it were on the market.

In general, the most expensive metropolitan Hispanic American–owned homes were in California. Although only 4 of the nation's top 50 metropolitan areas are in California (Anaheim–Santa Ana, Oxnard–Ventura, San Francisco, and San Jose), the median value of homes in those areas exceeded $200,000. Even so, the home values for Hispanic Americans in these metropolitan areas were still 20 to 25 percent lower than for their non-Hispanic White counterparts. The only top-50 metropolitan area in the country where the Hispanic American householders median home value was higher than that of non-Hispanic Whites was Jersey City, New Jersey ($165,000 compared to $160,000). Of the other 49 top metropolitan areas, the largest value gap between Hispanic American and non-Hispanic White median home values was in the Philadelphia–New Jersey area, where the median value of Hispanic Americans' homes was just over $30,000, while among non-Hispanic Whites the median value was $113,000.

Between 1992 and 1993, almost one in four Hispanic Americans moved; between 1993 and 1994, the number had dropped to just over one in five.

Households with more than one person per room are considered "crowded." Within metropolitan areas in 1990, Hispanic American households were far more likely than non-Hispanic White households to be crowded; in central cities, this discrepancy was even more pronounced (29 percent compared to 2 percent).

Metropolitan non-Hispanic White households contained a median 2.2 persons, while the Hispanic American metropolitan household median was 3.3 persons. In central cities, Hispanic American households averaged 3.19 persons, but in the suburbs the average jumped to 3.45. Among non-Hispanic White households, the comparable medians had a much smaller range (1.99 in central cities compared to 2.32 in the suburbs). In the top 50 metropolitan areas of the nation, the Salinas-Seaside-Monterey, California, MA and the Anaheim–Santa Ana, California, MA saw the largest Hispanic American households, each with medians of over four people; and the Los Angeles–Long Beach MA saw the most common occurrences of household crowding (almost half of the Hispanic American households in that area were crowded in 1990). In half of the top 50 metropolitan areas, more than one out of every four Hispanic American households lived in crowded conditions.

Hispanic American subgroups in suburbs generally mirror the geographic distribution of Hispanic Americans in the United States. For example, Caribbean, Central, and South American immigrants tend toward the Northern and Eastern suburbs, while Salvadorans move primarily to the Virginia and Maryland suburbs of Washington, D.C. Mexican Americans account for four out of five Hispanic Americans in the Los Angeles suburban areas, and Cuban Americans comprise more than half of Miami's Hispanic American suburban population. Puerto Rican Americans not only make up the majority of suburban Hispanic Americans in Philadelphia and Orlando, they also account for more than one-fourth of those in New York; Bergen-Passaic, New Jersey; Newark; Boston; Tampa–St. Petersburg; and Fort Lauderdale. The notable exception is Chicago, which is the only large northern midwestern metropolitan area with large numbers of Mexican Americans in its suburbs.

In 1990, 6 million of the nation's households had a Hispanic American householder. The vast majority of those (5.4 million) lived in a metropolitan area. Over half of the nation's Hispanic American households were established in central cities of metropolitan areas. Of the remainder, most lived in the suburbs (37 percent), while only a very few (10 percent) lived outside of metropolitan areas altogether. About 8 percent of all the metropolitan area householders were Hispanic American; in central cities the number of householders was about 11 percent, and in the suburbs the number was approximately 5 percent.

Of the seven metropolitan areas in the United States with a 40 percent or higher rate of Hispanic American householders per capita, six were in the South (including Texas), and four were in Texas alone. The Laredo, Texas, MA had the highest percentage of Hispanic American householders with 91 percent, followed by the McAllen–Edinburg–Mission, Texas, MA, at 76 percent, the Brownsville–Harlingen, Texas, MA at 72 percent, and the El Paso, Texas, MA at 60 percent.

In terms of numbers of people, the metropolitan areas with the most Hispanic American households were the Los Angeles–Long Beach MA (784,000), the New York City MA (584,000), the Miami–Hialeah MA (320,000), the Chicago MA (189,000), and the Houston MA (187,000). These five metropolitan areas combined accounted for almost two of every five Hispanic American households in the United States. More than four out of every five Hispanic Americans lived in one of the 50 metropolitan areas that had more than 17,000 Hispanic American households, and 40 of those 50 were in the West or the South (California and Texas together account for more than half of them: 16 in California, and 10 in Texas).

According to the 1990 census, about 43 percent of the nation's Hispanic Americans live in suburbs of metropolitan areas, up from about 40 percent in 1980. In just one decade, the number of Hispanic American suburbanites grew by 69 percent from 5.9 million to 8.7 million people. The suburbs gained about 15.3 million people during the decade, with Hispanic Americans accounting for nearly one-fourth of the total growth.

Metropolitan areas with large Hispanic American populations witnessed the greatest growth of Hispanic American suburbanites in the 1980s. Almost 600,000 Hispanic Americans moved to the suburbs of Los Angeles during the decade, a number larger than the total Hispanic American suburban population of any other area. The Riverside, California, MA and the Miami MA ranked second and third in terms of both number of people and percentage gain.

Among the Hispanic Americans who rent, the Nassau–Suffolk, New York, MA, the Anaheim–Santa Ana, California, MA, and the San Jose MA charged the highest prices of any other top 50 metropolitan area, ranging from about $700 per month to about $650. The least expensive metropolitan areas were the Laredo, Brownsville–Harlingen, Texas, MA, and the McAllen–Edinburg–Mission, Texas, MA, with rents under $225. Within metropolitan areas, Hispanic American renters paid a median of $405 compared to the non-Hispanic White rate of $414. Rent in the suburbs was higher than in central cities: $479 in suburbs for Hispanic Americans, more than the figure of $440 for non-Hispanic Whites; $373 in central cities for Hispanic Americans, less than the $392 average rent for non-Hispanic Whites.

Nativity *(See Chart 3.5)*

In 1990, almost 8 million Hispanic Americans then living in the United States were foreign-born; those from Mexico, Central America, South America, and the Caribbean represented about 43 percent of all the foreign-born people in the United States. Among the foreign-born Hispanic Americans, the proportions varied greatly among ethnic groups, from fewer than one in ten for Spanish Americans, to almost two-thirds for Central Americans.

In 1994, only 3 percent of all non-Hispanic Whites were born outside the United States, compared to 39 percent of Hispanic Americans. Nearly three-fourths of the Hispanic American population, however, were either U.S. born or naturalized citizens (compared to 97 percent of the non-Hispanic American population). Many Central Americans are relative newcomers and have not had time to go through the naturalization process, but keep in mind that everyone born in the Commonwealth of Puerto Rico is already an American citizen.

Almost two-thirds of all Hispanic Americans were born in the United States—including more than four out of every five Spanish Americans, over two-thirds of all Mexican Americans, one-fourth of South Americans, and about one in five Central Americans.

Citizenship

In 1994, 1.9 million Hispanic Americans were naturalized citizens, compared to 8.4 million who were *not* citizens. Among Mexican Americans, 878,000 were naturalized, while 5.3 million remained status-unchanged; 46,000 Puerto Rican Americans were naturalized, 28,000 were not; 375,000 Cuban Ameri-cans were naturalized, 416,000 were not; and among other Hispanic American groups, 455,000 people were naturalized, leaving 2.1 million not citizens. This represents 18.3 percent of the total Hispanic American population who were naturalized, and 81.7 percent who remained without citizenship status.

Foreign-Born

Whether pulled by the need to be reunited with families or pushed by political events occurring in the country of their birth, many Hispanic Americans moved to the United States between 1980 and 1990; more than half of the Hispanic American foreign-born population arrived since 1980. Prior to that, about 28 percent came between 1970 and 1979, only 15 percent between 1960 and 1969, and a mere 7 percent prior to 1960.

About one of every five Central Americans who were foreign-born arrived in the United States between 1970 and 1979. A full 70 percent arrived between 1980 and 1990, and the Central American immigrants represent the largest proportion of newly arrived Hispanic immigrants for that decade. In the 1960s, the largest contingency of immigrants were from Cuba. Between 1960 and 1969 (particularly in the early part of the decade, following the Cuban Missile Crisis), almost half of the Cuban foreign-born arrived here.

Immigration   *(See Chart 3.6)*

Before 1950, the largest proportion of legal immigrants to the United States was from Europe, but between 1950 and 1990 the nation witnessed a wave of immigration from Latin American countries. Between 1951 and 1960, of the 2.5 million legal immigrants, only one in five were Hispanic; from 1961 to 1970, one in three of the 3.3 million legal immigrants were from Latin America; during the 1970s, roughly four in ten of the 4.5 million legal immigrants were from Latin America, and by 1980, the number was up to about 47 percent of the total. From 1980 to 1990, nearly 3 million legal Hispanics came to the United States.

Age Distribution   *(See Charts 3.7 and 3.8)*

In 1994, the median age for Hispanic Americans was 10 years younger than it was for non-Hispanic Whites (26 years old compared to 36 years old). Among the Hispanic American groups, the median age ranged greatly, from 24 years for Mexican Americans to 43 years for Cuban Americans. Among Hispanic American males in general, the median age was 25, while for Hispanic American females it was 34.

Approximately 13 percent of non-Hispanic Americans (a shorthand term that includes non-Hispanic Whites, African Americans, Asian Pacific Americans, and all others who are not of Hispanic origin) were 65 years old or over, compared to only about 5 percent of Hispanic Americans. Nearly 40 percent of the Hispanic American popu-lation was under 20 years old (compared to the national average of 28 percent). This difference can be attributed to relatively high fertility rates among recent immigrants.

Elderly

In 1994, about one out of every five elderly Hispanics was living in poverty; that's two times the rate for non-Hispanic Whites.

In 1990, the United States was home to about 31 million elderly people of all races, and 1.1 million of them were Hispanic American; that accounts for only about 5 percent of Hispanic Americans. It is estimated that the proportion of Hispanic Americans who are elderly will climb to about 16 percent by the year 2050; that percentage includes an estimated more than 4 million

who will be more than 80 years old, and an estimate of 12 million total.

Educational Attainment *(See Charts 3.9 and 3.10)*

In 1993, 13 percent of the nation's 18-to-24-year-olds were in the "dropout pool," down from 15 percent a decade earlier. Among Hispanic Americans, the likelihood of dropouts was much greater than among African Americans and non-Hispanic Whites: one in three of all Hispanic Americans in the age group, compared to under one in six for African Americans and about one in eight for Whites. More than four out of five non-Hispanic Whites, three out of four African Americans, and fewer than two out of three Hispanic Americans were high school graduates.

In 1970, only three out of ten Hispanic Americans 25 years old and over had completed at least four years of high school, and fewer than 1 in 20 had completed four or more years of college. By 1980, about four out of ten Hispanic Americans had completed high school, and 1 out of 13 had completed four or more years of college.

By 1994, more than half of all Hispanic Americans aged 25 years old and over were high school graduates, compared to just over four out of ten in 1980. During the same time period, however, the proportion of Hispanic Americans who held bachelor's degrees remained unchanged (roughly 9 percent, or 1 in 11). Hispanic American adults, however, were less likely than non-Hispanic American adults to complete high school or college.

In 1993, similar to 20 years previous, the college enrollment rate of Hispanic American high school graduates stood at 36 percent.

In 1990, the high school completion rates among Hispanic American groups varied considerably. For example, persons who identified themselves as "Spanish" had a 77 percent graduation rate, compared to only 34 percent among Salvadorans. As with high school completion, the rates of college completion varied greatly, depending on the particular Hispanic American group, ranging from 20 percent among Spanish Americans to 5 percent among Salvadorans. The Hispanic Americans of South American origin tended to have higher educational attainments than those from Cuba or Mexico. Nearly one in five South American persons had a bachelor's or postgraduate degree, compared to only one in six Cuban Americans, and only 1 in 16 Mexican Americans.

In 1993, the distribution of degrees by field of study among Hispanic Americans was not substantially different from that of the general population, with the exception of the field of "education"; Hispanic Americans were less likely than average to have earned their highest degree in education.

Variations in Educational Attainment

In 1994, among Hispanic Americans 25 years old and over, about one in ten had less than a fifth-grade education, more than half were high school graduates or more, and about 1 in 11 had earned a bachelor's degree. Within the specific ethnic groups, there was a great deal of diversity. For example: among Mexican Americans, about one in seven have less than a fifth-grade education, nearly half are high school graduates or more, and 1 in 15 have a bachelor's degree or higher; among Puerto Rican Americans, Cuban Americans, Central and South Americans, the fifth-grade education rate was lower, but the high school and bachelor's degree rates were higher. Puerto Rican Americans with less than a fifth-grade education numbered roughly 1 in 14, Cuban Americans numbered about 1 in 18, and Central and South Americans numbered nearly 1 in 12. The high school graduate or more rates for Puerto Rican Americans ranked at three out of five, just over two-thirds among Cuban Americans, and slightly under two-thirds for Central and South Americans. For those holding bachelor's degrees or higher, Puerto Rican Americans numbered about 1 in 11, Cuban Americans were approximately one in six, and Central and South Americans were at about one in eight. When compared to non-Hispanic Whites, those with less than a fifth-grade education numbered about one in eight, but six out of seven were high school graduates, and nearly one-fourth had a bachelor's degree or more.

Among Hispanic Americans specifically, about half the population earned a high school diploma or higher in 1990, though the rates varied from a high of 77 percent among Spanish Americans to a low of 43 percent among Dominicans. And while almost 10 percent of the Hispanic American population received a bachelor's degree or higher in that same year, about 20 percent of Spanish Americans and South Americans earned bachelor's degrees, compared to only 6 percent of Mexican Americans.

Occupations *(See Charts 3.11 and 3.12)*

In 1992, 60 percent of all Hispanic American men between the ages of 25 to 54 years worked year-round, full-time, down from 67 percent in 1979. Among Hispanic American women in 1992, 37 percent worked year-round, full-time, up from 30 percent in 1979.

In 1994, two-thirds of all non-Hispanic Whites were in the labor force, and only 1 in 20 were unemployed. Nearly as many Hispanics were in the civilian labor force, but one in nine were unemployed. Specifically, two-thirds of all Mexican Americans were in the labor force, with one in nine unemployed; just over one-half of all Puerto Rican Americans were in the labor force with one in seven unemployed; almost six in ten Cuban Americans were in the labor force with 1 in 15 unemployed; and seven in ten Central and South Americans in the labor force with one in nine unemployed.

In 1994, one out of nine Hispanic American males held managerial and professional specialty jobs, compared to almost one in three non-Hispanic White males, 1 in 12 Mexican American males, one in seven Puerto Rican American males, one in five Cuban American males, and one in seven Central and South American males. One in seven Hispanic American males held technical, sales, and administrative support jobs, compared to one in five among non-Hispanic White males, just over one in eight for Mexican American males, almost one in five for Puerto Rican American males, almost one in four of all Cuban American males, and about one in seven Central and South American males. Service occupations were held by about 17 percent of the Hispanic American males, compared to only 9 percent among non-Hispanic White males, 16 percent among Mexican American males, 21 percent for Puerto Rican American males, about 15 percent for Cuban American males, and just over 20 percent for Central and South American males. Slightly more than 1 in 13 Hispanic American males worked in farming, forestry, and fishing, compared to 1 in 25 non-Hispanic White males, 1 in 10 Mexican American males, 1 in 60 Puerto Rican American males, 1 in 80 Cuban American males, and about 1 in 30 Central and South American males.

About one in five Hispanic American males were occupied in the precision production, craft, and repair trades, and the same was true of both non-Hispanic White males and Mexican American males. Puerto Rican American males and Central and South American males were only a little less likely to work in those fields, while Cuban American males were the least likely, at about one in seven. Finally, almost one-third of all Hispanic American males were operators, fabricators, and laborers, compared to fewer than one in five non-Hispanic White males, about one-third of all Mexican American males, one-fourth of all Puerto Rican American and Cuban American males, and a little less than one-third of the Central and South American males.

In 1994, about one in six Hispanic American females held managerial and professional specialty jobs, almost two out of five had technical, sales, and administrative support jobs, and nearly one-third had service occupations; but only 1 in 85 had farming, forestry, or fishing jobs, one in three had precision production, craft, and repair jobs, and about one in seven were operators, fabricators, and laborers. Among non-Hispanic White females, about one-third held managerial and professional specialty jobs, almost half had technical, sales, and administrative support jobs, nearly one in six had service occupations, only 1 in 85 had farming, forestry, and fishing jobs, 1 out of 50 had precision production, craft, and repair jobs, and about 1 in 16 were operators, fabricators, and laborers. Among Mexican American women, only one in seven held managerial and professional specialty jobs, almost two out of five had technical, sales, and administrative support jobs, nearly one-third had service occupations, 1 in 55 had farming, forestry, and fishing jobs, 1 out of 30 had precision production, craft, and repair jobs, and 1 in 7 were operators, fabricators, or laborers. Among Puerto Rican American women, about one in four held managerial and professional specialty jobs, almost half had technical, sales, and administrative support jobs, just over one in five had service occupations, 1 in 500 had farming, forestry, and fishing jobs, 1 out of 50 had precision production, craft, and repair jobs, and 1 out of 11 were operators, fabricators, and laborers. Among Cuban American women, only one in five held managerial and professional specialty jobs, nearly half had technical, sales, and administrative support jobs, about one in ten had service occupations, 0.6 percent had farming, forestry, and fishing jobs, 2 percent had precision production, craft, and repair jobs, and one in eight were operators, fabricators, and laborers. Finally, among Central and South American women, one in ten held managerial and professional specialty jobs, almost one-third had technical, sales, and administrative support jobs, over one-third had service occupations, none were listed as holding farming, forestry, and fishing jobs, 1 out of 30 had precision production, craft, and repair jobs, and one in six were operators, fabricators, and laborers

From the numbers above, it is clear that Hispanic Americans are far less likely than non-Hispanic Americans to be professionals or managers. Only about one in eight Hispanic American males held such a position in 1990, compared with over one in four non-Hispanic American males. During that time, more than one-fourth of all Hispanic American males 16 years old and over worked as operators, fabricators, and laborers, compared with fewer than one in five non-Hispanic American males.

Among Hispanic American women, the technical, sales, and administrative support positions provided the largest employment base, at almost two in five; however, there were still more non-Hispanic females in the field, at almost one-half. About one in six non-Hispanic females worked in service occupations, which provided employment for fully half of all working Hispanic American women.

Income *(See Chart 3.13)*

In 1993, the median income for non-Hispanic White males was $22,000. For Hispanic American males, it was $15,000; among the subgroups, the median figure ranged from $21,000 for Cuban Americans, to $19,000 for Puerto Rican Americans, to $15,000 for Central and South Americans, to $14,000 for Mexican Americans. Year-round, full-time income for non-Hispanic White males was $32,000. Among Hispanic American males, it was a median of $20,000, which varied from $24,000 for Puerto Rican Americans and Cuban Americans, to $19,000 for Mexican Americans, to $18,000 for Central and South Americans.

The 1993 median income for non-Hispanic White women was $15,000. For Hispanic American women, it was only $11,000, ranging from $24,000 for Cuban Americans, to $15,000 for Puerto Rican Americans, to $11,000 for Central and South Americans, to $10,000 for Mexican Americans. The income for year-round, full-time non-Hispanic White working women was $22,000. For Hispanic Americans it was $17,000, which ranged from $21,000 for Puerto Rican Americans, to $20,000 for Cuban Americans, to $16,000 for Mexican Americans, to $16,000 for Central and South Americans. When comparing the median wages of year-round, full-time Hispanic American women workers to the wages of their male counterparts, the women earned only 83 cents to the dollar. Among non-Hispanic White women and men, the women earned only 70 cents to the dollar.

Family Income

In 1990, the median family income for all Americans was $35,000; for Hispanic Americans it was only $25,000. Among Hispanic Americans, Dominicans had the lowest median family income ($20,000), Spanish Americans the highest ($37,000). Among all female householders with no husband present, the median income was $17,000; for comparable Hispanic American women, the median was only $12,000.

Between 1979 and 1992, the percentage of year-round, full-time Hispanic American civilian workers 16 years old and over who earned low incomes rose from 13.4 percent to 26.4 percent among males, and from 32.2 percent to 36.6 percent among females. During the same period, the percentage of comparable Hispanic American workers who earned high incomes only rose from 5.2 to 5.3 percent among men and 1.0 to 1.8 percent among women.

In 1993, the median household income for non-Hispanic Whites was $34,000; for Hispanic Americans it was only $23,000, ranging from $25,000 for Central and South Americans, to $24,000 for Mexican Americans and Cuban Americans, to $19,000 for Puerto Rican Americans. Puerto Rican American female householders with no husband present had the lowest median household income of all, at $9,000, while Cuban American and Spanish Americans female householders with no husband present had the highest incomes, $19,511 and $20,000, respectively.

The 1993 median incomes for non-Hispanic White, African American, Asian Pacific American, and Hispanic American households remained unchanged in real terms from their 1992 levels. The real median household income for all these groups was lower than in 1989.

The 1994 median income per capita for all races was $17,000; for non-Hispanic Whites, $18,000; for African Americans, $11,000; for Asian Pacific Americans, $17,000; and for Hispanic Americans, $9,000.

Market Power *(See Chart 3.14)*

In 1992, there were 720,000 Hispanic American–owned businesses in the United States, which generated $63 billion in sales and employed millions of workers. Hispanic American–owned businesses are growing twice as fast as that of general market companies.

Poverty

In 1990, more than two of every ten Hispanic American families lived in poverty (over 1 million); among the subgroups, one-third of all Dominican families, almost one-third of all Puerto Rican American families, about one in ten Spanish American families, one in nine Cuban American families, just over one in five Central American families, and one out of four Mexican American families lived below the poverty level. Among all Hispanic American individuals, the average poverty rate was about 22 percent, and the median duration of poverty was about five months.

Among Hispanic Americans specifically, the females, children, and elderly had higher proportional poverty rates then their non-Hispanic counterparts. While almost one-third of all Hispanic American women lived in poverty in 1990, only one in eight non-Hispanic women lived in poverty. The poverty levels for Hispanic American and non-Hispanic children under 18 years old were comparable (18 percent compared to 17 percent), but when comparing individuals 65 years old and over, twice as many Hispanic Americans as non-Hispanics in that age group lived in poverty (one-fourth versus one-eighth).

One year later in 1991, 12 percent of Hispanic Americans were chronically poor, and Hispanic Americans comprised 22 percent of the chronically poor. During that same year, 13 percent of those Hispanic Americans living in poverty managed to climb out of poverty. However, in 1993, almost one-third of all Hispanic American families still lived in poverty; they ranged from a low of 17 percent among Cuban Americans to a high of 35 percent among Puerto Rican Americans. The overall percentage is more than twice that of non-Hispanic families living in poverty (27 percent compared to 11 percent).

Hispanic American individuals were also at least twice as likely as non-Hispanic people to be poor; the overall rates in 1993 were 31 percent compared to 13 percent. Among Hispanic Americans under 18 years old, the rate was an astonishing 41 percent, and among Hispanic American people 18 to 64 years old, the rate dropped to 24 percent (for non-Hispanic individuals the rates were 20 and 11 percent, respectively). The poverty rates for elderly individuals were similar to the rates of the 18-to-64-year-olds.

In 1993, one in eight Hispanic American mothers between the ages of 15 to 44 years were recipients of the Women, Infants, and Children supplemental food program (WIC), compared to only 1 in 16 non-Hispanic mothers; approximately half of the Hispanic American WIC mothers were born outside of the United States. During the same period, nearly one in five Hispanic American mothers in the same age range were on Aid to Families with Dependent Children (AFDC). By comparison, only one in ten non-Hispanic mothers received AFDC. In terms of actual people, those numbers translate to about 784,000 Hispanic American mothers and 3 million non-Hispanic mothers. Although both Hispanic American and non-Hispanic mothers on AFDC averaged 20 years old when they had their first child, Hispanic American mothers had almost 0.7 more children than non-Hispanic mothers, and almost one-third of the Hispanic American mothers on AFDC were born outside the United States. The following year, one in four Hispanic American mothers was a food stamp recipient (1.1 million), compared to one in seven non-Hispanic mothers (4.2 million).

Between 1993 and 1994, poverty rates for non-Hispanic Whites and African Americans dropped, though there was no significant change for either Asian Pacific Americans or Hispanic Americans. While the number of poor African Americans dropped significantly between 1993 and 1994, the number of poor Hispanic Americans showed a significant increase. In March 1994, the unemployment rates among Hispanic Americans ranged from about 1 in 14 for Cuban Americans to about one in seven for Puerto Rican Americans. Overall, one in nine Hispanic Americans and 1 in 16 non-Hispanic Whites were unemployed.

Family Composition *(See Chart 3.15)*

In 1990, about one in eight children in the United States were Hispanic American. Of those, two-thirds were of Mexican American origin, with the others tracing their origins to Puerto Rico, Cuba, El Salvador, Colombia, Guatemala, Nicaragua, Ecuador, Peru, Honduras, or other Caribbean and Central and South American countries.

About four out of five Hispanic American preschoolers in 1990 lived in families of one to three children. Among Hispanic American adolescents, slightly over half lived in families of one to three children. Most Hispanic Americans lived in family households and 70 percent of those families were maintained by married couples. Only 1 in 11 were headed by a male with no wife present, while over one in five were headed by a female with no husband present. Depending on the specific Hispanic American subgroup, the family-type distribution varied greatly; for example, over three-fourths of all Cuban American and Spaniard families were maintained by married couples, while about 14 percent of Central American families were maintained by a male with no wife present. Families maintained by a female with no husband present were found primarily among Puerto Rican American and Dominican families.

Half of all Hispanic American children in 1990 had mothers with a high school diploma, and one-fourth of those children had mothers with less than nine years of education. Four out of ten Hispanic American children living with their fathers had fathers who worked part-time or not at all, and the same was true of Hispanic American children living with their mothers. The children living with mothers whose mothers worked full-time, however, were one in five.

In 1994, Hispanic Americans had 67.9 percent married-couple families, 25.2 percent female-householder-with-no-husband-present families, and 6.9 percent male-householder-with-no-wife-present families. By contrast, non-Hispanic Whites had 83.4 percent, 13 percent, and 3.7 percent; Mexican Americans had 71.7 percent, 20.3 percent, and 8 percent; Puerto Rican Americans had 51.7 percent, 43.5 percent, and 4.9 percent; Cuban Americans had 72.7 percent, 24.4 percent, and 3 percent; and Central and South Americans had 66.3 percent, 27.3 percent, and 6.4 percent.

In 1994, 34.8 percent of Hispanic Americans had never been married, 54.2 percent were married, 4.1 percent widowed, and 6.9 percent divorced. By comparison, 23.8 percent of non-Hispanic Whites had never married, 60.4 percent were married, 7 percent widowed, and 8.8 percent divorced. Mexican Americans had 34.8 percent never married, 55.3 percent married, 3.6 percent widowed, and 6.2 percent divorced. Puerto Rican Americans had 37.3 percent never married, 47.6 percent married, 5.5 percent widowed, and 9.6 percent divorced. Cuban Americans had 22 percent never married, 59.6 percent married, 7 percent widowed, and 11.4 percent divorced. Central and South Americans had 37.5 percent never married, 54.2 percent married, 3.8 percent widowed, and 4.6 percent divorced.

In 1994, single parents accounted for almost one-third (35 percent) of all Hispanic American family groups with children present, compared with 65 percent among African Americans and 25 percent among non-Hispanic Whites.

Housing *(See Charts 3.16–3.18)*

Among Hispanic American renters, Mexican Americans were more likely to move than any other group. During 1989 and later, nearly half of all Mexican American renters moved, compared only one-third of the Puerto Rican American or Cuban American renters.

In 1990, 2.5 million Hispanic Americans owned homes. Nearly two-thirds of them were Mexican American, with Puerto Rican Americans and Cuban Americans accounting for 8 percent each, and the remaining 21 percent among other Hispanic origin (including people whose origins are from Spain, the Spanish-speaking countries of Central and South America, and the Caribbean).

In 1991, more than one out of every seven Hispanic Americans households reported crowded living conditions; crowding is defined as more than one person per room in a house. At the same time, almost four out of five Hispanic American families could not afford to buy a median-priced home (compared to fewer than half of all non-Hispanic White families).

The 1991 median value of metropolitan homes owned by Hispanic American households was $85,000. For non-Hispanic White households in metropolitan areas, the median value was $91,000. Only four in ten Hispanic Americans were home owners, compared to two out of three metropolitan non-Hispanic White householders.

The highest number of Hispanic American households in 1991 were in the Los Angeles–Long Beach metropolitan area. Thirty-nine of the 50 largest metropolitan areas with the highest number of Hispanic American households were either located in the West or the South; California, with 15, and Texas, with 10, accounted for half of them.

Health

Between 1990 and 1992, during a 32-month period, one in ten Hispanic Americans were not covered by any health insurance, compared to only 1 in 30 non-Hispanic Whites; further, only half of those Hispanic Americans who *did* have health insurance were covered for the entire 32-month period, compared to four out of five non-Hispanic Whites with coverage.

Despite such programs as Medicaid and Medicare, almost one-third of the nation's poor had no health insurance of any kind during 1993; poor persons made up almost one-third of all uninsured Americans. Among poor persons, and all persons alike, Hispanic Americans were the most likely to lack coverage; while 14 percent of the nation lacked health insurance in 1993, fully one-third of Hispanic Americans lacked such coverage.

Similarly, between 1990 and 1992, one out of four Americans had a lapse in health insurance, but among Hispanic Americans, the number was almost one-half of their total numbers. Overall, in 1990 almost half of all Hispanic Americans lacked health insurance altogether, compared to one in five non-Hispanic Whites.

Language

The common bond among Hispanic Americans is, naturally, the Spanish language. In 1990, about one out of every seven children in the nation who were five years old and over spoke a language other than English at home; about half of all the non-English speakers in the country spoke Spanish. Nearly all the Hispanic American non-English speakers spoke Spanish, and almost four out of five Hispanic Americans spoke a language other than English at home. Among the Hispanic Americans who spoke Spanish at home, about half of them reported speaking English "very well," while the other half reported that they did not speak English "very well." A greater proportion of Dominicans and Central Americans than Puerto Rican Americans and Spanish Americans who spoke Spanish at home did not speak English "very well."

In 1990, 19 out of 20 Hispanic Americans aged five years and over who were born outside the United States spoke a language at home other than English, compared to only about two-thirds of all Hispanic Americans who were native-born.

Voter Turnout

In the November 1994 elections, the overall turnout was 45 percent when computed based on the number of residents. When the turnout rate is computed based on the number of citizens, however, the percentage rises to 48; it also significantly increases the turnout level among Hispanic Americans to over one-third. Thirty percent of all Hispanic Americans were registered to vote and 19 percent of them reported that they *did* vote. Among the 81 percent who did not vote, only 13 percent of them were registered, the other 54 percent were not U.S. citizens.

Agriculture

One percent of all American farm-owners in the United States in 1992 were Hispanic Americans.

Map 3.1 Hispanic Americans by State, 1990

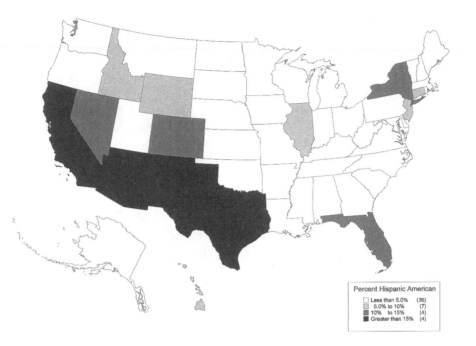

Percent Hispanic American

☐	Less than 5.0%	(36)
▨	5.0% to 10%	(7)
▩	10% to 15%	(4)
■	Greater than 15%	(4)

Map 3.2 Hispanic Americans by County, 1990

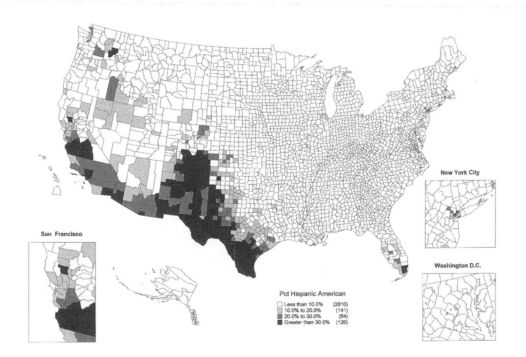

New York City

San Francisco

Washington D.C.

Pct Hispanic American

☐	Less than 10.0%	(2810)
▨	10.0% to 20.0%	(141)
▩	20.0% to 30.0%	(64)
■	Greater than 30.0%	(126)

Map 3.3 Mexican Americans by State, 1990

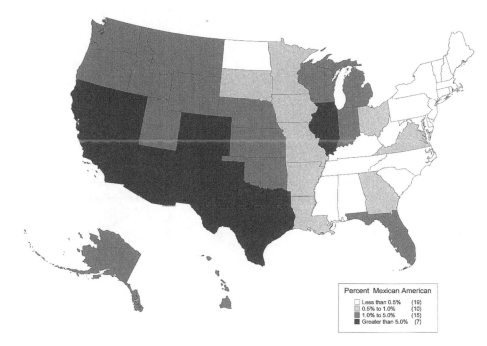

Percent Mexican American

☐ Less than 0.5%	(19)
0.5% to 1.0%	(10)
1.0% to 5.0%	(15)
■ Greater than 5.0%	(7)

Map 3.4 Mexican Americans by County, 1990

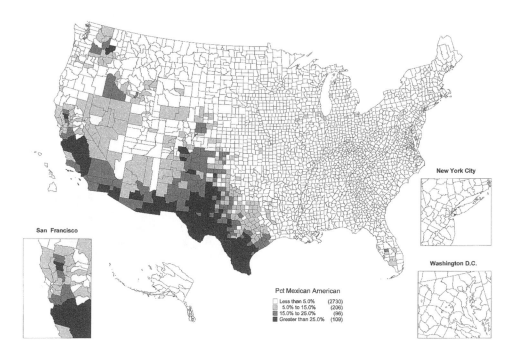

New York City

San Francisco

Washington D.C.

Pct Mexican American

☐ Less than 5.0%	(2730)
5.0% to 15.0%	(206)
15.0% to 25.0%	(96)
■ Greater than 25.0%	(109)

Map 3.5 Puerto Rican Americans by State, 1990

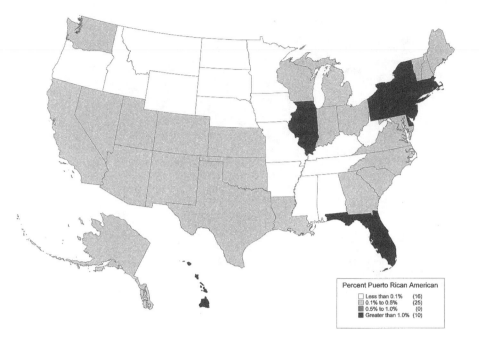

Map 3.6 Puerto Rican Americans by County, 1990

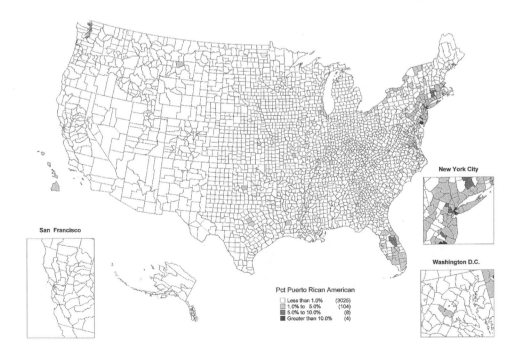

Map 3.7 Cuban Americans by State, 1990

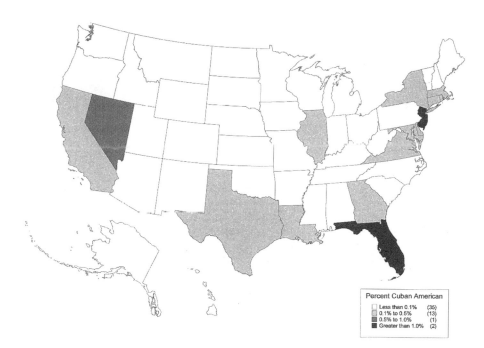

Map 3.8 Cuban Americans by County, 1990

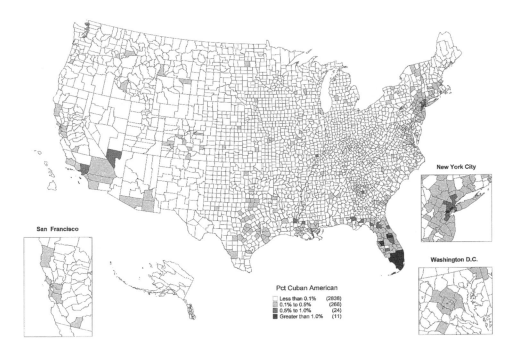

Map 3.9 Dominican Americans by County, 1990

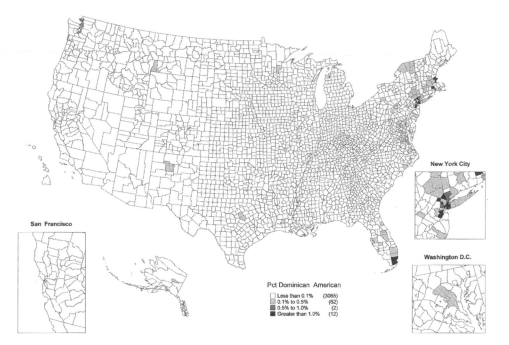

Map 3.10 El Salvadoran Americans by County, 1990

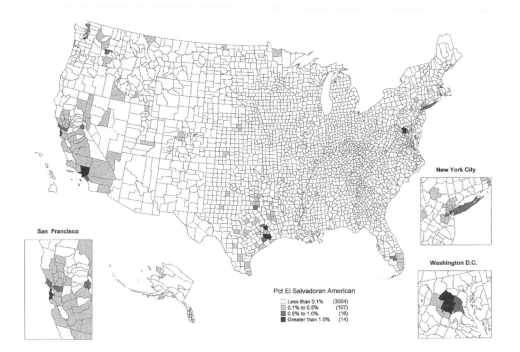

Map 3.11   Honduran Americans by County, 1990

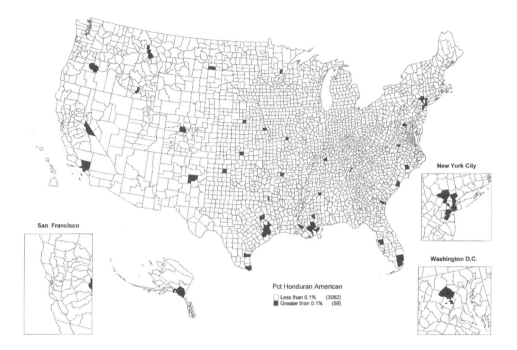

Map 3.12   Guatemalan Americans by County, 1990

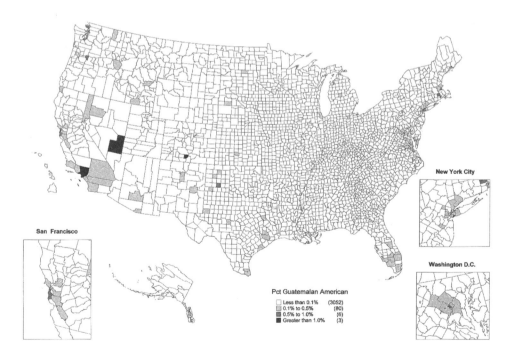

Map 3.13 Nicaraguan Americans by County, 1990

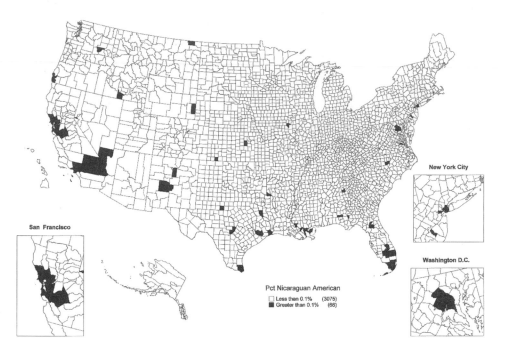

Map 3.14 Panamanian Americans by County, 1990

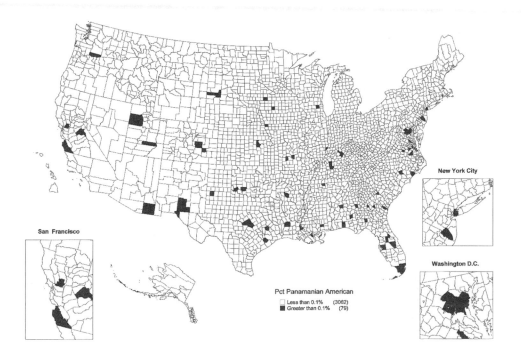

Chart 3.1 Projected Hispanic American Growth Rate, 1930–2050 (Millions)

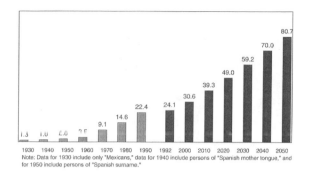

Note: Data for 1930 include only "Mexicans," data for 1940 include persons of "Spanish mother tongue," and for 1950 include persons of "Spanish surname."

Chart 3.2 Hispanic American Population Growth Rate, 1970–1990 (Percent)

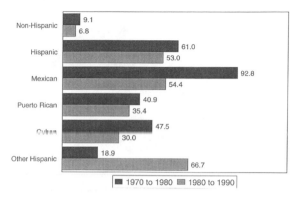

■ 1970 to 1980 ■ 1980 to 1990

Chart 3.3 Hispanic American Population by State, 1990 (Percent)

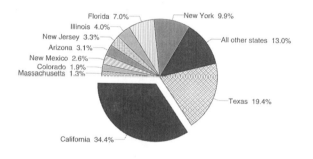

Chart 3.4 Nativity and Citizenship for Selected Hispanic American Origin Groups, 1990 (Percent)

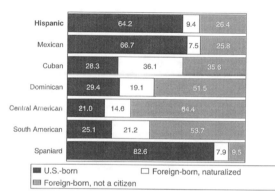

■ U.S.-born   □ Foreign-born, naturalized
■ Foreign-born, not a citizen

Chart 3.5   Hispanic American Population by Place of Origin, 1990 (Percent)

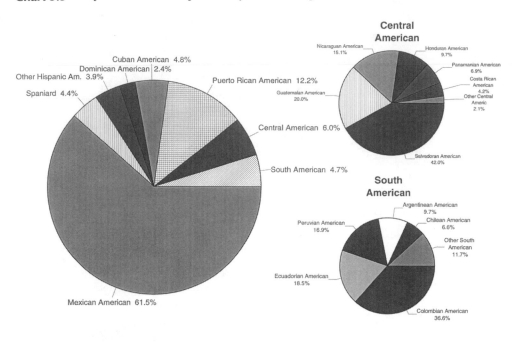

Cuban American 4.8%
Dominican American 2.4%
Other Hispanic Am. 3.9%
Spaniard 4.4%
Puerto Rican American 12.2%
Central American 6.0%
South American 4.7%
Mexican American 61.5%

Central American

Nicaraguan American 15.1%
Honduran American 9.7%
Panamanian American 6.9%
Costa Rican American 4.2%
Other Central Americ 2.1%
Guatemalan American 20.0%
Salvadoran American 42.0%

South American

Argentinean American 9.7%
Chilean American 6.6%
Other South American 11.7%
Peruvian American 16.9%
Ecuadorian American 18.5%
Colombian American 36.6%

Chart 3.6 Hispanic American Immigrants by Decade (Percent)

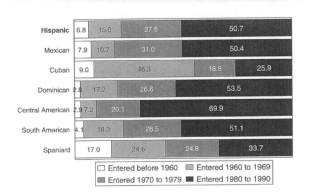

Hispanic	6.8	15.0	27.5	50.7
Mexican	7.9	10.7	31.0	50.4
Cuban	9.0	46.3	18.8	25.9
Dominican	2.8	17.2	26.6	53.5
Central American	2.9 7.2	20.1	69.9	
South American	4.1	18.3	26.5	51.1
Spaniard	17.0	24.6	24.8	33.7

☐ Entered before 1960   ▨ Entered 1960 to 1969
▨ Entered 1970 to 1979   ■ Entered 1980 to 1990

Chart 3.7 Resident Hispanic American Population by Age, 1990 (Percent)

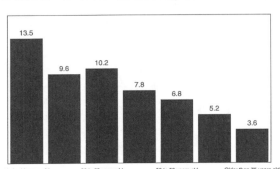

13.5
9.6
10.2
7.8
6.8
5.2
3.6

Under 19 years old
20 to 29 years old
30 to 39 years old
40 to 49 years old
50 to 59 years old
60 to 74 years old
Older than 75 years old

Chart 3.8 Hispanic and Non-Hispanic White Age Distribution, 1990 (Percent)

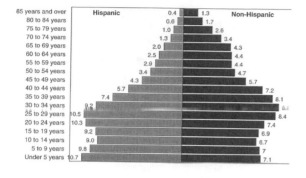

Chart 3.9 Hispanic American and Non-Hispanic White American Educational Attainment, 1970–1990 (Percent)

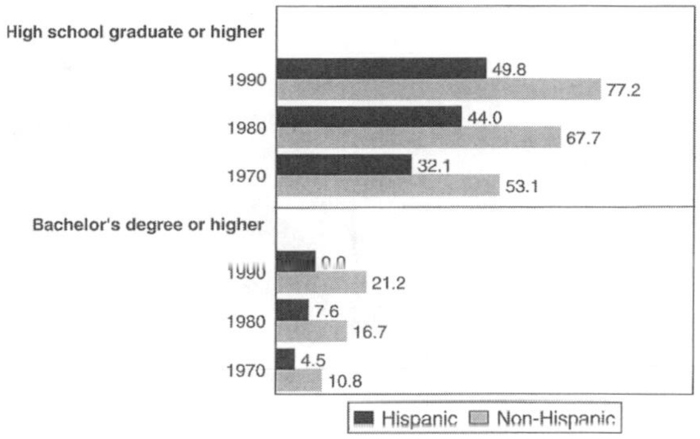

Chart 3.10 Educational Attainment for Selected Hispanic American Origin Groups, 1990 (Percent, 25 years and older)

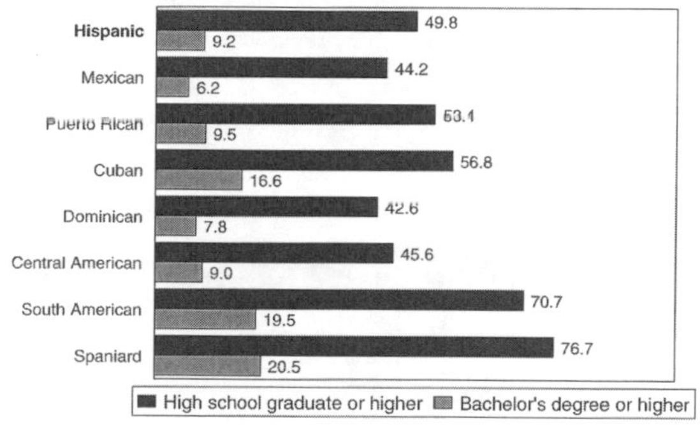

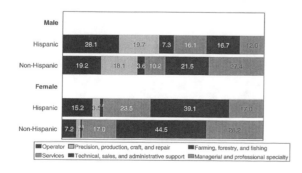

Chart 3.11 Hispanic American Occupational Distribution by Sex, 1994 (Percent, 16 years and older)

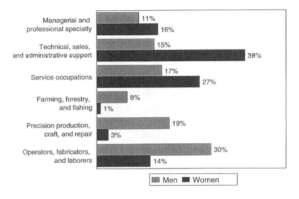

Chart 3.12 Major Occupations for Hispanic and Non-Hispanic White Americans by Sex, 1990 (Percent, 16 years and older)

Chart 3.13 Median Hispanic American Income by Family Composition, 1990 (Thousands, in 1989 dollars)

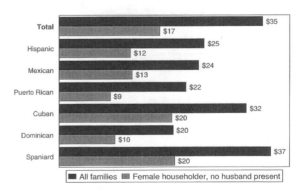

Chart 3.14 Hispanic American-Owned Firms, 1972–1988 (Thousands)

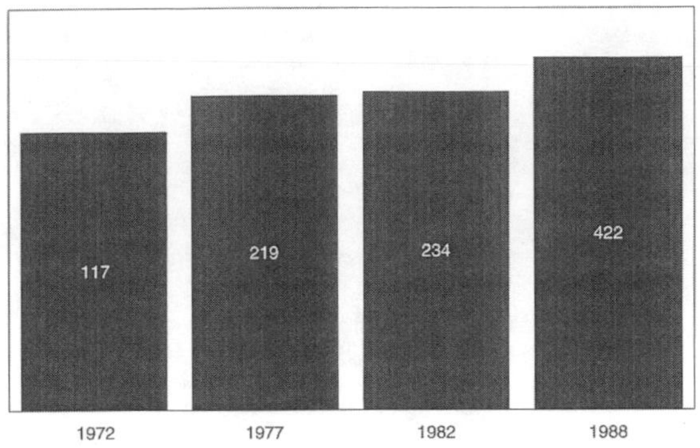

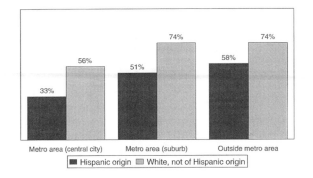

Chart 3.15 Hispanic American Composition by Place of Origin, 1990 (Percent)

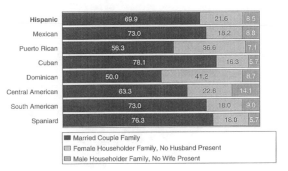

Chart 3.16 Hispanic American and Non-Hispanic White American Home Ownership, 1990 (Percent)

Chart 3.17 Crowded Living Conditions for Hispanic and Non-Hispanic White Americans, 1990 (Percent of households with more than one person per room)

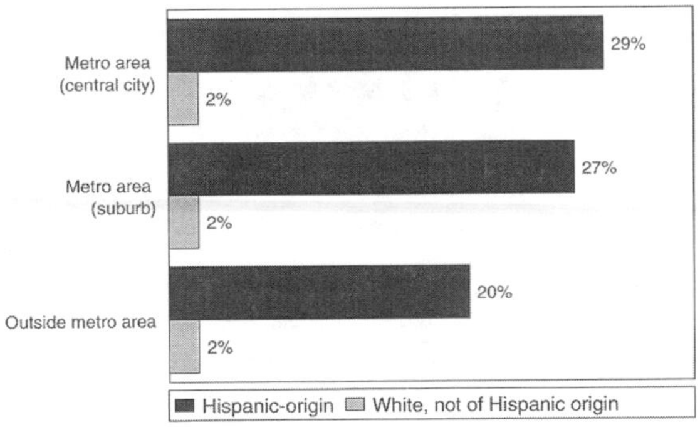

Chart 3.18 Hispanic and Non-Hispanic White Home Values, 1990 (Thousands)

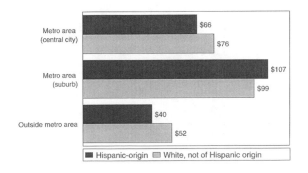

Chapter 4

Native Americans

Introduction

Native Americans, including American Indians, Eskimos (Inuit), and Aleuts, once constituted perhaps 75 million people in the Americas, prior to the late 15th century. Originally called "Indians," because Christopher Columbus mistook the natives of Hispaniola as people of the islands near India, today the Native Americans living in the United States represent a vast diversity of tribal backgrounds, languages, physical differences in phenotype (outward appearance), and cultures.

By the late 19th century, Native Americans had experienced such a population decline that many surmised that they had in fact died out or simply disappeared. Explorers and journalists of the day wrote about the "vanishing American" and his reduced state of socioeconomic and cultural resources after years of removal from his native home, his forced displacement into reservations, and, according to many, in effect the genocide visited on his people. Today, however, Native Americans are experiencing a surge in population and once more pose a significant presence in the American populace. Roughly 1 percent of the total United States population, nevertheless they remain one of the most impoverished of all ethnic or racial groups in the United States.

Population Growth *(See Charts 4.1 and 4.2)*

From 1890 to 1950, the Native American population increased by only about 129,000 people. Between 1950 and 1990, however, there were an additional 1.6 million Native Americans added to the population rolls, representing a 419 percent jump. Most of that growth occurred during the last two of these four decades. In 1970, the total Native American population in the United States was 827,000, by 1980 it had reached 1.4 million, and by 1990 nearly 2 million (consisting of 1.9 million American Indians, 57,000 Eskimos, and 24,000 Aleuts, for a total Native American population of 1.96 million). By July 1994 the U.S. Census Bureau estimated that there were 2.2 million Native Americans in the United States. If that growth rate stays constant, by 2050 there will be approximately 4.3 million Native Americans, still constituting almost 1 percent of the total population of the United States.

Natural increase is not the sole factor in the tremendous and relatively sudden increase among the Native American population. Two other factors that have contributed greatly to their apparent growth are the methodological improvements that the Census Bureau has made in the way it counts people on reservations, in trust lands, and in Native Alaskan villages, plus the greater likelihood for indigenous people (particularly those of mixed Indian and/or non-Indian parentage) to report themselves as being, simply, "American Indians." Other important factors in the growth of figures reported in the census include the continued use of self-identification for obtaining information on race, improvements on the question of race on census forms, and heightened promotion campaigns and outreach programs.

Regional Dispersion *(See Chart 4.3)*

More than any other ethnic minority, Native Americans are more likely to be concentrated in rural areas. This fact may in part be a remnant of resettlement of entire tribes on remote reservations in undesirable lands ("out of sight, out of mind" from the growing dominance of White explorers, pioneers, and eventually settlers). 1990 marked a change, with just under one-half of all Native Americans living outside metropolitan areas, compared to just over half a decade earlier. While the shift among Native American metropolitan concentrations is insignificant in terms of numbers, it nevertheless marks a substantial difference by comparison to other ethnic groups. For example, in the same year, 1990, only one in four non-Hispanic Whites, one in six African Americans, and one in ten Hispanic Americans lived in nonmetropolitan areas.

During that period, almost one-half of all Native Americans lived in the West, about 2 in 7 in the South, 1 in 6 in the Midwest, and only 1 in 15 in the Northeast. Between 1980 and 1990, the largest area of growth among Native Americans was the South, increasing from one in four to two in seven. By 1990, the four states with a Native American population exceeding 100,000 (in ranked order) were Oklahoma, California, Arizona, and New Mexico; these four states alone contained almost one-half of the total Native American population in the United States. In 1980, California had the largest number of Native Americans, though by 1990 it had changed places with Oklahoma; Arizona and New Mexico remained third and fourth, respectively, over the decade.

Metropolitan Concentration

In 1990, over half the Native American household-ers in the Unites States were concentrated in non-metropolitan areas and particularly in the West; about half of these householders were actual home owners, with a median housing value of about $63,000.

Native Americans in both 1980 and 1990 were a little less likely to live in a metropolitan area than in a nonmetropolitan area, but only by a very small percentage (49 percent metropolitan compared to 51 percent nonmetropolitan).

A majority of all Native Americans lived in the West in 1990; of the ten states with the largest number of Native American residents, only North Carolina, Michigan, and New York are east of the Mississippi River. The ten states with the largest number of Native Americans also were home to two-thirds of all Native Americans. Those states are: Oklahoma, 252,000; California, 242,000; Arizona, 204,000; New Mexico, 134,000; Alaska, 86,000; Washington, 81,000; North Carolina, 80,000; Texas, 66,000; New York, 63,000; and Michigan, 56,000.

U.S. Population *(See Chart 4.4)*

Between 1980 and 1990, the Native American population in the United States rose by more than one-third to a total of almost 2 million people. If the projections are accurate, by 2050 there may be as many as 4.3 million Native Americans.

While most Native American tribes had fewer than 10,000 people in 1990, there were 14 tribes with populations between 10,000 and 21,000. Those with over 100,000 people were the Cherokee, who reported 16 percent of the total Native American population; the Navajo, with 12 percent; and the Chippewa and Sioux, with 6 percent each. The tribes with populations between 50,000 and 100,000 were the Choctaw, Pueblo, and Apache. The Iroquois Confederacy, Lumbee, and Creek all had populations between 43,000 and 50,000.

State Populations *(See Chart 4.5)*

During the 1980s, a subgroup of Native Ameri-cans, the Alaska Natives, (encompassing Eskimos, Aleuts, and others), increased in popula-tion by one-third, from 64,000 at the beginning of the decade to 86,000 in 1990. Two percent of the total Native American population lived in Alaska Native Village Statistical Areas, defined as reserva-tions and areas with a largely Alaskan Native popu-lation. Eskimos and Aleuts were more geographically clustered than any other Native American group; just over two-thirds of their total numbers lived in Alaska.

There were 57,000 Eskimos and 24,000 Aleuts living in Alaska in 1990.

In 1990, among Native Americans as a whole, two in three lived in the ten states with the largest Native American populations. Of these ten states, only North Carolina, Michigan, and New York lie east of the Mississippi River. More than half of all Native Americans lived in a mere six states: Oklahoma, California, Arizona, New Mexico, Alaska, and Wash-ington. Oklahoma had the largest Native American population, with 10 percent of the total (just over

250,000 people), California was second and Arizona third (each with over 200,000 people), and New Mexico was fourth (Native Americans numbering over 130,000). Two of every five Native Americans lived in one of these four states.

The state with the largest numerical increase in the Native American population was Oklahoma, but the state with the highest percentage increase was Alabama. Between 1980 and 1990, the Native American population of Oklahoma rose to 83,000, while that of Alabama rose 118 percent. The two states in 1990 with the highest proportion of occupants who were Native Americans were Alaska (1 of every 6 persons) and New Mexico (1 of every 11).

Reservation Populations *(See Chart 4.6)*

Reservations and trust lands are areas of the United States that have boundaries established by treaty, by statute, and/or by executive order. As of 1990, there were 314 reservations and trust lands in the United States, and about one in five Native American lived on those lands (approximately half a million American Indians, 200 Eskimos, and 100 Aleuts).

The number of Native Americans who lived on reservations and trust lands varied greatly in 1990. Most reservations had fewer than 1,000 people, but there was one with more than 100,000 people (the Navajo Reservation and Trust Lands spread across portions of Arizona, New Mexico, and Utah), another with more than 10,000 people (Pine Ridge Reservation and Trust Lands in Nebraska and South Dakota), and eight with more than 7,000 people (Fort Apache, Arizona; Gila River, Arizona; Papago, Arizona; Rosebud, South Dakota; San Carlos, Arizona; Zuni Pueblo, Arizona and New Mexico; Hopi, Arizona; and Blackfeet, Montana). Seven of the preceding ten reservations and trust lands were either partially or entirely located in Arizona. The total number of Native Americans living on these ten reservations and trust lands accounted for almost half the Native Americans in the country who lived on reservations and trust lands.

In real numbers, the 1990 Native American population living on the ten largest reservations and trust lands totaled 218,000 American Indians, 25 Eskimos, and 5 Aleuts.

Fewer than half of all the occupied housing units in all reservations and trust lands had a Native American householder in 1990; but among the ten largest reservations, there were substantially more Native American householders: as high as 95 percent on the San Carlos, Gila River, and Papago reservations, and as low as 76 percent on the Rosebud Reservation.

The median number of people in Native American reservation and trust land households was 3.6 in 1990. Among the ten largest reservations and trust lands, the count ranged from 4.6 at the Zuni Pueblo Reservation to 3.5 at the Blackfeet Reservation. The Zuni Pueblo, Pine Ridge, San Carlos, and Fort Apache reservations and trust lands all had four or more persons per unit.

More than 20 percent of all housing units for Native Americans on reservations and trust lands in 1990 lacked adequate plumbing facilities. That is more than three times as many Native American homes not on reservations and trust lands with inadequate plumbing. Among the ten largest reservations and trust lands, the Navajo and Hopi reservations had the largest proportion of housing units that lacked complete facilities, while the Blackfeet Reservation had the lowest proportion.

Age Distribution *(See Charts 4.7–4.10)*

In 1990, about two of five Native Americans were 20 years old or younger, compared with the national average of around two out of seven, but only a very small proportion (about 1 in 12) Native Americans were 60 years old and over. This made the median age of the Native American population 26 years old, compared to the nation's overall median age of 33. One reason for the younger population among Native Americans is the higher-than-average fertility rates. Among Native Americans living on reservations and trust lands, the median age was only 22 years old.

In 1990, among the ten largest reservations and trust lands, only the Hopi had a median age comparable to the total Native American median of 26 years old. Rosebud and Pine Ridge both reported the youngest median age at approximately 19 years old.

Children

More than one-third of the Native American population in 1990 was under 20 years old (39 percent, compared to the national average of 29 percent).

Elderly

Nearly 1 in 12 Native Americans in 1990 was 60 years old or over; that's about half the proportion of the total population.

Educational Attainment (See Charts 4.11–4.13)

Between 1980 and 1990, the level of educational attainment for Native Americans improved significantly; however, when compared to the total population, the numbers were still considerably low. The school enrollment rates for all Native Americans three years old and over was one in four (one in three for those living on reservations and trust lands), compared to only one in five for the total U.S. population. However, when high school graduate statistics are examined, the numbers begin to change. For example, while a full two-thirds of the Native Americans 25 years and older in 1990 were high school graduates (up from just over one-half a decade earlier), the national average is three-fourths.

Among those Native Americans living on reservations and trust lands who were 25 years old and over in 1990, more than half were high school graduates or had some advanced education or degrees. On the ten largest reservations and trust lands, there was a considerable range. The Blackfeet and Hopi, for example, had about two-thirds graduates, while the Gila River Reservation had just over one-third, and the Navajo saw only two out of every five actually graduate from high school or higher. Interestingly, the two reservations that saw the lowest rates of high school graduation were ranked among the highest in proportional school enrollment rates. The other two reservations with the highest proportional school enrollment rates were Rosebud and Pine Ridge.

Native Americans are still less likely than the rest of the entire United States population to have completed a bachelor's degree or higher, with only about 1 in 11 Native Americans in 1990 compared to 1 in 12 in 1980. While this represents an increase within the ethnic group, it is still considerably lower than the one in five average for the total population.

Labor Force Participation (See Charts 4.14 and 4.15)

In 1990, the likelihood of a person 16 years old and over being a member of the U.S. labor force was about 65 percent. Overall, Native Americans were only slightly lower than that average, at 62 percent. Among comparable males, approximately three out of four were members of the labor force, compared to Native American males at about seven out of ten. At the same time, the proportion of Native American women who joined the labor force grew significantly in the decade between 1980 and 1990, to include more than half of all Native American women 16 years old and over. The national average for all women was only slightly higher (55 percent compared to 57 percent).

On the ten largest reservations and trust lands, the civilian labor force participation varied greatly among Native Americans 16 years old and over. The Zuni Pueblo reported the highest proportion of employees in the civilian labor force, while at the Blackfeet, Gila River, San Carlos, Pine Ridge, and Fort Apache reservations only about 69 percent of the Native American population was employed.

Occupations (See Chart 4.16)

In 1990, about 730,000 Native Americans were employed in a variety of civilian occupations. Fewer than one in five Native Americans were occupied in managerial and professional specialty occupations, compared with more than one in four among the general population, and just over one-quarter were in technical sales and administrative support occupations, compared to almost one-third of the general population. In four occupational categories, Native Americans had a higher percentage than the general population: 1 in 5 worked in service, compared to the general average of slightly more than

1 in 8; 1 in 30 Native Americans were in the farming, forestry, and fishing industries, compared to 1 in 40 among the general population; almost 1 in 7 Native Americans worked in a precision, production, craft, or repair field, compared to the average of 1 in 9; and nearly 1 in 5 were operators, fabricators, or laborers, compared to only 1 in 7 among the general population.

Income *(See Charts 4.17 and 4.18)*

The 1990 median family income for Native Americans was less than $22,000; that was less than two-thirds of the median income for the total U.S. population (over $35,000). Among married-couple Native American families, the income rose slightly to $28,000, which is about 71 percent of the median for all married-couple families (about $40,000). More than one-fourth of all Native American families were maintained by a single female householder, with no husband present. While the median family income for comparable families was slightly more than $17,000, for Native American single female householders it was just under $11,000.

The average per capita income of Native Americans living on reservations or trust lands in 1990 was significantly less than the overall United States average income. The combined per capita average on all reservations and trust lands was about $4,500. The Blackfeet and Hopi reservations had higher-than-average per capita incomes, at $4,700 and $4,600, respectively, while the Pine Ridge and Papago had the lowest, at $3,100 each.

Poverty *(See Charts 4.19 and 4.20)*

Native Americans are more likely to live in poverty than any other ethnic group in the United States, and consequently far more likely to live in poverty than the population as a whole. Among Native American married-couple families, more than 1 in 6 live below the poverty level, compared to 1 in 20 in the total population. For male householders with no wife present, more than one-third of all Native Americans live in poverty, compared to fewer than one in seven for the total population. More than half of all female Native American householders with no husband present are considered poor, compared with less than one-third of the total population.

The national poverty rate for individuals was about one in eight in 1990, and for families, approxi-

mately one in ten. Among Native Americans, that rate was closer to one in three for both individuals and families. Half of all the Native American families maintained by women with no husband present were living in poverty. Among the general population, by contrast, only one-third of all comparable families were poor.

On reservations and trust lands, the rates are even worse. Over half of all the Native Americans living on reservations or trust lands live in poverty. Among the ten largest reservations and trust lands, named earlier, the highest rates of poverty (two-thirds) can be found at the Pine Ridge and Papago reservations. The Hopi reservation has the lowest rate, with only half of its residents living below the poverty level.

Family Composition *(See Chart 4.21)*

Among the half-million Native American families in 1990, six in ten were married-couple families, compared to the national average of eight in ten. In 1980, five in seven Native American families were husband-and-wife families, compared to five in six as the national average. The proportion of Native American families maintained by a female householder with no husband present increased to about two in seven by 1990. The national average, again, was considerably lower, at one in six.

While the national average family size in 1990 was 3.2 persons, the average size of a Native American family was slightly larger, at 3.6 persons. However, Native American married-couple families were less likely than the national average of all married-couple families to have children under 18 years old (54 percent compared to 70 percent).

Reservation Housing Characteristics *(See Chart 4.22)*

Since so many Native Americans live on reservations, the housing characteristics of residences on reservations are particularly important to the quality of life of Native Americans. Below, we examine some of these major characteristics.

Structural Characteristics

While all houses in the United States vary in age and form, the housing characteristics of Native Americans living on reservations and trust lands in 1990 have a considerably different mix. Any home that was built between 1985 and 1990 was considered new, any home built before 1940 was considered old; while nearly one in five people in the country occupied old housing units, one in ten were in new units. For Native Americans overall, the numbers were almost identical to the national averages, but among Native Americans living on reservations and trust lands, they were almost twice as likely to live in a new unit (1 in 6) and less than half as likely to live in an old one (1 in 12). Of course, these averages varied by reservation. For example, on the Pascua Yaqui Reservation in Arizona, more than half of all the housing units were new, but on the Isleta Pueblo reservation in New Mexico, more than one in four homes were old.

An average of seven in ten homes in the United States are single-family units. Among reservation and trust land dwelling Native Americans, more than three out of four housing units are designed for single families, and for Native Americans not living on reservations or trust lands, only three in five houses are single-family units. At the Pascua Yaqui Reservation in Arizona, 98 percent of the Native American households consisted of single families, compared to New York's Cattaraugus Reservation, where only 53 percent were single families.

About 1 in 14 homes in the United States in 1990 were mobile homes. For Native Americans not living on reservations, about one in eight lived in mobile homes, but among reservation—or trust land–dwelling Native Americans, almost one in seven lived in mobile homes. The reservations where mobile homes were most common were Hoopa Valley, California (41 percent), and Cattaraugus, New York (39 percent). At the same time, while more than one-fourth of all Americans, and almost one-third of all Native Americans not living on reservations or trust lands, lived in multiunit structures (apartments), only 1 in 20 Native Americans on reservations lived in apartments.

Plumbing Facilities

Complete plumbing facilities means that a house has hot and cold piped water, a flush toilet, and a bathtub or shower. In 1940, almost half of the households in the United States lacked complete plumbing facilities; by 1970, that number had shrunk to only about 1 in 15 homes, and by 1990 had dwindled to only 1 in 100 households. But for Native Americans living on reservations in 1990, one in five households still lacked complete plumbing facilities: *twenty times* the national rate.

About seven in ten households on Native American reservations had water supplied by public systems or private companies, but fewer than half were hooked up to a public sewer. It is important to note that most reservations and trust lands are not in metropolitan areas, and that public sewers are less common overall. In a comparison to the national averages, more than three-fourths of all households, and almost the same number of Native Americans not living on reservations, were hooked up to public sewers, but among the households outside metropolitan areas, the percentages are the same as for reservations. Even though just under 50 percent of reservation and nonmetropolitan homes were connected to public sewers in 1990, the averages varied greatly by reservation. For example, on the Pascua Yaqui Reservation in Arizona, almost all homes were on the public sewage system, but in Hoopa Valley, California, and St. Regis Mohawk, New York, almost none were.

Outhouses (pit toilets), chemical toilets, and facilities in another structure are the most common means of sewage disposal without public sewer, cesspool, or septic tank. Only 3 percent of all households in nonmetropolitan areas and only 3 percent of Native American households not on reservations and trust lands have to use alternate sewage disposal means, though for Native Americans living on reservations or trust lands, the number ranged from below 1 percent in Colville, Washington; Isleta Pueblo, New Mexico; Mescalero Apache, New Mexico; and Pascua Yaqui, Arizona, to about 40 percent on the Navajo and Hopi reservations in Arizona, New Mexico, and Utah.

In all the households in the United States, only about 1 in 100 lack complete plumbing facilities, and even in houses outside of metropolitan areas, still fewer than 2 in 100 are so inconvenienced. Native Americans living off of reservations who lacked complete plumbing totaled about 3 in 100, but of those still on reservations or trust lands, about one out of every five lacked complete facilities; on the Navajo and Hopi reservations in Arizona and New Mexico, almost one-half of all housing units were so lacking. The rates were even worse for home owners, with just over one in four home owners living on reservations lacking facilities. Again, for those on the Navajo reservation, the numbers were higher than average (six in ten).

Crowded houses are those with more than one person per room. Nationally, only 1 in 1,000 live in crowded homes and lack complete plumbing facilities, but on reservations, nearly one in ten households are lacking in such facilities and crowded. Not surprisingly, the Navajo and Hopi reservations and trust lands in Arizona, New Mexico, and Utah have the highest rates of overcrowding and insufficient plumbing concurrently—almost one-third of the households. Again, the home owners fared worse than the renters. One-fifth of all owned homes in the United States that were crowded and lacked complete plumbing facilities were on reservations, and four out of five of those homes were on the Navajo or Hopi reservations.

Equipment and Fuels

Kitchen Facilities   Complete kitchen facilities include a sink with piped water, a range or cookstove, and a refrigerator. In 1990, only about 1 in 100 homes in the United States, but about 3 in 100 Native Americans homes not on reservations, lacked complete kitchen facilities. At the same time, nearly one in five Native American reservation households were so lacking. As always, the percentage varied greatly depending on the reservation; the Navajo Reservation and trust lands of Arizona, New Mexico, and Utah had rates of almost one-half, the Hopi and Papago reservations in Arizona saw about one-fifth, while the Northern Cheyenne and Fort Peck reservations straddling Montana and South Dakota had levels below the national average.

Telephones   In the United States in 1990, 1 in 20 homes were without telephones; in nonmetropolitan homes, that number was about 1 in 11. More than one-half of all Native American households on reservations during that same time did not have telephones in their homes. The largest percentage of "phone-lessness" occurred on the Gila River, Navajo, and San Carlos reservations in Arizona, with about three in four homes lacking phones.

Vehicles   Only one in five households on reservations in 1990 did not have a vehicle—a number not very much different than the national average of about one in eight, or the nonreservation-dwelling Native American average of one in six. More than one-third of the households on the Fort Apache and Papago reservations in Arizona were without a vehicle, but a number of other reservations actually had lower vehicle-less rates than the national average (such as the Warm Springs Reservation and Trust Lands in Arizona, with only 1 in 12 lacking a vehicle).

Home Heating Fuel   The leading household heating fuel nationally is utility gas, used by over half of all homes in America, as well as by almost half of all those Native American homes not on reservations. But among Native American households on reservations and trust lands, utility gas is only used by about one in six households. By far the most common source of heating fuel on reservations in 1990 was wood. Two-thirds of all reservation homes were heated by wood, compared to 1 in 25 homes in the United States, and 1 in 12 among nonreservation Native American homes.

Map 4.1 Native Americans by State, 1990

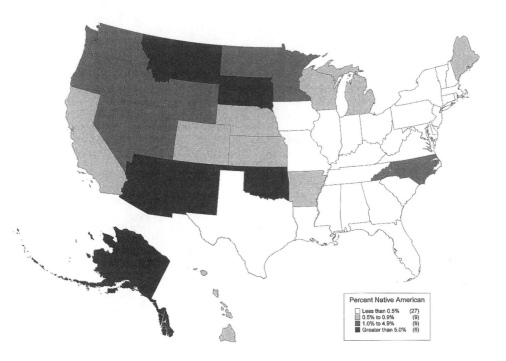

Percent Native American
Less than 0.5%   (27)
0.5% to 0.9%   (9)
1.0% to 4.9%   (9)
Greater than 5.0%   (6)

Map 4.2 Native Americans by County, 1990

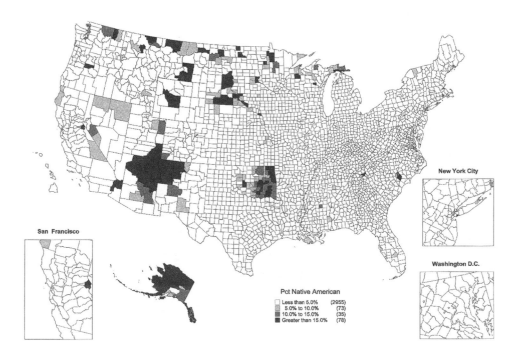

New York City

San Francisco

Washington D.C.

Pct Native American
Less than 5.0%   (2955)
5.0% to 10.0%   (73)
10.0% to 15.0%   (35)
Greater than 15.0%   (78)

Map 4.3 American Indians by State, 1990

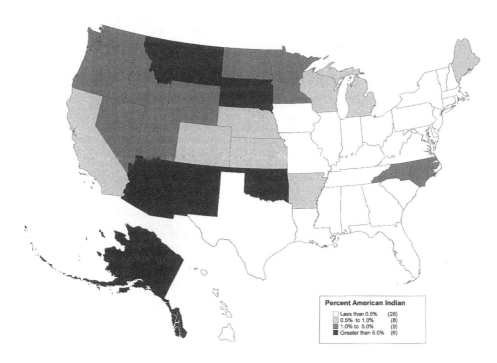

Percent American Indian

☐	Less than 0.5%	(28)
☐	0.5% to 1.0%	(8)
☐	1.0% to 5.0%	(9)
■	Greater than 5.0%	(6)

Map 4.4 American Indians by County, 1990

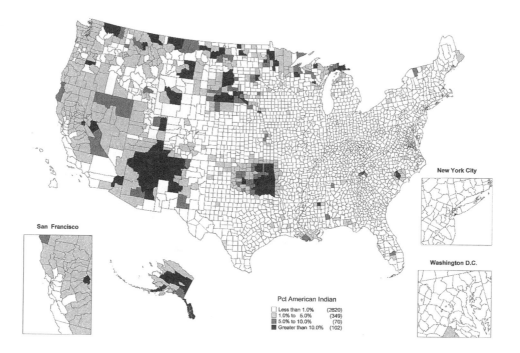

New York City

San Francisco

Washington D.C.

Pct American Indian

☐	Less than 1.0%	(2620)
☐	1.0% to 5.0%	(349)
■	5.0% to 10.0%	(70)
■	Greater than 10.0%	(102)

Map 4.5 Eskimo Americans by County, 1990

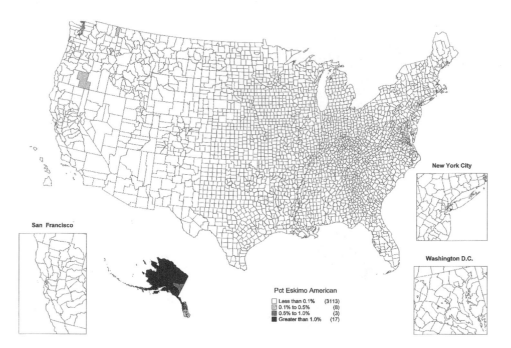

Map 4.6 Aleutian Americans by County, 1990

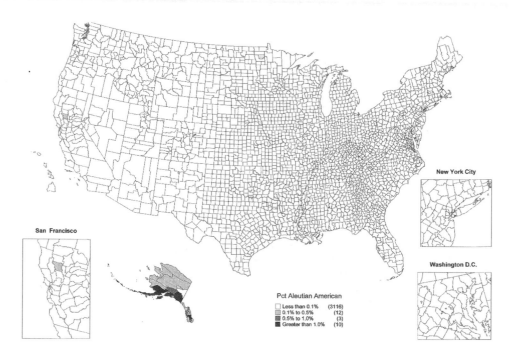

Chart 4.1 Native American Population, 1890–1990 (Thousands)

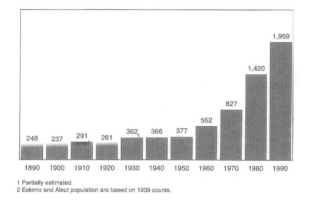

1 Partially estimated.
2 Eskimo and Aleut population are based on 1939 counts.

Chart 4.2 Native American Population Growth Rate, 1890–1990 (Thousands)

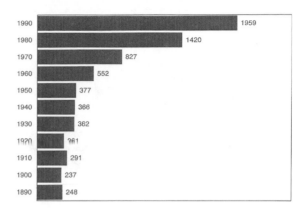

Chart 4.3 Native American Population by Type of Area, 1990 (Percent)

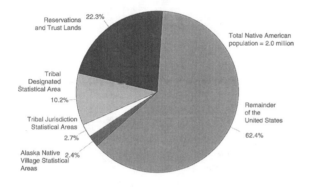

Chart 4.4 Ten Largest American Indian Tribes, 1990 (Thousands)

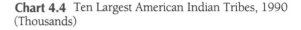
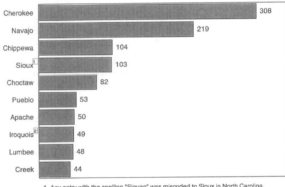

1. Any entry with the spelling "Siouan" was miscoded to Sioux in North Carolina.
2. Reporting and/or processing problems have affected the data for this tribe.

Chart 4.5 Top Ten States with the Largest Native American Populations, 1990 (Thousands)

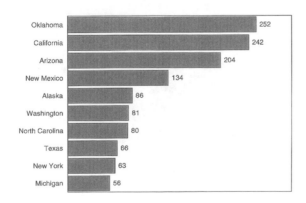

Chart 4.6 Reservations with the Largest Number of Native Americans, 1990 (Thousands)

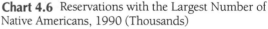
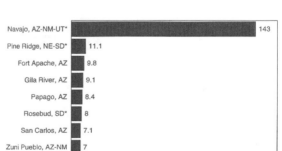

*Includes trust lands

Chart 4.7 Resident Native American Population by Age, 1990 (Percent)

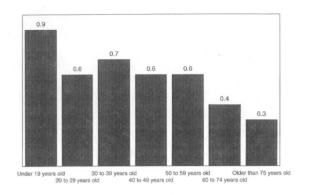

Chart 4.8 Native American Age Distribution, 1990 (Percent)

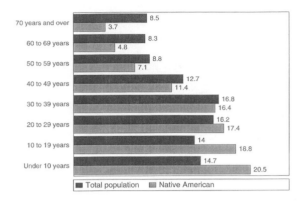

Chart 4.9 Native American Median Age, 1990

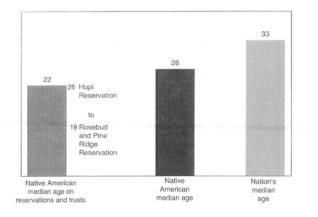

Chart 4.10 American Indian Median Age, 1990

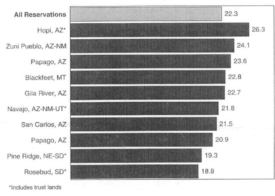

Chart 4.11 Native American Educational Attainment, 1990 (Percent, 25 years and older)

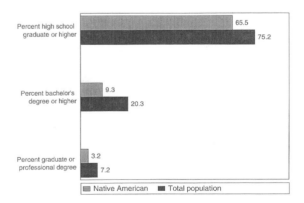

Chart 4.12 American Indian Educational Attainment, 1990 (Percent, 25 years and older)

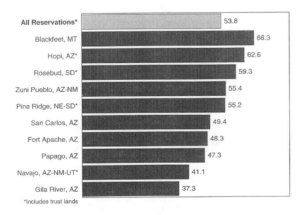

Chart 4.13 American Indian School Enrollment, 1990

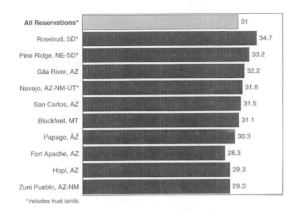

All Reservations* — 31
Rosebud, SD* — 34.7
Pine Ridge, NE-SD* — 33.2
Gila River, AZ — 32.2
Navajo, AZ-NM-UT* — 31.8
San Carlos, AZ — 31.5
Blackfeet, MT — 31.1
Papago, AZ — 30.3
Fort Apache, AZ — 28.3
Hopi, AZ — 29.3
Zuni Pueblo, AZ-NM — 29.0

*Includes trust lands.

Chart 4.14 Native American Labor Force Participation Rates by Sex, 1990 (Percent, 16 years and older)

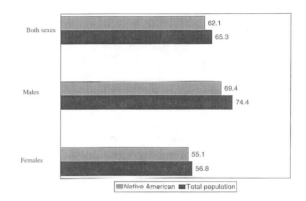

Both sexes — 62.1 / 65.3
Males — 69.4 / 74.4
Females — 55.1 / 56.8

■ Native American   ■ Total population

Chart 4.15 American Indian Employment Rates, 1990 (Percent, 16 years and older)

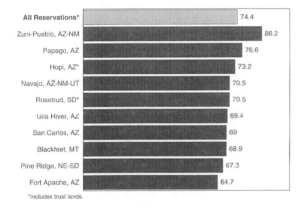

All Reservations* — 74.4
Zuni-Pueblo, AZ-NM — 86.2
Papago, AZ — 76.6
Hopi, AZ* — 73.2
Navajo, AZ-NM-UT — 70.5
Rosebud, SD* — 70.5
Gila River, AZ — 69.4
San Carlos, AZ — 69
Blackfeet, MT — 68.9
Pine Ridge, NE-SD — 67.3
Fort Apache, AZ — 64.7

*Includes trust lands.

Chart 4.16 Native American Occupational Distribution, 1990 (Percent, 16 years and older)

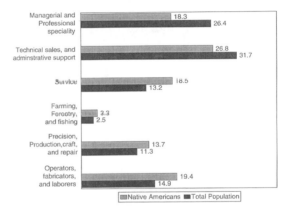

Managerial and Professional speciality — 18.3 / 26.4
Technical sales, and administrative support — 26.8 / 31.7
Service — 18.5 / 13.2
Farming, Forestry, and fishing — 3.3 / 2.5
Precision, Production, craft, and repair — 13.7 / 11.3
Operators, fabricators, and laborers — 19.4 / 14.9

■ Native Americans   ■ Total Population

Chart 4.17 Median Native American Income by Family Composition, 1990 (Thousands, in 1989 dollars)

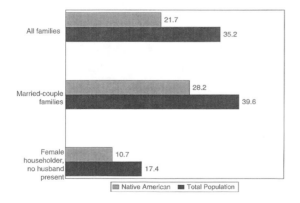

All families — 21.7 / 35.2
Married-couple families — 28.2 / 39.6
Female householder, no husband present — 10.7 / 17.4

■ Native American   ■ Total Population

Chart 4.18 American Indian Per Capita Income, 1990

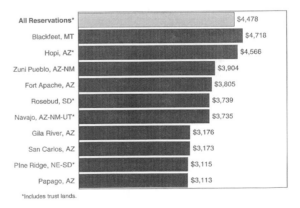

All Reservations* — $4,478
Blackfeet, MT — $4,718
Hopi, AZ* — $4,566
Zuni Pueblo, AZ-NM — $3,904
Fort Apache, AZ — $3,805
Rosebud, SD* — $3,739
Navajo, AZ-NM-UT* — $3,735
Gila River, AZ — $3,176
San Carlos, AZ — $3,173
Pine Ridge, NE-SD* — $3,115
Papago, AZ — $3,113

*Includes trust lands.

Chart 4.19 Native American and Total Population Poverty Rates by Family Composition, 1990 (Percent)

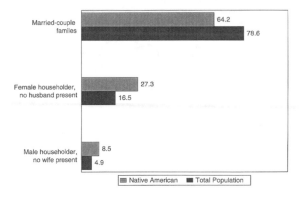

Chart 4.20 American Indian Poverty Rates, 1989 (Percent)

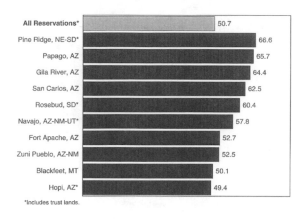

Chart 4.21 Native American and Total Population Family Composition, 1990 (Percent)

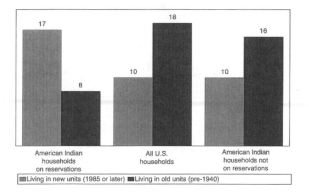

Chart 4.22 Percentage of American Indian Old and New Homes, 1990

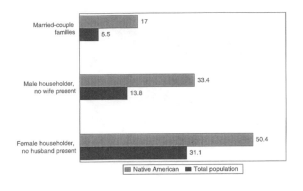

Chapter 5

Non-Hispanic Whites/ European Americans

Introduction

Non-Hispanic Whites,[1] as the term is used in this book and by the U.S. Census Bureau, include people from Canada, France, Germany, Greece, Ireland, Italy, Netherlands, Poland, Portugal, the former republics of the U.S.S.R., the member countries of the United Kingdom, Yugoslavia, other European nations, Iran, Israel, other Middle Eastern nations, and Australia (though not including aboriginal peoples from that continent).

Population Growth

Between 1980 and 1990, non-Hispanic Whites living in the United States experienced the lowest growth rate of any racial group in the country: a mere 6 percent. By the year 2000, it is estimated that the non-Hispanic White population will be less than 72 percent of the nation's total, and by 2050 less than 53 percent. Although they now make up almost three-fourths of today's total population, they are expected to contribute only about 35 percent of the growth between 1990 and 2000, decreasing to 23 percent between 2000 and 2010, and 14 percent between 2010 and 2030.

Metropolitan Concentration

In 1990, more than three-fourths of the non-Hispanic White, African American, and Asian Pacific American populations lived in metropolitan areas located throughout the United States.

U.S. Population

In the United States in 1990, eight of every ten people were self-identified as Whites, or counted as Whites by Census Bureau analysts or by follow-up studies. (In the remainder of this chapter, for reasons of brevity and readability, the terms *White* and *non-Hispanic White* are used interchangeably. In certain categories, however, where statistics are available, the overall term *Whites* may be contrasted with the subgroup of *non-Hispanic Whites*.)[2]

In 1990, the White population numbered 199,686,000. It is expected that the total number of Whites living in the United States by the year 2020 will be 255 million. Of the 40 million Whites who are expected to swell the nation's population between 1993 and 2020, 89 percent will live in the South and the West.

The White population will be expected to increase in California, Texas, and Florida by 30 percent or more. Pennsylvania will likely add no more members to its White population, while New York will lose a small portion (0.4 percent).

In 1994, the breakdown of the White population by age was the following: 0–14 years, 20.4 percent; 15–29 years, 20.1 percent; 30–44 years, 24.8 percent; 45–59 years, 16.7 percent; 60–74 years, 12.3 percent; and for those aged 75 and over, it was 5.8 percent.

The median age of Whites in the United States in 1994 was 33.2 years old.

In 1994, 27.9 percent of the United States population were White males under the age of 19. Of the population that ranged from 20 to 64 years old, 60.4 percent were White males. Those White males 65 years and over totaled 11.6 percent.

In the same year, 25.5 percent of the United States population were White females under the age of 19; 58.6 percent were between 20 and 64 years old; and 15.7 percent were aged 65 and older.

Age Distribution *(See Chart 5.1)*

Children

Of all the nation's children under 18 years old in 1990, totaling approximately 63.5 million, about two-thirds of them were of non-Hispanic White origin.

Among the children whose mothers were part-time workers in 1990, just under half were non-Hispanic Whites.

Among non-Hispanic White children who lived with their fathers in 1990, about one-fourth had fathers who only worked part-time or did not work at all.

In 1990, under 1 in 20 White children of non-Hispanic origin had mothers with fewer than nine years of education.

In 1990, the chances that children had a mother who held a bachelor's degree were twice as high for Whites as for African Americans.

In 1992, the likelihood that a custodial mother was White was 70 percent, but the likelihood of a custodial father who was White was 85 percent.

The number of White children living with only one parent rose by 3 percent during the 1980s. And by 1990 about one-fourth of White children lived in a home with one parent—or no parent.

A "traditional" family is defined as one in which the father works full-time and the mother is a home-maker. (Many working couples might disagree strongly with this definition, which seems to hark back to the idealized TV family of the 1950s; such definitions are used as ammunition in struggles over resources among community action organizations, political pressure groups, and elected officials and constituents alike.) Using this definition, in the 1980s and 1990s non-Hispanic White children were more likely than any other racial group to live in traditional families, but the number of 1-year-old non-Hispanic White children living in a traditional family declined from about one-third to one-fourth between 1980 and 1990. Part of this may be attributable to the fact that within that racial group the number of two-parent families in which *both* the mother and the father worked full-time rose significantly (from 5.2 percent to 12.7 percent) between 1980 and 1990.

Non-Hispanic White children are generally less likely than African American or Hispanic American children to be living in poverty. In 1990, for example, non-Hispanic White children were almost three times as likely as the other two groups of children to live in high-income families, and about one-third less likely than the other groups to live in low-income families.

In 1990, about nine out of ten non-Hispanic White preschoolers (that is, who have not entered kindergarten) lived in families with one to three children. For adolescents the rate was just under eight out of ten who lived in such families.

Elderly

Due in part to high survival rates and low recent fertility rates, the non-Hispanic White population had the highest proportion of elderly people among all racial groups in 1990. In addition, the number of White immigrants to the United States has declined since the 1960s; if these factors remain relatively constant, by 2050 an even larger proportion of the White population will be elderly.

In 1994, 29.8 million of the nation's elderly were Whites; of those people, despite Social Security, Medicare, Medicaid, and other assistance or supplemental income programs, one in nine of the White elderly lived in poverty.

Educational Attainment

In 1993, just under one in eight Americans belonging to the public school "dropout pool" (those who did not complete high school itself or high school equivalency courses) were non-Hispanic Whites, compared to one in six African Americans and one in three Hispanic Americans. The dropout pool itself only comprised a little more than one in eight of those between 18 and 24 years old, up from about one in six in 1983.

In 1993, five in six of all non-Hispanic Whites, three in four of all African Americans, and just under two in three of all people of Hispanic origin between

18 to 24 years old were high school graduates. For Whites, that means that the high school completion rate has remained relatively constant since 1973.

In 1993, among those Whites who had completed high school and who were between the ages of 18 and 24 years, about three in seven were enrolled in college or university (compared to only one in three in 1970), and almost one in three already held a degree or degrees beyond high school.

In 1994 the educational attainment of non-Hispanic Whites in the United States was as follows: 0.8 percent have lower than a fifth grade education; 5.4 percent have an education from fifth to eighth grade; 8.9 percent have an education between the ninth and twelfth grades; 84.9 percent have graduated from high school with a diploma; and 28 percent hold degrees beyond high school.

While in 1994 just over 50 percent of Whites had earned no college degree; 17.9 percent did move on to some college; 7.3 percent attained an associate's degree; 16 percent earned a bachelor's degree; and 8.3 percent were awarded some type of advanced degree.

Of those non-Hispanic Whites in 1994 who were between the ages of 25 and 34, 0.3 percent have less than a fifth-grade education; 1.2 percent have attended school from fifth to eighth grade; 7.5 percent have attended from ninth to twelfth grade; and 91 percent have graduated from high school. Of that same age group of Whites, 43.7 percent have not acquired a college education, though 20.1 percent have some college credits; 9.3 percent have an associate's degree; 21 percent have a bachelor's degree; and 6 percent have an advanced degree of some sort.

In 1994, 83 percent of Whites over the age of 35 had graduated with a high school diploma, while 9.4 percent attended school only from ninth to twelfth grade; 6.7 percent went solely from fifth to eighth grade; and only 0.9 percent got as far as the fifth grade.

Also in 1994, 52.5 percent of Whites over 35 years of age had no college degree, while 17.2 percent had some college; 6.7 percent had associate's degrees; 14.5 had bachelor's degrees; and 9.1 percent held advanced degrees.

Labor Force Participation

In 1992, 72.3 percent of all non-Hispanic White men worked year-round, full-time. In 1979, that number was 76.7 percent, which means that there has been a decrease by 4.4 percentage points. Among non-Hispanic White women in 1992, 47.6 percent worked year-round, full-time, compared to only 34.8 percent in 1979, for an increase of 12.8 percentage points.

Of those 93,483,000 non-Hispanic Whites—both male and female—over the age of 16 years of age in 1994, 28,200,000 were in managerial and professional positions; 29,502,000 held technical, sales, and administrative support positions; 11,406,000 were in service jobs; 10,132,000 worked in the areas of precision production, craft, and repair; 11,771,000 were operators, fabricators, and laborers, and 2,472,000 were in the farming, forestry, and fishing industries.

In 1994, of those 50,093,000 White males over the age of 16, 14,691 were in managerial and professional fields; 10,624,000 worked within technical, sales, and administrative support; 4,490,000 were in service occupations; 9,082,000 were either operators, fabricators, or laborers; and 1,949,000 were in the farming, forestry, and fishing industries.

Also in 1994, 29.3 percent of White males of all ages were in either managerial or professional fields; 21.2 percent worked in the area of technical, sales, and administrative support; 9 percent worked in service-oriented jobs; 18.5 percent worked in the field of precision production, craft, or repair; 18.1 percent were operators, fabricators, and laborers; while 3.9 percent labored within the fishing, forestry, and farming industries.

Net Worth and Income

The net worth (i.e., wages, salary, benefits, and assets) of non-Hispanic White households in 1990 in the United States as a whole was more than ten times that of African American households, and almost ten times that of Hispanic households. In numerical terms, the net worth of White households was $45,750, compared to $4,418

for African American households, and $4,656 for Hispanic households.

Among civilian workers aged 16 and over who work year-round, full-time, 11.6 percent of White men had low earnings (in the bottom fifth of the income distribution of the U.S. adult population) in 1992, compared to 7.2 percent in 1979.

This represents an increase of 4.4 percentage points. There was also an increase in the percentage of low-earning White women between 1979 and 1992; however, it was only 1.3 percentage points, from 19.8 percent to 21.1 percent.

On the flip side, among civilian workers aged 16 and over who had high earnings (in the highest fifth of income distribution) in 1992, White men saw a gain of 0.5 percentage point since 1979, from 15.9 percent to 16.4 percent. White women's averages also climbed during that time span, from 1.3 percent to 3.8 percent, marking a 2.4 percentage point change.

Per Capita Income

The per capita median income in the Unites States in 1994 for all races was $16,555, which represents an overall increase of 2.3 percent from 1993 (after adjusting for inflation). For Asian Pacific Americans, there was no detectable increase, though the per capita amount was slightly higher than overall, at $16,902. For non-Hispanic Whites only, it was higher still, at $17,611, which may be accounted for in part by the 2.2 percent increase in income. Among African Americans, despite the 5.3 percent increase, the income level was somewhat lower than the median, at $10,650, and for those of Hispanic origin, the per capita income not only remained unchanged, but it was also significantly lower than the nation's mean, at $9,435.

In 1994 the rate for unemployed Whites declined 0.8 percentage points to 4.9 percent.

Family Income

The 1993 median income for Asian Pacific Americans was $38,347; for non-Hispanic Whites $32,960; for Hispanics it was $22,886; and for African Americans, $19,532. While the real median household income was lower in 1993 for all these groups than it was in 1989, the level remained statistically unchanged in real terms controlling for cost of living increases from 1992 levels.

The median income for a non-Hispanic White householder in 1994 was $35,126, a substantial change from the 1993 figure.

Poverty

More than one-quarter of the non-Hispanic Whites who were poor in 1991 were not poor the next year. However, between 1992 and 1993, there was no significant change in the poverty rates for any racial group in the United States. Almost one in eight Whites, over one in three African Americans, just under one in three persons of Hispanic origin, and just under one in six Asians and Pacific Islanders lived in poverty during that period. Despite these percentages, the actual number of poor persons was higher for Whites and Hispanics than for any other racial group (up by 967,000 and 534,000 people, respectively).

In 1994, 11.7 percent of Whites lived below the poverty level.

Also in 1994, 7.2 percent of White families lived below the poverty line, as opposed to African Americans, who made up 27.3 percent of those living in poverty.

Between 1993 and 1994, poverty rates dropped for both Whites and African Americans, and the number of poor African Americans dropped greatly. But there was no significant change for Asians and Pacific Islanders, or for people of Hispanic origin (in fact, the number of poor Hispanics showed in increase). The average length of poverty among non-Hispanic Whites in 1994 was 4.1 months.

Poverty rates for Whites were 11 percent, compared to African Americans, whose poverty rate was 33 percent, and Hispanics, whose rate was 22 percent.

Even though as a racial group non-Hispanic Whites have the lowest rate of poverty, they account for the highest numbers of poor people. In 1990, Whites made up more than two-thirds of the population considered poor in the United States; more than half of those were long-term poor (defined by as living in poverty for more than six years).

About one out of every nine White mothers of childbearing age was a food stamp recipient in 1994.

About one of every four African American mothers of childbearing age were recipients of Aid to Families with Dependent Children (AFDC) in 1993, compared to only approximately 1 in 14 among corresponding White mothers. During the same time period, about 1 in 10 African American mothers were receiving aid from the Women, Infants, and Children program (WIC), compared to 1 in 16 White mothers. In real numbers, 1.5 million AFDC recipients were African American and 2.1 million were White; 600,000 WIC recipients were African American, and 1.7 million were White. Despite the rate differences, the number of children in the families were comparable.

Family Composition

In 1994, one-sixth of all non-Hispanic White single parents were fathers, compared to only half that rate among African American single parents. One-fourth of all White families with children present were headed by a single parent, compared to just under two-thirds of all African American families and over one-third of all Hispanic origin families.

Health Care

In 1995, 22 percent of Whites did not receive health insurance coverage for up to one month; 6 percent of African Americans also lacked such coverage, and 50 percent of persons of Hispanic origin lacked it.

In 1995, 92 percent of Whites had at least one month of health insurance.

In 1993 while Hispanic Americans had the largest proportion of noncoverage in the United States for health insurance, at 31.6 percent African Americans and non-Hispanic Whites lacked such coverage at the identical rate: 14.2 percent.

Housing

About two-thirds of all non-Hispanic Whites were home owners in 1991, with nearly half of all non-Hispanic White home owners living in the suburbs. The median value in 1990 of a non-Hispanic White home owner's house was $82,000. Among non-Hispanic White families 1991, nearly half couldn't afford a median-priced home.

Moving

The overall rate of moving to a different home among Whites in 1994 was about one-sixth of the population, compared to just under one-fifth of all African Americans, and nearly one-fourth of those of Hispanic origin.

Voter Turnout

In the 1994 congressional elections, the overall voter turnout was 45 percent. Among non-Hispanic Whites, there was a 47 percent showing at the polls. In the November 1994 elections, 46.9 percent of all Whites voted, out of only 64.2 percent registered. Among the 53.1 percent who did not or could not vote, 32.5 percent were registered, and 11.8 percent were not U.S. citizens.

Endnotes

1   Since 1790, the U.S. government has recognized the racial category "White," making Americans belonging to that majority group distinct from racial minorities. In 1848, under the treaty of Guadelupe Hidalgo, the United States was faced with the need to provide citizenship status to those of Castilian and Spanish heritage who were living in the West in what formerly was Mexico. Because the Naturalization Act of 1790 stated that only "free white males" could become citizens of the United States, this required the U.S. government to confer the status of "White" on this population. After that point, future social scientists and demographers—principally in the 1970s and later decades—would make an important distinction between "non-Hispanic Whites" and "Hispanic Whites." Non-Hispanic Whites, typically considered by many Hispanic Americans as "Anglos," are usually associated with those whose ancestry stems from Europe, excluding the Iberian peninsula (Spain and Portugal). Hispanic Whites, by contrast, refer to persons who identify their ancestry or origin as Spain or areas on the Iberian peninsula. Thus, persons of Portuguese, Basque, Castillian, and Spanish descent would be considered by the U.S. Census Bureau as Hispanic. Many persons who consider themselves "Latino" make a distinction between "Hispanic" and "Latino," as well. Latinos refer to persons of Spanish ancestry as well as mixed-Spanish ancestry who were raised in the crucible of experience in the Americas. By this measure, Portuguese, Spaniards, Basques, and non-aboriginal Brazilians are not "Latino," but rather they are considered as "Hispanic." The distinction has been made by many to differentiate the experiences of Latinos, or of many racial minority groups, from those of Hispanics, who constitute more of a cultural or linguistic minority group.

2   Roughly over half of the so-called plain-White population refuse to state a fill-in-the-box racial category on the decennial census. Many, instead, write in "American," "Heinz 57," "human being," or other oddities. In 1990, the Census Bureau tabulated many of the individuals who identified themselves as "American." Most are concentrated in the South, south of the Mason-Dixon line, and are of primarily Scotch-Irish-English extraction.

Map 5.1 Non-Hispanic White Americans by State, 1990

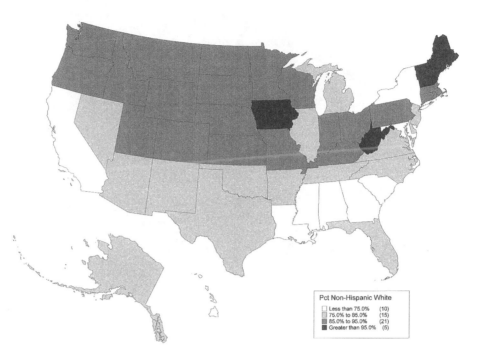

Pct Non-Hispanic White

☐ Less than 75.0% (10)
▨ 75.0% to 85.0% (15)
▨ 85.0% to 95.0% (21)
■ Greater than 95.0% (5)

Map 5.2 Non-Hispanic White Americans by County, 1990

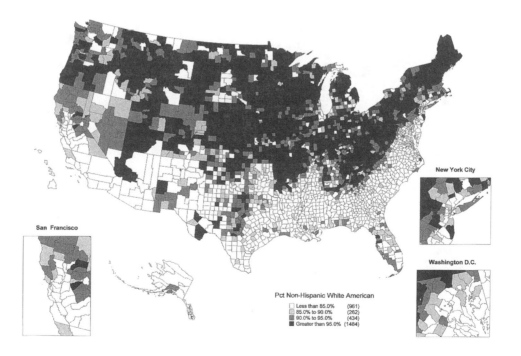

New York City

San Francisco

Washington D.C.

Pct Non-Hispanic White American

☐ Less than 85.0% (961)
▨ 85.0% to 90.0% (262)
▨ 90.0% to 95.0% (434)
■ Greater than 95.0% (1484)

Map 5.3 Northern European Americans by State, 1990

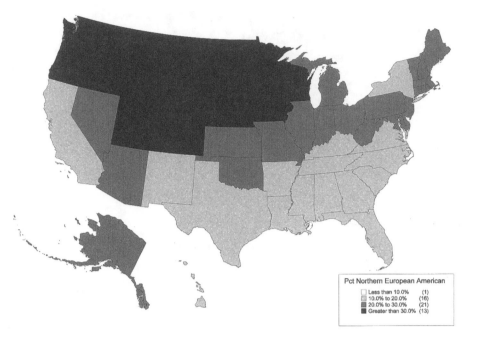

Pct Northern European American

☐ Less than 10.0%	(1)
☐ 10.0% to 20.0%	(16)
◼ 20.0% to 30.0%	(21)
◼ Greater than 30.0%	(13)

Map 5.4 Northern European Americans by County, 1990

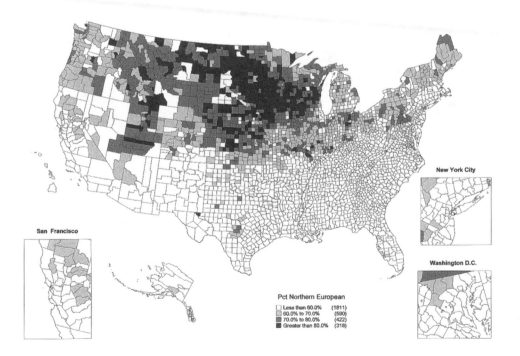

New York City

San Francisco

Washington D.C.

Pct Northern European

☐ Less than 60.0%	(1811)
☐ 60.0% to 70.0%	(580)
◼ 70.0% to 80.0%	(422)
◼ Greater than 80.0%	(318)

Map 5.5 Irish Americans by State, 1990

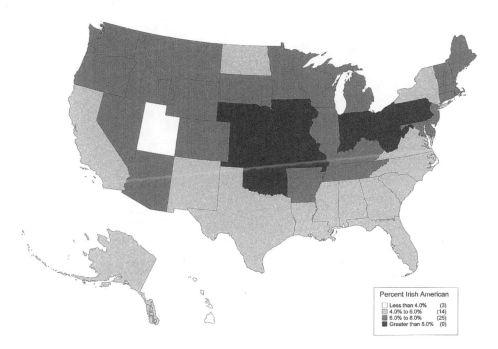

Map 5.6 Irish Americans by County, 1990

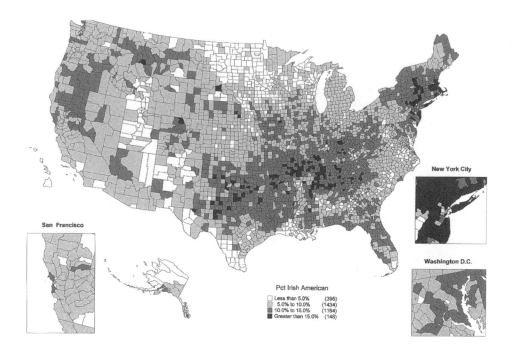

Map 5.7 English Americans by State, 1990

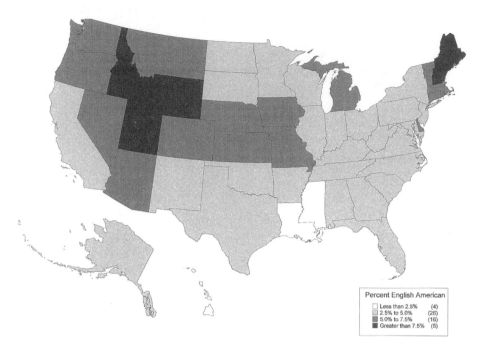

Percent English American

☐	Less than 2.5%	(4)
	2.5% to 5.0%	(26)
	5.0% to 7.5%	(16)
■	Greater than 7.5%	(5)

Map 5.8 English Americans by County, 1990

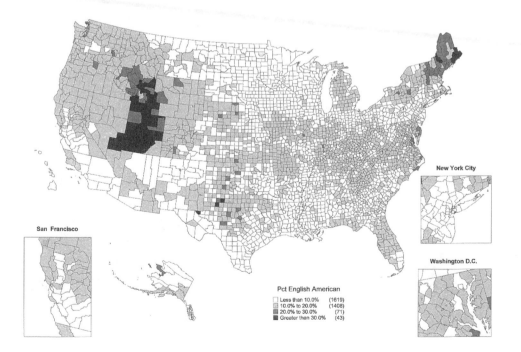

New York City

San Francisco

Washington D.C.

Pct English American

☐	Less than 10.0%	(1619)
	10.0% to 20.0%	(1408)
	20.0% to 30.0%	(71)
■	Greater than 30.0%	(43)

Map 5.9 German Americans by State, 1990

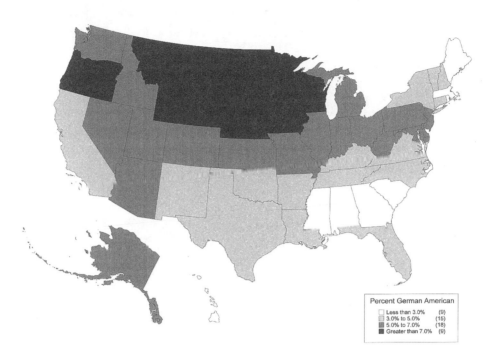

Percent German American

☐	Less than 3.0%	(9)
☐	3.0% to 5.0%	(15)
☐	5.0% to 7.0%	(18)
■	Greater than 7.0%	(9)

Map 5.10 German Americans by County, 1990

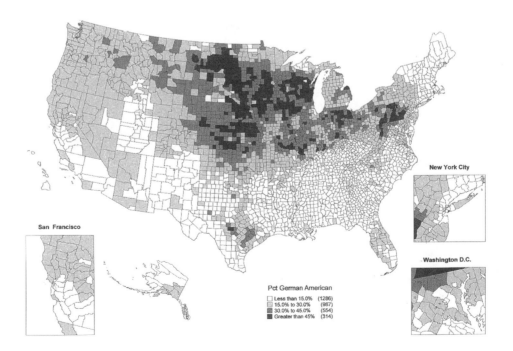

New York City

San Francisco

Washington D.C.

Pct German American

☐	Less than 15.0%	(1286)
☐	15.0% to 30.0%	(987)
☐	30.0% to 45.0%	(554)
■	Greater than 45%	(314)

Map 5.11 French Americans by State, 1990

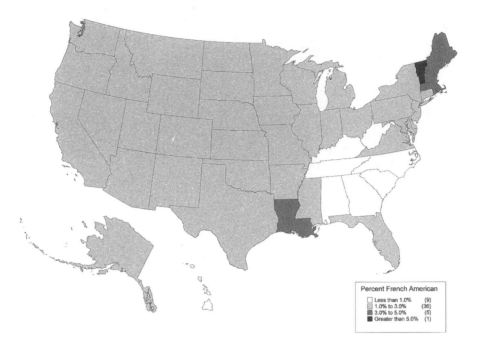

Percent French American
- ☐ Less than 1.0%   (9)
- ▨ 1.0% to 3.0%   (36)
- ▨ 3.0% to 5.0%   (5)
- ■ Greater than 5.0% (1)

Map 5.12 French Americans by County, 1990

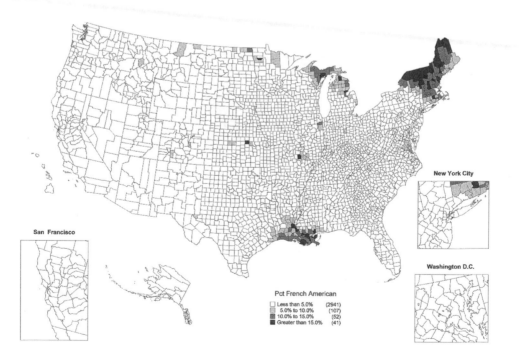

Pct French American
- ☐ Less than 5.0%   (2941)
- ▨ 5.0% to 10.0%   (107)
- ▨ 10.0% to 15.0%   (52)
- ■ Greater than 15.0% (41)

Map 5.13   Scotch-Irish Americans by State, 1990

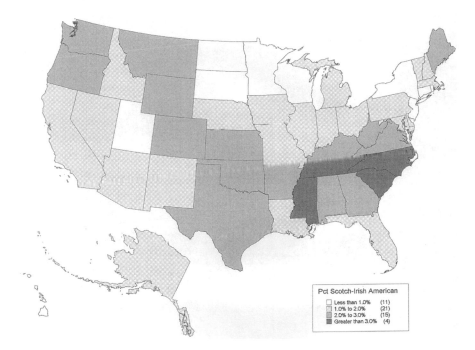

Pct Scotch-Irish American
	Less than 1.0%	(11)
	1.0% to 2.0%	(21)
	2.0% to 3.0%	(15)
	Greater than 3.0%	(4)

Map 5.14   Scotch-Irish Americans by County, 1990

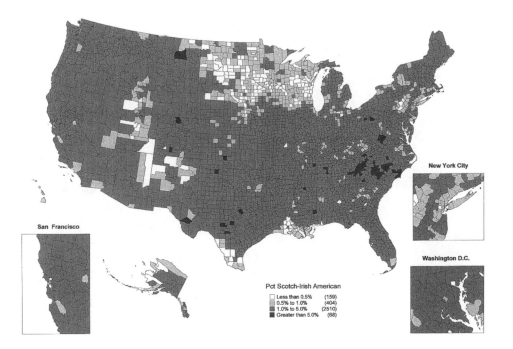

New York City

San Francisco

Washington D.C.

Pct Scotch-Irish American
	Less than 0.5%	(159)
	0.5% to 1.0%	(404)
	1.0% to 5.0%	(2510)
	Greater than 5.0%	(68)

Map 5.15   Scotch Americans by State, 1990

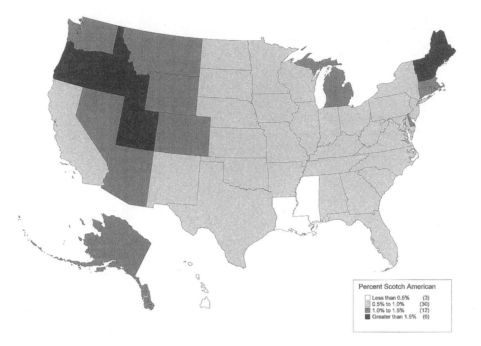

Percent Scotch American

Less than 0.5%   (3)
0.5% to 1.0%   (30)
1.0% to 1.5%   (12)
Greater than 1.5%   (6)

Map 5.16   Scotch Americans by County, 1990

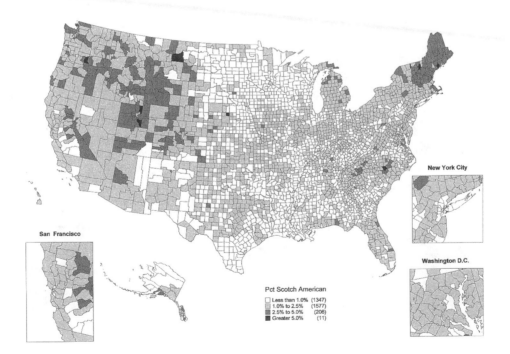

Pct Scotch American

Less than 1.0%   (1347)
1.0% to 2.5%   (1577)
2.5% to 5.0%   (206)
Greater 5.0%   (11)

New York City

San Francisco

Washington D.C.

Map 5.17   Scandinavian Americans by State, 1990

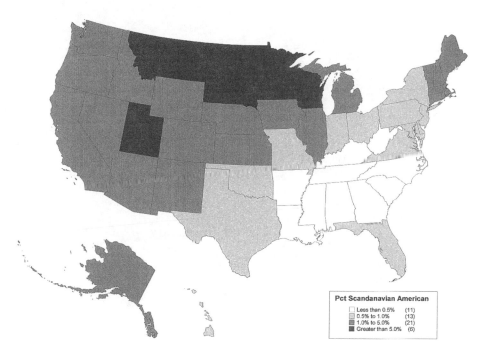

Pct Scandanavian American

☐ Less than 0.5%   (11)
▢ 0.5% to 1.0%   (13)
▨ 1.0% to 5.0%   (21)
■ Greater than 5.0%   (6)

Map 5.18   Scandinavian Americans by County, 1990

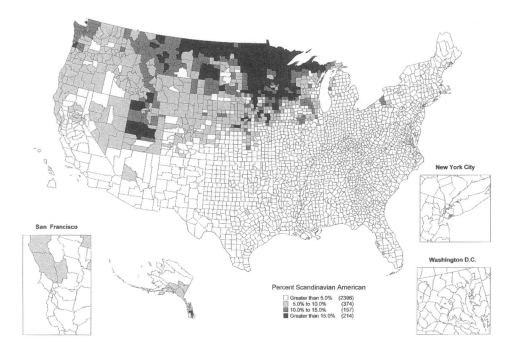

New York City

San Francisco

Washington D.C.

Percent Scandinavian American

☐ Greater than 5.0%   (2396)
▢ 5.0% to 10.0%   (374)
▨ 10.0% to 15.0%   (157)
■ Greater than 15.0%   (214)

Map 5.19 Welsh Americans by State, 1990

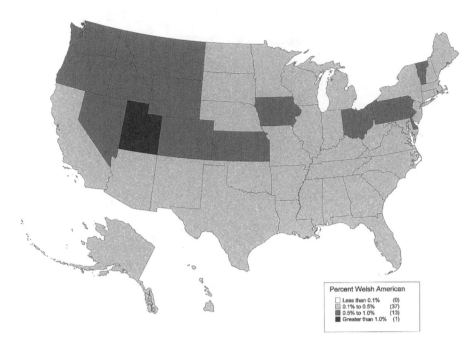

Map 5.20 Welsh Americans by County, 1990

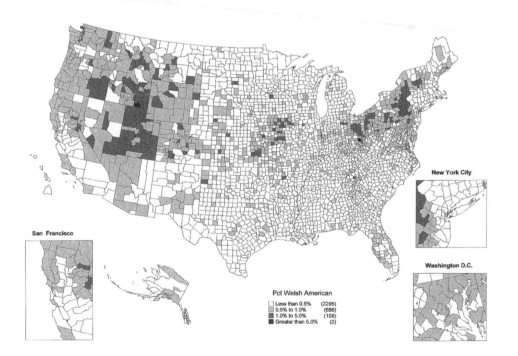

Map 5.21 Southern, Central, and Eastern European Americans by State, 1990

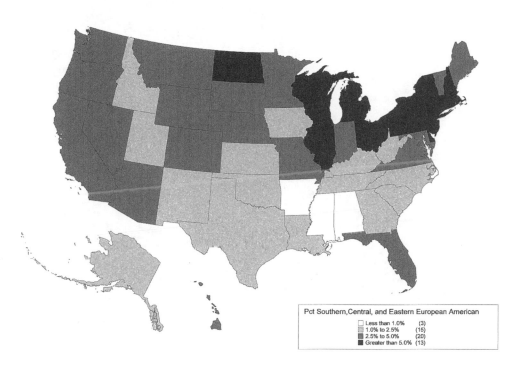

Pct Southern, Central, and Eastern European American
- ☐ Less than 1.0%   (3)
- ▨ 1.0% to 2.5%   (15)
- ▨ 2.5% to 5.0%   (20)
- ■ Greater than 5.0%   (13)

Map 5.22 Southern, Central, and Eastern European Americans by County, 1990

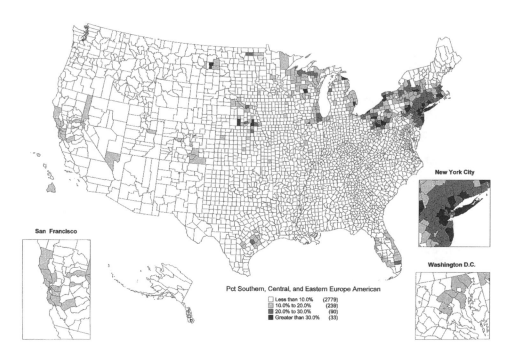

San Francisco

New York City

Washington D.C.

Pct Southern, Central, and Eastern Europe American
- ☐ Less than 10.0%   (2779)
- ▨ 10.0% to 20.0%   (239)
- ▨ 20.0% to 30.0%   (90)
- ■ Greater than 30.0%   (33)

Map 5.23 Italian Americans by State, 1990

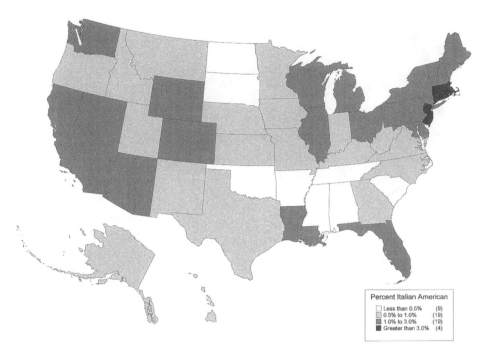

Map 5.24 Italian Americans by County, 1990

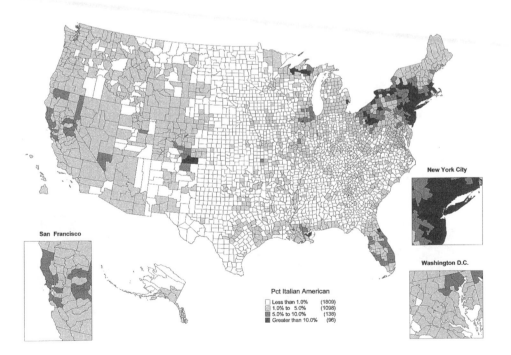

Map 5.25 Polish Americans by State, 1990

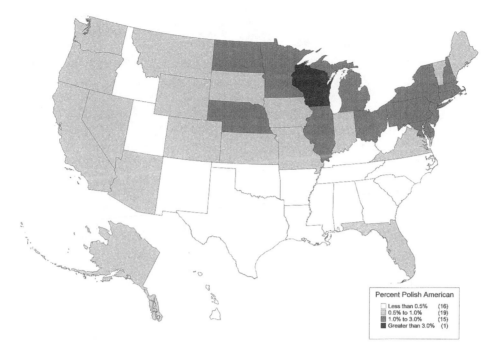

Percent Polish American
- ☐ Less than 0.5% (16)
- ☐ 0.5% to 1.0% (19)
- ◼ 1.0% to 3.0% (15)
- ◼ Greater than 3.0% (1)

Map 5.26 Polish Americans by County, 1990

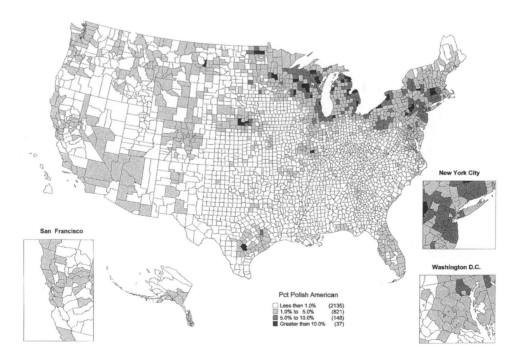

New York City

San Francisco

Washington D.C.

Pct Polish American
- ☐ Less than 1.0% (2135)
- ☐ 1.0% to 5.0% (821)
- ◼ 5.0% to 10.0% (148)
- ◼ Greater than 10.0% (37)

Map 5.27 Greek Americans by State, 1990

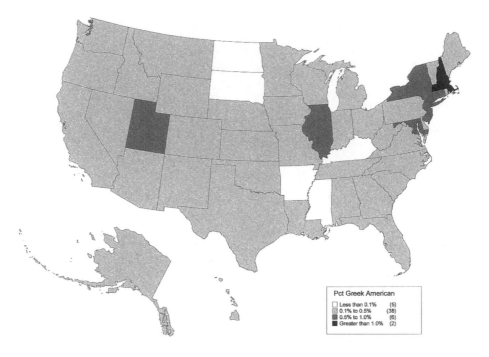

Pct Greek American
☐ Less than 0.1%   (5)
▨ 0.1% to 0.5%   (38)
▨ 0.5% to 1.0%   (6)
■ Greater than 1.0% (2)

Map 5.28 Greek Americans by County, 1990

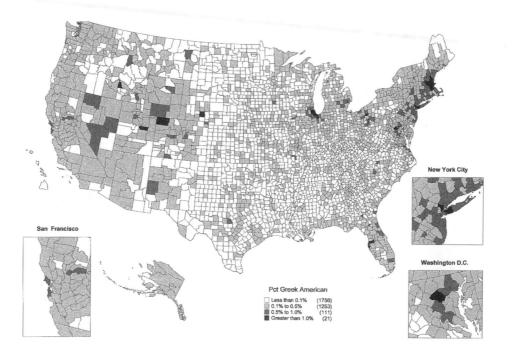

New York City

San Francisco

Washington D.C.

Pct Greek American
☐ Less than 0.1%   (1756)
▨ 0.1% to 0.5%   (1253)
▨ 0.5% to 1.0%   (111)
■ Greater than 1.0%   (21)

Map 5.29 Russian Americans by State, 1990

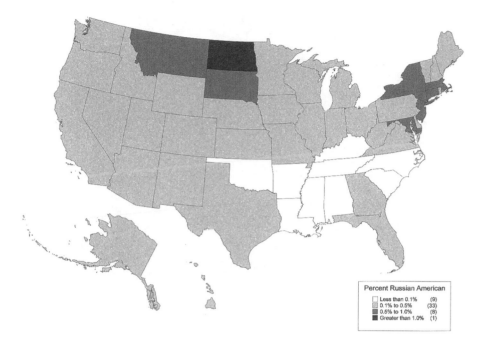

Percent Russian American

Less than 0.1%   (9)
0.1% to 0.5%   (33)
0.5% to 1.0%   (8)
Greater than 1.0%   (1)

Map 5.30 Russian Americans by County, 1990

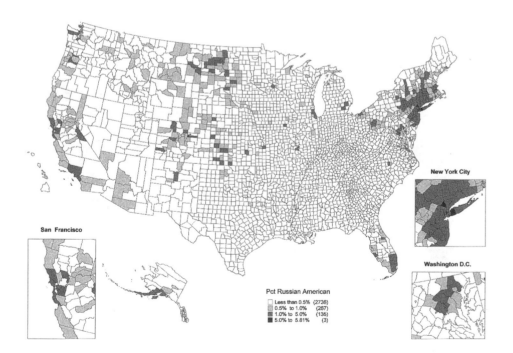

New York City

San Francisco

Washington D.C.

Pct Russian American

Less than 0.5%   (2736)
0.5% to 1.0%   (267)
1.0% to 5.0%   (135)
5.0% to 5.81%   (3)

Map 5.31 Hungarian Americans by State, 1990

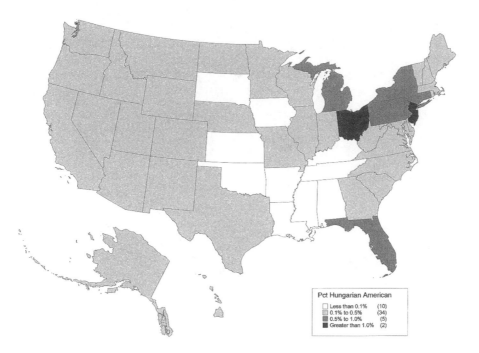

Pct Hungarian American

☐	Less than 0.1%	(10)
☐	0.1% to 0.5%	(34)
▨	0.5% to 1.0%	(5)
■	Greater than 1.0%	(2)

Map 5.32 Hungarian Americans by County, 1990

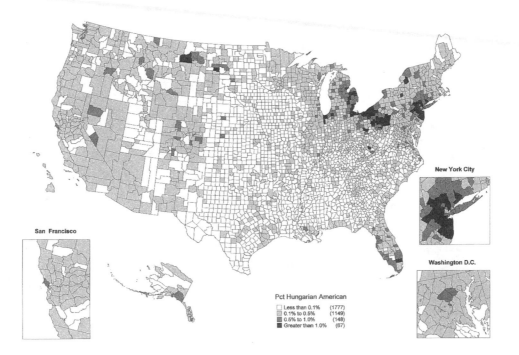

New York City

San Francisco

Washington D.C.

Pct Hungarian American

☐	Less than 0.1%	(1777)
☐	0.1% to 0.5%	(1149)
▨	0.5% to 1.0%	(148)
■	Greater than 1.0%	(67)

Map 5.33 Portuguese Americans by State, 1990

Map 5.34 Portuguese Americans by County, 1990

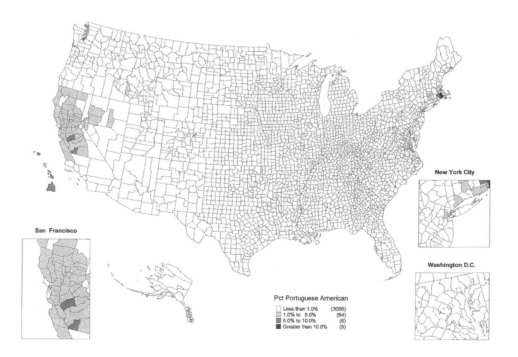

Chart 5.1 Resident Non-Hispanic White Population
by Age, 1990

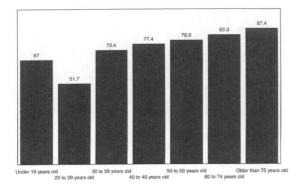

A Comparison of American Race and Ethnic Social and Economic Status

Introduction *(See Chart 6.1)*

In the past two decades, the nation has become increasingly more diverse racially and ethnically. America's minority populations—defined to include African Americans; American Indian, Eskimo, and Aleut (Native Americans); Asians and Pacific Islanders (Asian Pacific Americans); and Hispanic Americans—have grown much more rapidly than the population as a whole. This growth reflects higher birth rates among those already living there and, most strikingly, the increased immigration of Asians and Hispanics.

Between 1980 and 1990, the rate of increase among most racial groups in the United States was rapid: African Americans grew by 13 percent, Native Americans grew by 38 percent, Asian Pacific Americans grew by an astonishing 108 percent, while Whites grew by a mere 6 percent. The result of such growth is a nation that is increasingly racially diverse.

As a consequence, non-Hispanic Whites, who represented nearly 84 percent of the U.S. population in 1970, dropped to 80 percent in 1980 and to just over 75 percent in 1990. The trends are even more visible in many large urban areas and a few states: 6 of the nation's largest 10 cities, and 14 cities with over half a million persons, were ranked as "majority minority" in the 1990 census; New Mexico, with a minority population of almost 50 percent, nearly joined the District of Columbia (73 percent) and Hawaii (69 percent) as a "majority minority" state in 1990, while California (43 percent) is expected to do so by the year 2000. The U.S. Census Bureau projects that if current trends continue, the non-Hispanic White share of the population would steadily fall to 60 percent in 2030 and to 53 percent in 2050. The nation would thus approach a "majority minority" population around the middle of the next century.

But what's so new about these developments? After all, this is scarcely the first time that people from different nations and cultures have represented a large and growing segment of this "nation of immi-

grants." Why does the growth of racial and ethnic diversity seem to penetrate to the very heart of what the United States is, or could become?

Few of us can pinpoint or articulate what creates these feelings, but they almost certainly arise from the moral tension and discomfort that surrounds the public discourse about race in America. Moreover, there is a painful absence of shared understandings about how we see the issues of both race and inferiority in America. Uncomfortable as they make us, our feelings and fears seem to revolve closely around questions of racial or cultural inferiority and superiority.

Although today's increasingly racial and ethnic diversity shares much with the great European immigration that gave us our national self-image as a "melting pot," we perceive a difference that we are not sure we can overcome. As the term "minority" itself suggests, the nation sees members of minority groups very differently than the way it views its European immigrants. While many European immigrants faced hostility, prejudice, and discrimination on these shores, they were seldom assigned legally subordinate status.

Only America's non-Whites were considered sufficiently different and inferior to be so distinguished and subordinated, and thus denied the rights guaranteed to other Americans. For African Americans, of course, the inferior status assigned was slavery, plus, soon after the end of the Civil War, "Jim Crow" segregation. The United States Supreme Court fully recognized and sanctioned racial segregation in 1896, when it upheld, in *Plessy v. Ferguson*, Lousiana's law requiring separate railway carriages for African Americans (then called Negros), and through it, separate facilities in all areas of life, including public schools. For American Indians, the peoples we now term Native Americans, inferior status was imposed by a long history as a conquered people, symbolized most dramatically by the Trail of

Tears and by many Indian tribes' often-coerced relocation from their historical tribal lands to reservations, under the flag of the Indian Removal Act of 1830. (This, despite the Supreme Court's recognition of their right as sovereign nations to refuse to be relocated.) For Asian immigrants, their inferior status assignment was the status, defined by the very first Congress in 1790, of "aliens ineligible for citizenship." This status was used in state and federal laws from 1850 until a century later to limit immigration from Asia and to prevent Asians who did emigrate from owning or leasing land in the United States. Indeed, Asian-born persons were denied citizenship until as late as 1952—long after the 14th Amendment had guaranteed that same right to the group we now call African Americans.

Perception and Reality

According to a recent study reported by Patricia Leibowitz in the *New York Times* (1996), non-Hispanic (or White) Americans think that 14.9 of the nation's people are Hispanic (while the actual number is 9.5). And White Americans think that 10.8 of the nation is Asian (compared to the actual figure, 3.1). And they think that 23.8 of the nation is African American (versus the actual figure of 11.8). Most paradoxically, White Americans think the nation is only 49.9 "White" (whereas the reality is that 74 percent of its people are White).

Racial Classification

The set of racial classifications used by the U.S. Census Bureau, in its gathering and analysis of statistics, provides standards on race—as well as on categories of Hispanic Americans—for statistical reporting to be used by all federal agencies. The race and Hispanic-origin categories are defined as follows.

American Indian, Eskimo, and Aleut (Native American)

A person having origins in any of the aboriginal (or native) peoples of North America who maintains a cultural identification through tribal affiliation or community recognition.

Asian and Pacific Islander (Asian Pacific American)

A person having origins in any of the original peoples of the Far East, Southeast Asia, the Indian subcontinent, or the Pacific Islands. This area includes, for example, China, India, Japan, Korea, the Philippine Islands, Samoa, and the Hawaiian Islands (later, the state of Hawaii).

Black (African American)

A person having origins in any of the Black racial groups of Africa.

Hispanic

A person of Mexican, Puerto Rican, Cuban, Central or South American or other Spanish culture or origin, regardless of race.

White

A person having origins in any of the original peoples of Europe, North Africa, or the Middle East.

Population Growth *(See Charts 6.2–6.4)*

Between 1980 and 1990, rapid growth among most racial groups created more pronounced racial diversity in the Unites States. The rate of increase during the decade for each of the main groups was as follows: African Americans, 13 percent; Native Americans, 38 percent; and Asian Pacific Americans, 108 percent—all of them exceeding the rate of increase for non-Hispanic Whites, at 6 percent. Consequently, each racial group *except* Whites constituted a larger share of the total population in 1990 than it did in 1980. Despite this general shift, about eight of every ten U.S. residents in 1990 were White.

Asian Pacific Americans actually have the highest percentage growth of any U.S. minority, increasing today by 3.5 percent annually, but that is from a much smaller base of people than Hispanic Americans represent, whose population is rising at almost the same rate, about 3.4 percent annually. By contrast, African Americans are increasing by 1.3 percent annually, and Whites by 1.41 percent.

The federal report from which these statistics are drawn, entitled "U.S. Population Estimates by Age, Sex, Race and Hispanic American: 1990–1995," also shows that Asian Pacific Americans are adding about 300,000 people annually, while African Americans are adding some 400,000. Native Americans added roughly 25,000 people annually.

The current Hispanic American birth rate is equal to that of Asian Pacific Americans and is 10 percent higher than of African Americans (21 and 19 births per 1,000 population, respectively). Birth rates for all three minorities are higher than for non-Hispanic Whites but are expected to decline steadily and slowly.

Estimates are that four of every ten persons who will likely be added to the population through net immigration from 1995 to 2050 would be Hispanic, three in ten would be Asian and Pacific Islander, two in ten would be non-Hispanic White, and one in ten would be African American.

During 1994, the Hispanic American population grew by 897,000 people (a 3.5 percent increase). At the same time, the non-Hispanic White population added 813,000 people, an increase of 0.4 percent. The Asian Pacific American population grew by 336,000 (3.8 percent); the African American population grew by 484,000 (1.5 percent); the Native American population grew by 33,000 (1.5 percent); and the overall White population (including both Hispanic and non-Hispanic Whites) grew by 1.62 million (0.8 percent).

By the year 2000, the non-Hispanic White proportion of the U.S. population is projected to decrease to less than 72 percent, with about 13 percent African American, 11 percent Hispanic American, 4 percent Asian Pacific American, and 1 percent Native American.

By 2050, less than 53 percent of the population would be non-Hispanic White, 16 percent would be African American, 23 percent would be Hispanic American, 10 percent Asian Pacific American, and 1 percent Native American.

Although non-Hispanic Whites make up almost 75 percent of the total population, they would contribute only 35 percent of the total population growth between 1990 and 2000. This percentage of growth would decrease to 23 percent between 2000 and 2010 and decrease further to 14 percent from the years 2010 to 2030. The African American population, on the other hand, would double its present size to 62 million by 2050. The Asian Pacific American population would increase too by 2050, more than five times its current size, to 41 million.

Although nearly three-quarters of the population was non-Hispanic White in 1995, this group would contribute only about one-quarter of the total population growth in the next ten years. From 2030 to 2050, the non-Hispanic White group would contribute nothing to the nation's population growth—because it would decline in size. The non-Hispanic White share of the U.S. population would steadily fall from 74 percent in 1995 to 72 percent in 2000, 64 percent in 2020, and 53 percent in 2050.

By the middle of the 21st century, the African American population would nearly double its 1995 size, to 62 million. After the year 2016, more African Americans than non-Hispanic Whites would be added to the population each year.

The races or ethnic groups with the highest rates of increase would be Hispanic Americans and Asian Pacific Americans, both with annual growth rates that may exceed 2 percent until 2030. In comparison, even at the peak of the Baby Boom era of the 1940s and 1950s, the total U.S. population never grew by more than 2 percent in a year.

Federal projections are that, every year from now to 2050, the race/ethnic group adding the largest number of people to the population would be the Hispanic Americans. In fact, after 2020 the Hispanic American population is projected to add more people to the United States every year than would all other race/ethnic groups combined. By 2010, in fact, the Hispanic American population may become the second-largest race/ethnic group.

Each year from 1997 to 2050, more than half of America's population growth will occur among the nation's Hispanic American and Asian Pacific American populations. Four of every ten persons added to the population through net immigration from 1995 to 2050 would be Hispanic American, three in ten would be Asian and Pacific Islander, two in ten would be non-Hispanic White, and one in ten would be African American. Another 8.4 million persons, or 4 percent of the population, will be members of races other than White or African American; persons of "other races" include Asian Pacific Americans and Native Americans.

Metropolitan and Nonmetropolitan Concentrations (See Charts 6.5 and 6.6)

More than three-quarters of the White, African American, and Asian Pacific American populations lived in metropolitan areas throughout the nation in 1990. Asian Pacific Americans were the most likely to be metropolitan dwellers (94 percent). In contrast, the Native American population was about as likely to live in nonmetropolitan areas (49 percent) as in metropolitan areas (51 percent).

In 1990, 49 percent of the Native American population lived outside of metropolitan areas. Only 16 percent of African Americans, 24 percent of non-Hispanic Whites, and 10 percent of Hispanic Americans lived in nonmetropolitan areas.

Ancestry (See Chart 6.7)

In the 1990 census, the most frequently reported ancestry in the United States was German. Nearly one-quarter of the American people (58 million) considered themselves to be of German or part- German ancestry. The next largest ethnic groups, in rank order, were Irish, English, African American, and Italian. In all, 33 different ancestry groups had at least 1 million people. About 5 percent of the respondents reported the general category "American." Most people reported only one ancestry group; however, a substantial segment reported a mixed background. Nationally, about 60 percent of the population reported only one ancestry; another 30 percent also wrote in a second ancestry. About 10 percent did not report any ancestry.

In over half of the states in 1990, more people reported they had German roots than any other ancestry. African American was the most frequently reported ancestry in the second highest number of states (seven), all of which were in the South. Irish and English were the largest ancestry groups in five states each, located in the South and Northeast for Irish, and in the Northeast and West for English.

Regional Concentrations by Ancestry (See Charts 6.8 and 6.9)

In 1990, individual ancestry groups showed striking variations in their patterns of regional distribution within the United States. These differences often reflected initial settlement patterns, especially for the newer immigrant groups. Of the largest European ancestries, French, Scottish, and Welsh were distributed evenly among the four regions of the North, South, West, and Midwest. Other large European groups were more concentrated. For example, more than half of the nation's Italians lived in the Northeast region, and over half of the Norwegians and Czechs were clustered in the Midwest. About 47 percent of the Scotch-Irish were concentrated in the South, while 45 percent of those with Danish ancestry lived in the West.

The regional concentrations of persons of Hispanic ancestry depended on their specific country of origin. For instance, the Northeast contained 86 percent of the country's Dominicans, 66 percent of its Puerto Ricans, and 63 percent of Ecuadorians. The South was home to 69 percent of Cubans and 51 percent of Nicaraguans. About 62 percent of both Salvadorans and Guatemalans and 57 percent of Mexicans lived in the West.

Persons from the West Indies ancestry groups were concentrated in the Northeast: 59 percent of the nation's Jamaicans and 55 percent of Haitians lived there. Among the larger ancestry groups from Southwestern Asia, over half of the Armenians and Iranians resided in the West, and 43 percent of the Syrians lived in the Northeast. Asian and Pacific Islander ancestry groups were found largely in the West. The West was home to 87 percent of the country's Hawaiians, 72 percent of its Japanese, 59 percent of its Cambodians, and 55 percent of its Chinese and Vietnamese.

Ancestry groups of 100,000 or more people with at least 35 percent in a region of the United States are as follows (the percentage is given in parentheses):

West: Armenian (53), Cambodian (59), Chinese (55), Danish (45), Filipino (68), Guatemalan (62), Hawaiian (87), Iranian (52), Japanese (72), Korean (44), Laotian (52), Mexican (57), Nicaraguan (38), Portuguese (41), Salvadoran (62), Taiwanese (47), Thai (43), Vietnamese (55).

Midwest: Czech (52), German (39), Norwegian (52), Polish (37), Swedish (40), Swiss (36).

South: Acadian/Cajun (91), African American (54), Cuban (69), Haitian (41), Honduran (40), Native American (47), Nicaraguan (51), Scotch-Irish (47).

Northeast: Colombian (49), Dominican (86), Ecuadorian (63), French Canadian (45), Greek (37), Haitian (55), Hungarian (36), Italian (51), Jamaican (59), Peruvian (38), Polish (37), Portuguese (49), Puerto Rican (66), Russian (44), Slovak (40), Syrian (43).

Educational Attainment *(See Charts 6.10–6.15)*

Levels of educational attainment varied considerably between different racial groups. In 1993, the percentage of high school graduates in the age range between 18 and 24 was 83 percent for non-Hispanic Whites, 75 percent for African Americans, and 61 percent for Hispanic Americans. In the same age range, the percent of high school graduates who went on to college was 42 percent for non-Hispanic Whites, 33 percent for African Americans, but 36 percent for Hispanic Americans.

In 1993, 13 percent of 18-to-24-year-olds were in the dropout pool, down from 15 percent ten years earlier. Hispanic Americans were far more likely to have dropped out of school (33 percent) than African Americans (16 percent) or Whites (12 percent).

In 1993, more students remained in school. The annual high school dropout rate for persons aged 14 to 24 enrolled in grades 10 through 12 declined from 6.3 percent in 1973 to 4.2 percent in 1993.

More of the nation's preschoolers are enrolled in some form of school. Nursery school enrollment has more than doubled from 1.3 million in 1973 to 3.0 million in 1993, owing in part to the increasing educational levels and labor force participation rates of mothers.

Educational attainment differences among non-Hispanic Whites, African Americans, and Hispanic Americans were substantial: 28 percent of Whites held degrees beyond high school, compared with 16 percent of African Americans and 13 percent of Hispanic Americans. In addition, the proportion of Hispanic Americans without a high school diploma (40 percent) was much greater than the proportion of either Whites (18 percent) or African Americans (27 percent).

High school completion rates for African Americans rose significantly from 67 percent in 1973 to 75 percent in 1993. There was no change for either Whites (83 percent) or Hispanics (61 percent).

Among undergraduate college students, about six in ten African Americans as well as Whites were enrolled in a four-year college, while only about five in ten Hispanics were enrolled in a four-year college.

The proportion of African American young adults, aged 18 to 24, who were high school dropouts in 1993 was only slightly higher than that for Whites (16 percent versus 12 percent). Hispanic Americans, however, had a substantially higher dropout rate, at 33 percent.

While non-Hispanic Whites had the highest level of high school completion for those age 25 and above, persons *other* than Whites or African Americans, such as Asians and Pacific Islanders, had the highest completion level for bachelor's degrees.

Educational Attainment of Mothers

In 1990, non-Hispanic African American children were one-half as likely as non-Hispanic White children to have a mother with a bachelor's degree, and the proportion for Hispanic Americans was much smaller.

Non-Hispanic African American children also were substantially less likely than non-Hispanic White children to have a mother with a high school diploma, and only 50 percent of Hispanic children had mothers with this much education.

One-quarter of Hispanic children had mothers with less than nine years of education, compared with fewer than 1 in 20 non-Hispanic White children and non-Hispanic African American children.

Marital Status *(See Chart 6.16)*

In 1994, single parents accounted for almost two-thirds (65 percent) of all African American family groups with children present, compared with 35 percent among Hispanic Americans and 25 percent among non-Hispanic Whites.

One significant trend is that of fathers playing a larger role in taking care of their children. In 1991, 20 percent of preschoolers were cared for by their fathers while their mothers were at work, up from 15 percent in 1988. Single fathers were twice as common among Whites (16 percent of all White single parents) as among African Americans (8 percent of all African American single parents).

The proportion of single-parent families has increased dramatically, however. The percent of all parent-child family groups maintained by single parents rose from 13 percent in 1970 to 30 percent in 1993. Nearly three-quarters of these single parents either had never married or were divorced.

The proportion of adolescents in families with one to three children was 78 percent for non-Hispanic Whites, 64 percent for non-Hispanic African Americans, and 56 percent for Hispanics.

The proportion living in "traditional" families declined from 34 percent to 20 percent for non-Hispanic Whites, from 8 percent to 4 percent for non-Hispanic African Americans, and from 21 percent to 15 percent for Hispanics.

In 1994, there were 1.3 million interracial married couples, 296,000 of whom were African American/White; 909,000 couples were White/Other (that is, other than African American); and 78,000 interracial married couples were African American/Other (other than White).

Labor Force Participation   (See Chart 6.17)

The proportion of adults who worked year-round, full-time among White men in 1992 and 1979 was, respectively, 72.3 and 76.7 percent, showing a 4.4 percent decline. In comparison, between 1992 and 1979, White women dramatically increased their labor force participation. In 1992, the proportion was 47.6 percent, as compared to 34.8 in 1979, demonstrating a remarkable 12.8 percent increase.

In 1992, African American men showed a greater percentage decline in labor force participation as compared to White men and a lower increase in labor force participation among African American women when compared to White women. Exactly 56.6 percent of African American men, compared to 62.1 percent in 1979, worked year-round, full-time, marking a 5.5 percent decline in labor force participation. Among African American women, the proportion was 48.2 percent in 1992, compared to 39.9 percent in 1979, showing a 8.3 percent increase.

Hispanic American men and women showed a similar pattern in the proportion working year-round, full-time, when compared to non-Hispanic Whites and African Americans. Of Hispanic American men, 60.3 percent worked year-round, full-time, in 1992, compared to 67.2 percent in 1979, indicating a 6.9 percent decline in labor force participation. Among Hispanic American women, the proportion was 36.6 percent in 1992, compared to 29.9 percent in 1979, showing a 6.7 percent increase.

Both non-Hispanic African American children and Hispanic children living with fathers were somewhat less likely than non-Hispanic White children living with fathers to have a father who worked.

By 1990, the proportion of children living with mothers who were full-time workers was 27 percent for non-Hispanic Whites, 30 percent for non-Hispanic African Americans, and 21 percent for Hispanics.

The proportion living with mothers who were part-time workers was substantially larger, at 47 percent for non-Hispanic Whites and at 41 percent for both non-Hispanic African Americans and Hispanics.

Women of every racial group increased their labor force participation rates between 1980 and 1990. In that decade, Asian Pacific American women and African American women had the highest labor force participation rates. American Indian, Eskimo, and Aleut women had the lowest. The range of variation among the race groups diminished between 1980 and 1990, however.

Family Income   (See Chart 6.18)

In 1993 the median household incomes for non-Hispanic Whites ($32,960), African Americans ($19,532), Asian Pacific Americans ($38,347), and Hispanic Americans ($22,886) remained unchanged in real terms from their 1992 levels. The real median household income for all these groups was lower than in 1989.

The 1994 median income for householders classified as White was $34,028; for non-Hispanic Whites, it was $35,126; for African Americans, $21,027; for

Other Races, $32,283; for Asian and Pacific Islanders, $40,482; and for Hispanic Americans, $23,421.

Household income is dropping. Median household income was $31,241 in 1993, down 1 percent in real terms from 1992, when it was $31,553. In central cities of metropolitan areas of one million or more persons, the real median income of households declined 3.2 percent, from $27,498 in 1992 to $26,622 in 1993.

Earnings of year-round, full-time workers have declined. Real median earnings of year-round, full-time workers declined both for men and for women from 1992 to 1993.

Non-Hispanic White children in 1990 were about three times more likely than either non-Hispanic African American children and Hispanic children to live in families with high incomes.

For children in two-parent families, the chances of living at comfortable or high income levels reached 74 percent for non-Hispanic Whites, but only 57 percent for non-Hispanic African Americans and even less, 44 percent, for Hispanics.

Among mother-only families, non-Hispanic children were most likely to be in low-income families, at 69 percent, compared with 46 percent for non-Hispanic White children.

The poverty rate for children in 1990 was 18 percent, but it was three or four times larger for non-Hispanic African Americans and Hispanics than for non-Hispanic Whites.

Nine percent of children in two-parent families were poor, but children in father-only families were more than twice as likely to be poor, and children in mother-only families were more than five times as likely to be poor.

Among children in two-parent families, the Hispanic poverty rate was more than three times greater than for non-Hispanic White children, while the rate for non-Hispanic African Americans was about two times the rate for non-Hispanic Whites.

The poverty rate for Hispanic and non-Hispanic African American children in mother-only families was much greater than for non-Hispanic Whites in mother-only families.

For non-Hispanic African American children and for Hispanic children in families with only one employed parent, the proportions experiencing poverty were substantially higher than for non-Hispanic Whites.

Poverty rates were lower for non Hispanic White than for non-Hispanic African American and Hispanic children, if they lived with two parents.

Whether they lived with two parents or only their mother, if children had only one working parent and the parent was a full-time worker, the poverty rate was two to three times greater for both non-Hispanic African Americans and Hispanics than it was for non-Hispanic Whites.

The median duration of poverty was longer for African Americans (5.8 months) than for non Hispanic Whites (4.1 months). And for Hispanics, it was five months.

Per Capita Income

The 1994 median income per capita for all races was $16,555; for Whites, it was $17,611; for African Americans, $10,650; for Asian and Pacific Islanders, $16,902; and for Hispanic Americans, $9,435.

Immigration   (See Chart 6.19)

In California, 45 percent of all immigrants over the age of 65 received Supplemental Security Income (SSI) in 1990, compared with only 9 percent of native-born seniors. Among elderly Chinese immigrants, the figure was 55 percent.

During the 1980s, the countries from which the largest number of U.S. immigrants came included Mexico (22.6 percent), the Philippines (7.5 percent), China (4.7 percent), Korea (4.5), and Vietnam (3.8 percent).

In 1994, 8.7 percent of the population of the United States was foreign-born—nearly double the percent who were foreign-born in 1970 (4.8 percent). This foreign-born population is not distributed evenly throughout the country. California is home to

7.7 million foreign-born persons—representing more than one-third of all immigrants to the U.S. and nearly one-quarter of all California residents. New York ranks second with 2.9 million, while Florida ranks third with 2.1 million foreign-born. Three other states have over one million foreign-born residents: Texas, Illinois, and New Jersey.

By 1994, about 20 percent of the foreign-born population came to the U.S. in the previous five years (4.5 million between 1990 and 1994, compared to 4.8 million for the decade of the 1970s). Nearly as many came per year during the 1980s (8.3 million) as in all of the preceding five years. The remainder of the foreign-born came to the U.S. prior to 1970.

More than 6 in 10 of the foreign-born population are White, about 1 in 5 are Asian or Pacific Islander, and only 1 in 14 are African American. Nearly half (46 percent) of all foreign-born persons are considered Hispanic American.

Of the Asian and Pacific Islanders living in the United States, 62 percent are foreign-born, and most of the immigrants (92 percent) entered this country since 1970. Although 39 percent of Hispanic Americans are foreign-born and most have lived in the United States long enough to qualify for naturalization, only 18 percent are in fact naturalized citizens.

Of the 22.6 million foreign-born persons living in the United States in 1994, 6.2 million came from Mexico. That country was by far the country of origin with the largest number of immigrants. The next largest group was from the Philippines—1 million. Of the 4.5 million most recent immigrants, over one-quarter (1.3 million) came from Mexico and an additional 243,000 came from Russia, after the breakup of the Soviet Union. Other countries with large numbers of recent immigrants include Vietnam, the Dominican Republic, the Philippines, India, and El Salvador.

Earnings *(See Charts 6.20–6.22)*

White households had a net worth of $45,740, about ten times that of both African American households ($4,418) and Hispanic households ($4,656). (The latter two figures are not statistically different.)

The percentages of year-round, full-time civilian workers aged 16 and over with *low* earnings, in 1992 and 1979, are:

- White men, 1992, at 11.6 percent, compared to 7.2 percent in 1979, making a +4.4 percentage point change
- White women, 1992, at 21.1 percent, compared to 19.8 percent in 1979, making a +1.3 percentage point change
- African American men, 1992, at 19.4 percent, compared to 14.0 percent in 1979, making a +5.4 percentage point change
- African American women, 1992, at 26.9 percent, compared to 24.3 percent in 1979, making a +2.6 percentage point change
- Hispanic American men, 1992, at 26.4 percent, compared to 13.4 percent in 1979, making a +13.0 percentage point change
- Hispanic American women, 1992, at 36.6 percent, compared to 32.3 percent in 1979, making a +4.3 percentage point change

By contrast with the above, the percentages of year-round, full-time civilian workers aged 16 and over with *high* earnings, in 1992 and 1979, are:

- White men, 1992, at 16.4 percent, compared to 15.9 percent in 1979, making a +0.5 percentage point change
- White women, 1992, at 3.8 percent, compared to 1.3 percent in 1979, making a +2.5 percentage point change

- African American men, 1992, at 5.1 percent, compared to 4.2 percent in 1979, making a +0.9 percentage point change
- African American women, 1992, at 1.6 percent, compared to 0.5 percent in 1979, making a +1.1 percentage point change
- Hispanic American men, 1992, at 5.3 percent, compared to 5.2 percent in 1979, making a +0.1 percentage point change
- Hispanic American women, 1992, at 1.8 percent, compared to 1.0 percent in 1979, making a +0.8 percentage point change

There was no significant change between 1992 and 1993 in poverty rates for non-Hispanic Whites (12.2 percent), African Americans (33.1 percent), Hispanic Americans (30.6 percent), or Asian Pacific Americans (15.3 percent). However, the number of poor persons was higher for both Whites (up by 967,000) and Hispanics (up by 534,000).

The 1993 median income for the different races is as follows: White ($32,960), African American ($19,532), Asian and Pacific Islander ($38,347) and Hispanic ($22,886). The real median household income for all these groups is lower than in 1989.

The per capita income for all persons increased by 2.3 (+/- 1.2) percent between 1993 and 1994 (after adjusting for inflation). Increases were also evident in the White population, at 2.2 (+/- 1.4) percent, while for the African American population it was 5.3 (+/- 3.5) percent. The per capita income for the Asian and Pacific Islander and Hispanic American populations, however, remained unchanged.

Poverty rates dropped between 1993 and 1994 for Whites and African Americans but showed no significant change for Hispanic Americans or Asian Pacific Americans. While the number of poor African

Americans dropped significantly between 1993 and 1994, the number of poor Hispanics showed a significant increase.

White households had a net worth of $45,740, about ten times that of either African American households ($4,418) or Hispanic households ($4,656). (The latter two figures are not statistically different.)

Over one-quarter (26 percent) of Whites who were poor in 1991 were not poor the next year. By comparison, 13 percent of African Americans and a similar proportion of Hispanics exited poverty. Notably, exit rates have worsened for African Americans: only 17 percent of those who were poor in 1990 escaped poverty in 1991.

African Americans and Hispanics' chronic poverty rates were 16 and 12 percent, respectively, much higher than the 3 percent for Whites. Even so, Whites still comprised a majority (55 percent) of the chronically poor. Another 40 percent were African American while 22 percent were Hispanic.

The median number of months for which their state of poverty lasted (among those who became poor after October 1990), by selected demographic characteristics, are as follows: from October 1990 through August 1993, all persons, 4.3 months; Whites, 4.1 months; African Americans, 5.8 months; Hispanics, 5.0 months.

The median gross income of families or primary individuals who owned their homes was $36,485 in 1993. About 5.4 million of the nation's 61.3 million home owners maintained low-income households that were below the household poverty level.

The median annual income of renters in 1993 was $18,957 (about half that of home owners). Income levels were generally higher inside metropolitan statistical areas (MSAs), particularly suburbs, than outside these areas. For renters residing in central cities, the median income was $17,152. Among those in suburbs of MSAs, income was 35 percent higher, or $23,173. Renters living outside MSAs had the lowest level of income, or a median income of $14,886. For all renters together, about 8.4 million, or 25 percent, were low-income, with levels below the household poverty level.

Health Care *(See Charts 6.23 and 6.24)*

A growing number of people in the United States live without health insurance coverage. An estimated 39.7 million people went without health insurance coverage during the entire 1993 calendar year, 1.1 million more than in 1992.

The proportions of persons who spent at least one month without insurance were: non-Hispanic Whites, 22 percent; African Americans, 36 percent; and Hispanic Americans, 50 percent.

Ninety-two percent of non-Hispanic Whites had at least one month of private insurance coverage, while 73 percent of African Americans and 70 percent of Hispanic-origin persons had at least one month of such coverage (the latter two figures are not statistically different).

In 1993 there were almost 1.1 million child victims in substantiated cases of abuse or maltreatment, up from 801,000 in 1990.

Poverty *(See Charts 6.25 and 6.26)*

The poverty rate for people under 65 years of age throughout the nation as a whole was 15 percent in 1992.

For non-Hispanic Whites over 65, the poverty rate was 11 percent; for African Americans, it was 33 percent; and for elderly Hispanics, 22 percent. The poverty rate increases with age. Women over 65, in general, had a 16 percent poverty rate, whereas men over 65 had a rate of 9 percent. Women do, however, have a higher life expectancy than men (79 years as opposed to 72). And elderly women are more likely to be widowed, while elderly men are more likely to be married.

Of course, factors such as age, sex, race, ethnicity, marital status, living arrangements, educational attainment, former occupation, and work history all affect poverty levels among the elderly. The better educated the elderly are, the healthier they are, and the better off they are economically.

There was no significant change between 1992 and 1993 in the poverty rates for Whites (12.2 percent), African Americans (33.1 percent), persons of Hispanic American descent (30.6 percent), or Asians and Pacific Islanders (15.3 percent). However, the number of poor persons in the latter year was higher for both Whites (up by 967,000) and Hispanics (up by 534,000).

Poverty rates dropped between 1993 and 1994 for Whites and African Americans but showed no significant change for Hispanic Americans or Asians and Pacific Islanders. While the number of poor African Americans dropped significantly between 1993 and 1994, the number of poor Hispanics showed a significant increase.

Of all the population subgroups looked at, only African Americans lost ground in the likelihood of escaping poverty. For those who were poor in the previous year, their exit rate dropped from 17.4 percent in 1991 to 13.0 percent in 1992.

The median duration of poverty was longer for African Americans (5.8 months) than for Whites (4.1 months). For Hispanics, it was five months, not statistically different from the other groups.

In 1994, about 13 percent of the nation's 4.2 million foreign-born mothers lived on food stamps, and about three-quarters of all foreign-born mothers on food stamps were not U.S. citizens.

In 1993, about one in four African American mothers of childbearing age (1.5 million) were recipients of Aid to Families with Dependent Children (AFDC), higher than the 7 percent (less than one in ten) of corresponding White mothers (2.1 million). Despite these differences in beneficiary rates, African American AFDC mothers did not have significantly more children than their White counterparts.

In 1993, nearly one in five Hispanic mothers (784,000) aged 15 to 44 were on AFDC. By comparison, about 1 in 10 (3 million) non-Hispanic mothers were AFDC recipients. Although both Hispanic and non-Hispanic mothers on AFDC were an average of 20 years old when they had their first child, Hispanic women had almost 0.7 more children than non-Hispanic women. About three in ten Hispanic mothers surviving on AFDC were born outside the United States.

In 1993, about 9 percent (392,000) of the nation's 4.2 million foreign-born mothers aged 15 to 44 were on AFDC, not statistically different from the 11 percent (3.4 million) of U.S.-born mothers who were AFDC recipients. Native- and foreign-born mothers on AFDC each had higher fertility rates than their counterparts who were not AFDC participants. Incidentally, about three-quarters of all foreign-born mothers on AFDC were not citizens of the United States.

In 1993, about 1 in 16, or 1.7 million, White mothers of childbearing age were recipients of support from the Women, Infants, and Children supplemental food program (WIC). This compares to one in ten, or 600,000, African American mothers receiving WIC. Despite the different WIC recipiency rates, African American and White WIC mothers had about the same number of children.

In 1993, one in eight, or 500,000, Hispanic mothers 15 to 44 years old were on WIC. By comparison, about 1 in 16, or 1.9 million, mothers not of Hispanic American ethnicity were WIC recipients. It should be noted that approximately one-half of the Hispanic WIC mothers were born outside the United States.

About 8 percent, or 338,000, of the nation's 4.2 million foreign-born mothers aged 15 to 44 were WIC participants. Their participation rate was not significantly different from that of native-born mothers (7 percent). In addition, foreign-born WIC mothers were older than their native-born counterparts (29 years versus 26 years). About three-quarters of all foreign-born WIC mothers were not United States citizens.

More Americans in the 1990s are on public assistance than in previous decades. The average monthly number of persons participating in at least one major federal public assistance program in 1991 was 30.9 million, up from 28.5 million in 1990.

More people are poor, too. The number of Americans living below the poverty level increased from 38.0 million in 1992 to 39.3 million in 1993. This was the fourth straight year that the number of persons living in poverty has increased.

The nation's poverty rate has not changed. In 1993, 15.1 percent of all Americans were poor, a rate that was not statistically different from the previous year.

Home Ownership (See Chart 6.27)

While 47 percent of White families couldn't afford a median-priced home, 78 percent of African American and a similar percent of Hispanic families (79 percent) were unable to buy.

While the overall home ownership rate declined during the 1980s for the first time since 1940, ownership rates actually increased for Whites, for American Indians, Eskimos, and Aleuts, and for Asian and Pacific Islanders. Ownership rates declined, however, for both African Americans and Hispanic Americans.

Asian Pacific American metro households paid the highest contract rent for housing ($495 a month), followed by non-Hispanic Whites ($414), Hispanic-origin persons ($405), and African Americans ($329).

Home ownership rates are at record highs. Sixty-five percent of the country's homes were owned in 1993, the highest home ownership rate since 1985.

The home ownership rate for married-couple families in 1993 was 79 percent, its highest level since 1988.

Forty-nine percent of non-Hispanic White householders lived in the suburbs. Three out of five African American householders were central city residents. Among Native Americans, 55 percent were highly concentrated in nonmetropolitan areas in the West. And 99 percent of Hispanic householders lived in metropolitan areas—52 percent in cities and 38 percent in suburbs.

About 68 percent of White householders were home owners with the median value of homes at $82,000 in 1991. About 43 percent of African American householders were owners, with a median home value of $55,400. Some 53 percent of Native American householders were owners, with a median home value of $62,900. About half of Asian Pacific American householders were owners, with a median home value of $195,900. Two in five Hispanic householders were owners, with a median home value of $80,900.

Family Composition *(See Charts 6.28 and 6.29)*

More families throughout the nation are being maintained by women without a husband. The proportion rose considerably from 11 percent of all families in 1970, to 18 percent in 1994. Such families constituted 48 percent of African American families and 14 percent of White families in the latter year.

A large proportion of births occurred out of wedlock: about 26 percent of babies born in 1994 were so born. Of African American women who gave birth in 1994, 66 percent were unmarried, compared with 19 percent of White women and 28 percent of Hispanic women.

Elderly

Compared with other race groups or with Hispanics, the White population had the highest proportion of elderly in 1990. This is because Whites have higher survival rates to 65 years old, and lower recent birth rates. Also, the White population of immigrants has declined over the past 30 years. In 2050, an even larger proportion of the White population may be elderly.

From 1990 to 2050, the percentage of elderly in the African American population could nearly double, from 18 percent to 15 percent.

Among Native Americans the proportion of elderly could more than double, from nearly 6 percent to just over 12 percent.

The elderly constituted 6 percent of the Asian Pacific American population in 1990 and could reach 16 percent of this group in 2050.

Only 5 percent of persons of Hispanic American origin were elderly in 1990. This could triple to 15 percent by 2050.

In 1990, of the 31 million elderly people of all races, 28 million were White; 2.5 million were African American; about 114,000 were Native American; and about 454,000 were Asian Pacific American. There were 1.1 million elderly Hispanic Americans in 1990.

There were more than 600,000 persons of races other than White who were 80 years old and over in 1990.

In 2050, there will likely be 79 million elderly Americans. While the number of elderly Whites could more than double to 62 million in 2050, the number of elderly African Americans could nearly quadruple to over 9 million.

The number of Native American elderly would be 562,000. The number of Asian Pacific American elderly would approach 7 million.

The number of elderly Hispanic Americans in 2050, 12 million, would be 11 times as many as in 1990.

The number of persons 80 years old and over would increase at a faster rate. The number of Hispanics 80 years old and over would increase from about 200,000 in 1990 to more than 4 million in 2050.

Moving

Non-Hispanic Whites (16 percent) have lower overall rates of moving than either African Americans (19.6 percent) or Hispanic Americans (22.4 percent).

Voter Turnout

Voter turnout for non-Hispanic Whites in 1994 was 47 percent, compared with 37 percent for African Americans and 19 percent for persons of Hispanic American origin. Asian Americans voted at levels of about 18 percent.

Voter turnout for Whites 18 years and over was 47 percent, compared with 37 percent for African Americans and only 19 percent for Hispanic Americans. Asian Americans voted at levels similar to Hispanic Americans, at a rate of only 18 percent.

By the year 2000 the African American population will number 22.9 million persons, representing 12 percent of the voting age population. Whites will represent 165.2 million persons, accounting for 84 percent of the voting age population. Another 8.4 million persons, or 4 percent of the population, will be races other than White or African American; persons of such other races include Asian or Pacific Islander, American Indian, Eskimo, and Aleut. Hispanics will number 18.6 million, or 9 percent of the electorate.

Map 6.1 "American" Americans by State, 1990

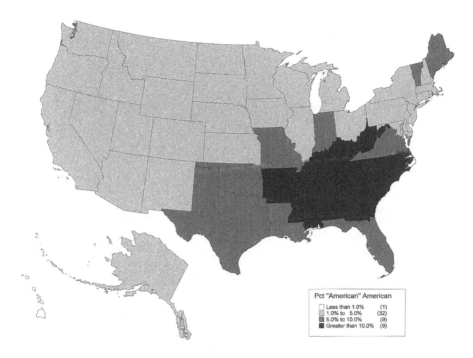

Map 6.2 "American" Americans by County, 1990

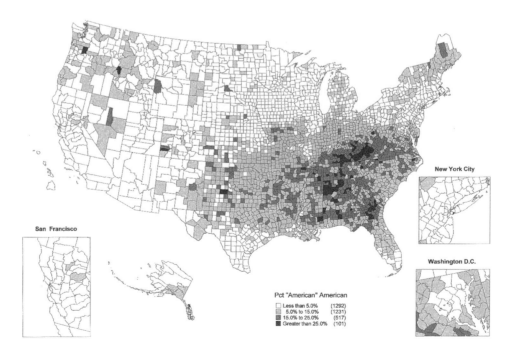

Map 6.3 Arab Americans by State, 1990

Percent Arab American
- ☐ Less than 0.1%   (45)
- ■ Greater than 0.1%   (6)

Map 6.4 Arab Americans by County, 1990

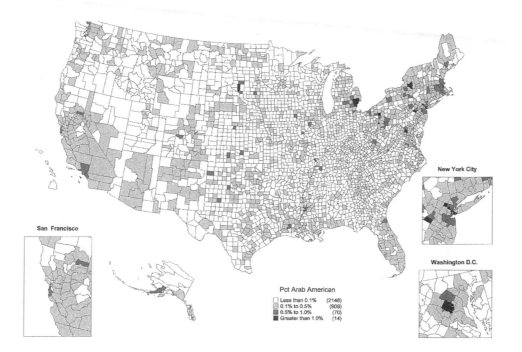

New York City

San Francisco

Washington D.C.

Pct Arab American
- ☐ Less than 0.1%   (2148)
- 0.1% to 0.5%   (909)
- 0.5% to 1.0%   (70)
- ■ Greater than 1.0%   (14)

Map 6.5 Multiethnic Americans by State, 1990

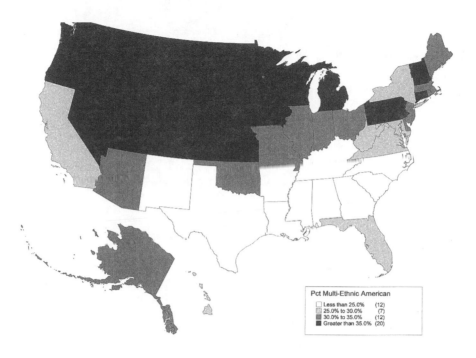

Map 6.6 Multiethnic Americans by County, 1990

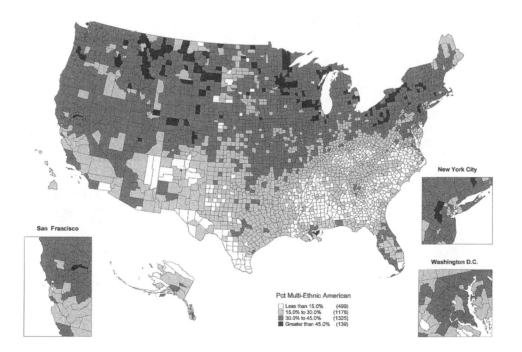

Chart 6.1 U.S. Population by Race, 1990 (Percent)

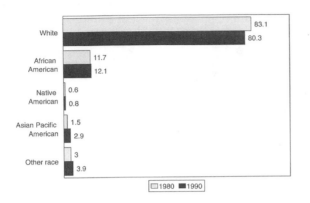

Chart 6.2 U.S. Population by Race, 1790–2050 (Thousands)

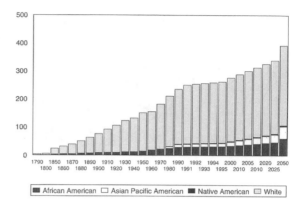

Chart 6.3 U.S. Population by Race, 1970–2050 (Percent)

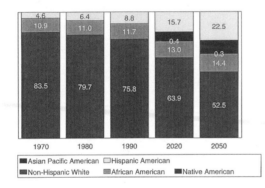

Note: Bar segments for 2 percent or less are not labeled separately on figure.

Chart 6.4 Resident Population by Hispanic and Non-Hispanic Origin, 1995 and 2050 (Projected) (Percent)

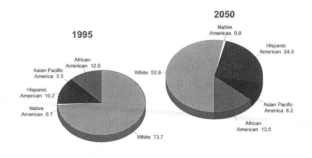

Chart 6.5 U.S. Metropolitan and Non-Metropolitan Residence by Race, 1990 (Percent)

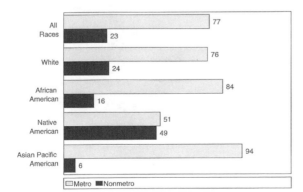

Chart 6.6 Selected Metropolitan Areas Minority Populations, 1990 (Percent)

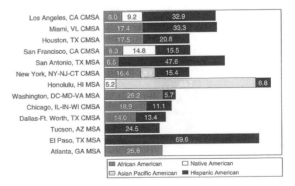

Chart 6.7 Top Fifteen U.S. Ancestry Groups, 1990 (Millions)

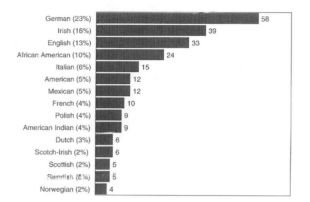

Chart 6.8 U.S. Regional Population by Race, 1990 (Percent)

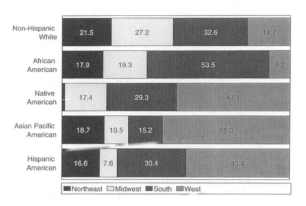

Chart 6.9 Regional U.S. Population by Race, 1990 (Thousands)

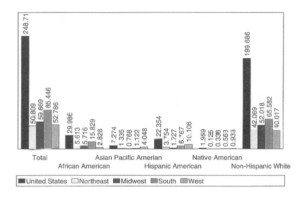

Chart 6.10 Educational Attainment by Race, 1990 (Percent)

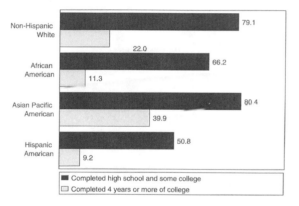

Chart 6.11 Educational Attainment by Race and Sex, 1990 (Percent receiving bachelor's degree)

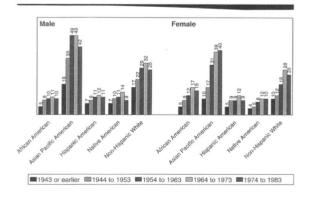

Chart 6.12 Educational Attainment by Race, 1940 and 1990 (Percent, 25 years and older)

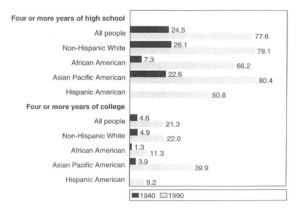

Chart 6.13 College Completion Rates by Race and Sex (Percent, 25 years and older)

Chart 6.14 Associate's and Bachelor's Degrees Earned by Race, 1990 and 1992 (Percent)

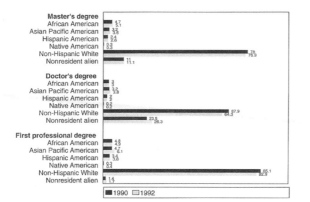

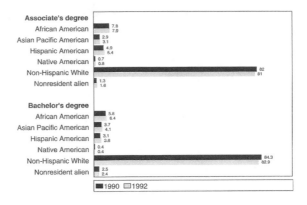

Chart 6.15 Graduate Degrees Earned by Race, 1990 and 1992 (Percent)

Chart 6.16 Percentage of Children Living in Two-Parent Families, 1970, 1980, and 1990

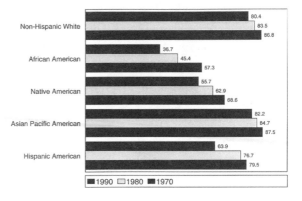

Chart 6.17 Occupational Distribution of the Civilian Labor Force by Race and Sex, 1990 (Percent, 16 years and older)

Chart 6.18 Income Brackets by Race, 1990 (Thousands)

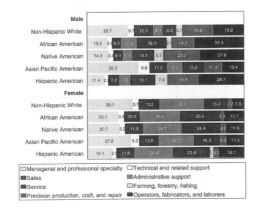

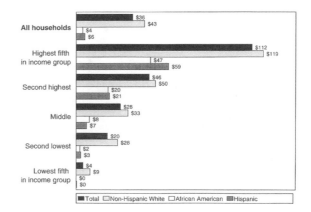

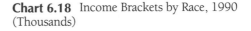

Chart 6.19 Legal Immigration by Area of Origin, 1952–1990 (Thousands)

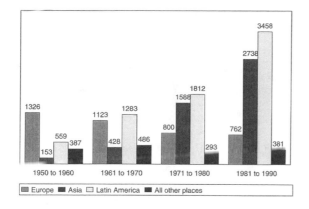

Chart 6.20 Male Income by Race, 1990 (Percentage of non-Hispanic White earnings, 35–44 years old)

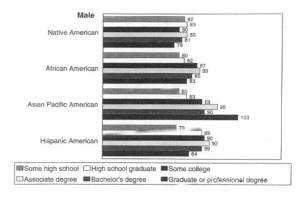

Chart 6.21 Female Income by Race, 1990 (Percentage of non-Hispanic White earnings, 35–44 years old)

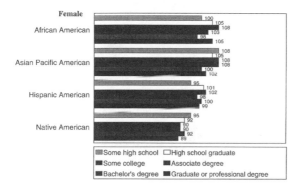

Chart 6.22 Minority Owned Firms, 1988 (Thousands)

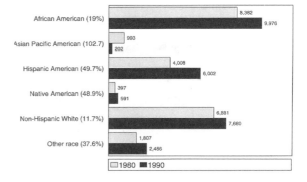

Chart 6.23 AIDS Deaths by Race, 1982–1994

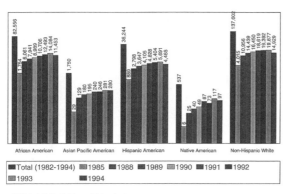

1-AIDS stands for Acquired Immunodeficiency Syndrome

Chart 6.24 Victims of Child Abuse and Neglect by Race, 1993 (Percent)

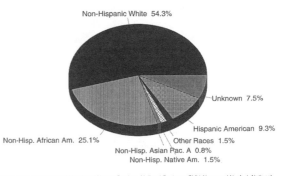

Source: U.S. Department of Health and Human Services, National Center on Child Abuse and Neglect, National Child Abuse and Neglect Data System, Working Paper 2, 1991 Summary Data Component, May 1993; Child Maltreatment - 1992, May 1994; and Child Maltreatment - 1993, April

Chart 6.25 Poverty Rates for Families, Persons, and Children by Race, 1990 (Percent)

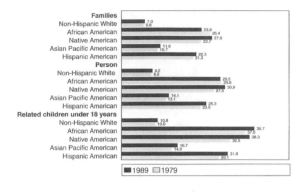

Chart 6.26 AFDC Recipients by Race, 1990

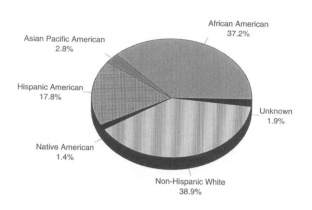

Chart 6.27 U.S. Housing Tenures by Race, 1980 and 1990 (Percent)

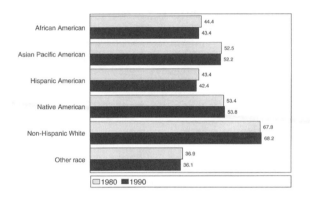

Chart 6.28 Birth Rate by Race, 1992 (Per 1,000 population)

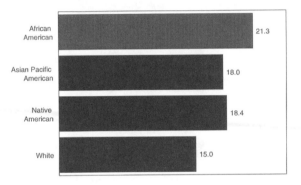

Chart 6.29 Family Composition by Race, 1970, 1980, and 1990 (Percent)

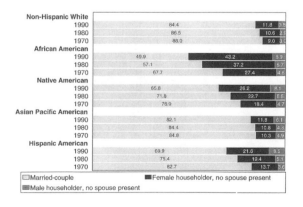

For Further Reading

Acuna, Rudolfo. *Occupied America: A History of Chicanos.* 2d ed. New York: Harper and Row, 1981.
_____. *Ethnic Identity: The Transformation of White America.* New Haven: Yale University Press, 1990.

Alba, Richard D. *Italian Americans: Into the Twilight of Ethnicity.* Englewood Cliffs, N.J.: Prentice-Hall, 1985.

American Jewish Committee. *American Jewish Year Book 1990.* New York: American Jewish Committee.

Anderson, Charles H. *White Protestant Americans.* Englewood Cliffs, N.J.: Prentice-Hall, 1970.

Ashton, Elwyn T. *The Welsh in the United States.* Hove, Sussex: Caldra House, 1984.

Bailyn, Bernard. *Voyagers to the West: A Passage in the Peopling of America on the Eve of the Revolution.* New York: Knopf, 1986.

Battistella, Grazano, ed. *Italian Americans in the 80s: A Sociodemographic Profile.* Staten Island, N.Y.: Center for Migration Studies, 1989.

Bean, Frank D., and Marta Tienda. *The Hispanic Population of the United States.* New York: Russell Sage Foundation, 1987.

Bennett, Claudette E., Barbara Martin, and Kymberly DeBarros. *We the Americans: Blacks.* Washington, D.C.: U.S. Department of Commerce, Economics and Statistics Administration, U.S. Bureau of the Census, Sept. 1993.

Billigmeier, Robert H. *Americans from Germany: A Study in Cultural Diversity.* Belmont, Calif.: Wadsworth Publishing, 1974.

Blalock, Hubert M., Jr. *Race and Ethnic Relations.* Englewood Cliffs, N.J.: Prentice-Hall, 1982.

Bouvier, Leon F. *Peaceful Invasions: Immigration and Changing America.* Lanham, Md.: University Press of America, 1992.

Campbell, Paul R. *Population Projections for States, by Age, Sex, Race, and Hispanic Origin: 1993 to 2020.* Current Population Reports, Series P25–1111. Washington, D.C.: U.S. Bureau of the Census, 1994.

Carver, Craig M. *American Regional Dialects.* Ann Arbor: University of Michigan Press, 1987.

Chavez, Linda. *Out of the Barrio: Toward a New Politics of Hispanic Assimilation.* New York: Basic Books, 1991.

Crispino, James A. *The Assimilation of Ethnic Groups: The Italian Case.* Staten Island, N.Y.: Center for Migration Studies, 1980.

Cuddy, D. L., ed. *Contemporary American Immigration: Interpretive Essays.* Boston: Twayne Publishers, 1982.

Davis, Jerome. *The Russian Immigrant.* Reprint, New York: Arno Press and *The New York Times,* 1969.

Day, Jennifer Cheeseman. *Population Projections of the United States by Age, Sex, Race, and Hispanic Origin: 1995 to 2050.* Current Population Reports, Series P25–1130. Washington, D.C.: U.S. Bureau of the Census, 1996.

Del Pinal, Jorge. *We the American: Hispanics.* Washington, D.C.: U.S. Bureau of the Census, U.S. Government Printing Office, Sept. 1993.

Deloria, Vine, Jr., and Clifford M. Lytle. *American Indians, American Justice.* Austin: University of Texas Press, 1983.

Desbarats, J. "Indochinese Resettlement in the United States." *Annals of the Association of American Geographers* 75:4(1985): 522–538.

Dinnerstein, Leonard, and David M. Reimers. *Ethnic Americans: A History of Immigration.* 3d ed. New York: Harper and Row, 1988.

Espiritu, Yen Le. *Asian American Panethnicity: Bridging Institutions and Identities.* Philadelphia: Temple University Press, 1992.

Fallows, Marjorie R. *Irish Americans: Identity and Assimilation.* Englewood Cliffs, N.J.: Prentice-Hall, 1979.

Farley, Reynolds, and Walter R. Allen. *The Color Line and the Quality of Life in America.* New York: Russell Sage Foundation, 1987.

Fitzpatrick, Joseph P. *Puerto Rican Americans: The Meaning of Migration to the Mainland.* 2d ed. Englewood Cliffs, N.J.: Prentice-Hall, 1987.

Foner, Nancy. *New Immigrants in New York.* New York: Columbia University Press, 1987.

Fugita, Stephen S., and David J. O'Brien. *Japanese American Ethnicity: The Persistence of Community.* Seattle: University of Washington Press, 1991.

Gans, Herbert. *The Urban Villagers.* 2d ed. New York: Free Press, 1983.

Gardner, Robert W., Bryant Robey, and Peter C. Smith. "Asian Americans: Growth, Change, and Diversity." *Population Bulletin* 40(Oct.): 1–43.

Glass Ceiling Commission. *Good for Business: Making Full Use of the Nation's Human Capital. The Environmental Scan.* Washington, D.C.: U.S. Government Printing Office, 1995.

Glazer, Nathan, and Daniel Patrick Moynihan. *Beyond the Melting Pot: The Negroes, Puerto Ricans, Jews, Italians, and Irish of New York City*. Cambridge, Mass.: MIT Press, 1963.

Grebler, Leo, Joan W. Moore, and Ralph C. Guzman. *The Mexican-American People: The Nation's Second Largest Minority*. New York: Free Press, 1970.

Greeley, Andrew M. *That Most Distressful Nation: The Taming of the American Irish*. Chicago: Quadrangle Books, 1972.

Hacker, Andrew. *Two Nations: Black and White, Separate, Unequal*. New York: Scribners, 1992.

Haines, David W. *Refugees as Immigrants: Cambodians, Laotians, and Vietnamese in America*. Totowa, N.J.: Rowman and Littlefield, 1989.

Halich, Wasyl. *Ukrainians in the United States*. Reprint, New York: Arno Press and *The New York Times*, 1970.

Herbert, Will. *Protestant-Catholic-Jew*. Garden City, N.Y.: Doubleday, 1960.

Hertzberg, Arthur. *The Jews in America: Four Centuries of an Uneasy Encounter*. New York: Simon and Schuster, 1989.

Higham, John. *Strangers in the Land*. New York: Atheneum, 1973.

Hurh, Won Moo, and Kwang Chung Kim. *Korean Immigrants in America*. Rutherford, N.J.: Farleigh Dickinson University Press, 1984.

Jiobu, Robert M. *Ethnicity and Assimilation*. Albany, N.Y.: State University of New York Press, 1988.

Katsup, A. *The Swedish Heritage in America*. Minneapolis: Swedish Council of America, 1975.

Kim, Illsoo. *New Urban Immigrants: The Korean Community in New York*. Princeton: Princeton University Press, 1981.

Kitano, Harry H. L., and Roger Daniels. *Asian Americans: Emerging Minorities*. Englewood Cliffs, N.J.: Prentice-Hall, 1976.

Krantz, Les. *America by the Numbers*. Boston: Houghton Mifflin, 1993.

Landry, Bart. *The New Black Middle Class*. Berkeley: University of California Press, 1987.

Leyburn, James G. *The Scotch-Irish: A Social History*. Chapel Hill: University of North Carolina Press, 1962.

Lieberson, Stanley. *A Piece of the Pie: Blacks and White Immigrants since 1880*. Berkeley: University of California Press, 1980.

Lieberson, Stanley, and Mary C. Waters. *From Many Strands: Ethnic and Racial Groups in Contemporary America*. New York: Russell Sage Foundation, 1988.

Light, Ivan, and Edna Bonacich. *Immigrant Entrepreneurs: Koreans in Los Angeles 1965–1982*. Berkeley: University of California Press, 1988.

Lopata, Helena Z. *Polish Americans: Status Competition in an Ethnic Community*. Englewood Cliffs, N.J.: Prentice-Hall, 1976.

Lopez, Adalberto, ed. *The Puerto Ricans: Their History, Culture, and Society*. Cambridge, Mass.: Schenkman, 1980.

Luebke, Frederick C. *Germans in the New World: Essays in the History of Immigration*. Urbana: University of Illinois Press, 1990.

Marger, Martin N. *Race and Ethnic Relations: American and Global Perspectives*. 3d ed. Belmont, Calif.: Wadsworth Publishing, 1994.

Marshall, Jonathan. "Study Backs Fears About Immigrants." *San Francisco Chronicle*. Feb. 26, 1996, D1 and D3.

Massey, Douglas S., and Nancy A. Denton. *American Apartheid: Segregation and the Making of the Underclass*. Cambridge: Harvard University Press, 1993.

McKee, J. O., ed. *Ethnicity in Contemporary America: A Geographical Appraisal*. Dubuque, Iowa: Kendall/Hunt, 1985.

Meinig, D. W. "The Mormon Culture Region: Strategies and Patterns in the Geography of the American West, 1847–1964." *Annals of the Association of American Geographers*. 55:2(1965): 191–220.

Moore, Joan W., and Harry Pachon. *Hispanics in the United States*. Englewood Cliffs, N.J.: Prentice-Hall, 1985.

Naff, Alixa. *The Arab Americans*. New York: Chelsea House Publishers, 1988.

National Urban League. *The State of Black America*. New York: National Urban League, 1994.

Nelli, Humbert S. *From Immigrants to Ethnics: The Italian Americans*. New York: Oxford University Press, 1983.

Novak, Michael. *The Rise of the Unmeltable Ethnics*. New York: Macmillan, 1972.

Office of Management and Budget. *Advance Notice of Proposed Review and Possible Revision of OMB's Statistical Policy Directive No. 15, Race and Ethnic Standards for Federal Statistics and Administrative Reporting; and Announcement of Public Hearings on Directive No. 15*. Washington, D.C.: Executive Office of the President, Office of Management and Budget, Office of Information and Regulatory Affairs, 1984.

O'Hare, William P. "America's Minorities—The Demographics of Diversity." *Population Bulletin* 4:47(4), 1992.

Omi, Michael, and Howard Winant. *Racial Formation in the United States: From the 1960s to the 1980s.* 2d ed. New York: Routledge, 1992.

Paisano, Edna L., Deborah L. Carroll, June H. Cowles, Kymberly A. DeBarros, Kenya N. Miles, and Leigh E. Zarbourgh. *We the American: Pacific Islanders.* Washington, D.C.: U.S. Bureau of the Census, U.S. Government Printing Office, 1993.

Paisano, Edna L., Deborah L. Carroll, June H. Cowles, Kymberly A. DeBarros, Ann J. Robison, and Kenya N. Miles. *We the Americans: Asians.* Washington, D.C.: U.S. Bureau of the Census, U.S. Government Printing Office, 1993.

Parrillo, Vincent N. *Strangers to These Shores: Race and Ethnic Relations in the United States.* 4th ed. New York: Macmillan, 1993.

Perlmutter, Philip. *A History of Ethnic, Religious, and Racial Prejudice in America.* Ames: Iowa State University Press, 1991.

Pido, Antonio J. A. *The Filipinos in America.* New York: Center for Migration Studies, 1986.

Pinkney, Alphonso. *Black Americans.* 3d ed. Englewood Cliffs, N.J.: Prentice-Hall, 1987.

Polenberg, Richard. *One Nation Divisible: Class, Race, and Ethnicity in the United States since 1938.* New York: Penguin, 1980.

Portes, Alejandro, and Robert L. Bach. *Latin Journey: Cuban and Mexican Immigrants in the United States.* Berkeley: University of California Press, 1985.

Rodriguez, Clara. *Puerto Ricans: Born in the U.S.A.* Boston: Unwin and Hyman, 1989.

Samora, Julian, and Patricia Vandel Simon. *A History of the Mexican-American People.* South Bend, Ind.: University of Notre Dame Press, 1977.

Sandberg, Neil. *Ethnic Identity and Assimilation: The Polish American Community.* New York: Praeger, 1974.

Schlesinger, Arthur M., Jr. *The Disuniting of America: Reflections on a Multicultural Society.* New York: Norton, 1992.

Schuman, Howard, Charlotte Steeh, and Lawrence Bobo. *Racial Attitudes in America: Trends and Interpretations.* Cambridge: Harvard University Press, 1991.

Shibutani, Tamotsu, and Kian M. Kwan. *Ethnic Stratification: A Comparative Approach.* New York: Macmillan, 1965.

Silberman, Charles E. *A Certain People: America's Jews and Their Lives Today.* New York: Summit Books, 1985.

Smith, Denise I., Cynthia M. Taeuber, and Louisa Miller. *We the American: Women.* Washington, D.C.: U.S. Bureau of the Census, U.S. Government Printing Office, 1993.

Snipp, C. Matthew. *American Indians: The First of This Land.* New York: Russell Sage Foundation, 1989.

Soloutos, Theodore. *The Greeks in the United States.* Cambridge: Harvard University Press, 1964.

Sowell, Thomas, ed. *Essays and Data on American Ethnic Groups.* Washington, D.C.: Urban Institute, 1978.

Sowell, Thomas. *Ethnic America: A History.* New York: Basic Books, 1981.

Steinberg, Stephen. *The Ethnic Myth: Race, Ethnicity, and Class in America.* Updated ed. New York: Atheneum, 1989.

Takaki, Ronald. *A Different Mirror: A History of Multicultural America.* Boston: Little, Brown and Company, 1993.

_____. *Strangers from a Different Shore: A History of Asian Americans.* Boston: Little, Brown and Company, 1989.

Taylor, Charles A., ed. *Guide to Multicultural Resources: 1993/1994.* Fort Atkinson, Wisc.: Highsmith Press, 1993.

Thernstrom, Stephan A., ed. *Harvard Encyclopedia of American Ethnic Groups.* Cambridge: Harvard University Press, 1980.

Thomas, W. I., and Florian Znaniecki. *The Polish Peasant in Europe and America.* Vol. 1. New York: Knopf, 1918.

Thornton, Russell. *American Indian Holocaust and Survival: A Population History Since 1942.* Norman: University of Oklahoma Press, 1987.

Time Special Issue. *The New Face of America: How Immigrants are Shaping the World's First Multicultural Society. Time Magazine,* fall 1993.

U.S. Bureau of the Census. *1992 Census of Agriculture.* Washington, D.C.: U.S. Government Printing Office, 1992.

_____. *1992 Survey of Minority-Owned Business Enterprises, Black.* Washington, D.C.: U.S. Government Printing Office, 1996.

_____. *1992 Survey of Minority-Owned Business Enterprises, Hispanic.* Washington, D.C.: U.S. Government Printing Office, 1996.

_____. *1993 Survey of Income and Program Participation (SIPP).* Washington, D.C.: U.S. Government Printing Office, 1993.

_____. *65+ in the United States.* Series P23-190. Washington, D.C.: U.S. Government Printing Office, 1996.

_____. *America's Racial and Ethnic Groups: Their Housing in the Early Nineties.* H121/94-3. Washington, D.C.: U.S. Government Printing Office, 1993.

_____. *Asian and Pacific Islanders in the United States: 1990.* CP-3-5. Washington, D.C.: U.S. Government Printing Office, 1993.

_____. *Census and You*. Jan. /Feb. 1996. 31:1/2. Washington, D.C.: U.S. Government Printing Office, 1996.

_____. *Census and You*. March 1996. 31:3. Washington, D.C.: U.S. Government Printing Office, 1996.

_____. *Census and You*. April 1996. 31:4. Washington, D.C.: U.S. Government Printing Office, 1996.

_____. *Census and You*. May 1996. 31:5. Washington, D.C.: U.S. Government Printing Office, 1996.

_____. *Census and You*. June 1996. 31:6. Washington, D.C.: U.S. Government Printing Office, 1996.

_____. *Characteristics of the Black Population: 1990*. CP-3-6. Washington, D.C.: U.S. Government Printing Office, 1991.

_____. *Current Population Reports: Estimates of the Population of the United States to December 1, 1994*. P25–1128. Washington, D.C.: U.S. Government Printing Office, 1995.

_____. *Current Population Reports: The Foreign-Born Population—1994*. Washington, D.C.: U.S. Government Printing Office, 1995.

_____. *Current Population Reports: What's It Worth? Fields of Training and Economic Status: 1993*. Washington, D.C.: U.S. Government Printing Office, 1995.

_____. *Current Population Survey: March 1994*. Washington, D.C.: U.S. Government Printing Office, 1994.

_____. *Educational Attainment in the United States: March 1991 and 1990*. Current Population Reports P-20-462. Washington, D.C.: U.S. Government Printing Office, 1992.

_____. *Educational Attainment in the United States: March 1993 and 1992*. P20-676. Washington, D.C.: U.S. Government Printing Office, 1993.

_____. *Historical Statistics of the United States*. Washington, D.C.: U.S. Government Printing Office, 1973.

_____. *How We're Changing, Demographic State of the Nation: 1996*. P23-191. Washington, D.C.: U.S. Government Printing Office, 1996.

_____. *Marital Status and Living Arrangements: March 1992*. Current Population Reports P20-468. Washington, D.C.: U.S. Government Printing Office, 1992.

_____. *Marital Status and Living Arrangements: March 1994*. P20-484. Washington, D.C.: U.S. Government Printing Office, 1995.

_____. *Marital Status and Living Arrangements: March 1994*. Series P20-484. Washington, D.C.: U.S. Government Printing Office, 1996.

_____. *Our Nation's Housing in 1993*. Washington, D.C.: U.S. Government Printing Office, 1995.

_____. *Population Profile of the United States, 1991*. Current Population Reports P-23-173. Washington, D.C.: U.S. Government Printing Office, 1991.

_____. *Population Profile of the United States, 1995*. Current Population Reports P-23-189. Washington, D.C.: U.S. Government Printing Office, 1995.

_____. *Population Projections of the United States by Age, Sex, Race, and Hispanic Origin: 1995–2050*. Current Population Reports P-23-1130. Washington, D.C.: U.S. Government Printing Office, 1996.

_____. *Projections of the Number of Households and Families in the United States: 1995 to 2010*. Series P25-1129. Washington, D.C.: U.S. Government Printing Office, 1996.

_____. *School Enrollment—Social and Economic Characteristics of Students, October 1993*. P20-479. Washington, D.C.: U.S. Government Printing Office, 1994.

_____. *Statistical Abstract of the United States, 1995*. Washington, D.C.: U.S. Government Printing Office, 1995.

_____. *Statistical Brief: America's Income—Changes Between the Censuses*. Washington, D.C.: U.S. Government Printing Office, 1993.

_____. *Statistical Brief: Asian and Pacific Islander Americans: A Profile*. Washington, D.C.: U.S. Government Printing Office, 1993.

_____. *Statistical Brief: Black Americans: A Profile*. Washington, D.C.: U.S. Government Printing Office, 1993.

_____. *Statistical Brief: Blacks in America—1992*. Washington, D.C.: U.S. Government Printing Office, 1994.

_____. *Statistical Brief: Dollars for Scholars—Postsecondary Costs and Financing*. Washington, D.C.: U.S. Government Printing Office, 1994.

_____. *Statistical Brief: Election '96—Counting the American Electorate*. Washington, D.C.: U.S. Government Printing Office, 1996.

_____. *Statistical Brief: Financing Our Residential Property*. Washington, D.C.: U.S. Government Printing Office, 1994.

_____. *Statistical Brief: Getting a Helping Hand*. Washington, D.C.: U.S. Government Printing Office, 1995.

_____. *Statistical Brief: Health Insurance Coverage: Who Had Gaps Between 1990 and 1992*. Washington, D.C.: U.S. Government Printing Office, 1993.

_____. *Statistical Brief: Health Insurance Coverage—1993*. Washington, D.C.: U.S. Government Printing Office, 1994.

_____. *Statistical Brief: Health Insurance Coverage—1994*. Washington, D.C.: U.S. Government Printing Office, 1995.

_____. *Statistical Brief: Home Equity Lines of Credit—A Look at the People Who Obtain Them*. Washington, D.C.: U.S. Government Printing Office, 1995.

_____. *Statistical Brief: Home Sweet Home—America's Housing, 1973 to 1993*. Washington, D.C.: U.S. Government Printing Office, 1995.

_____. *Statistical Brief: House Beautiful—Patterns of Home Maintenance*. Washington, D.C.: U.S. Government Printing Office, 1994.

_____. *Statistical Brief: Housing in Metropolitan Areas—Black Households*. Washington, D.C.: U.S. Government Printing Office, 1995.

_____. *Statistical Brief: Housing in Metropolitan Areas—Asian or Pacific Islander Households*. Washington, D.C.: U.S. Government Printing Office, 1995.

_____. *Statistical Brief: Housing in Metropolitan Areas—Hispanic Origin Households*. Washington, D.C.: U.S. Government Printing Office, 1995.

_____. *Statistical Brief: Housing in Metropolitan Areas—Movers and Stayers*. Washington, D.C.: U.S. Government Printing Office, 1994.

_____. *Statistical Brief: Housing in Metropolitan Areas—Single-Parent Families*. Washington, D.C.: U.S. Government Printing Office, 1994.

_____. *Statistical Brief: Housing of American Indians on Reservations—Equipment and Fuels*. Washington, D.C.: U.S. Government Printing Office, 1995.

_____. *Statistical Brief: Housing of American Indians on Reservations—Plumbing*. Washington, D.C.: U.S. Government Printing Office, 1995.

_____. *Statistical Brief: Housing of American Indians on Reservations—Structural Characteristics*. Washington, D.C.: U.S. Government Printing Office, 1995.

_____. *Statistical Brief: Income and Job Mobility in the Early 1990's*. Washington, D.C.: U.S. Government Printing Office, 1995.

_____. *Statistical Brief: Just What the Doctor Ordered. The Effects of Health Insurance Coverage on Doctor and Hospital Visits*. Washington, D.C.: U.S. Government Printing Office, 1994.

_____. *Statistical Brief: Mothers Who Receive AFDC Payments—Fertility and Socioeconomic Characteristics*. Washington, D.C.: U.S. Government Printing Office, 1995.

_____. *Statistical Brief: Mothers Who Receive WIC Benefits—Fertility and Socioeconomic Characteristics*. Washington, D.C.: U.S. Government Printing Office, 1995.

_____. *Statistical Brief: Our Scholastic Society*. Washington, D.C.: U.S. Government Printing Office, 1994.

_____. *Statistical Brief: Poverty Areas*. Washington, D.C.: U.S. Government Printing Office, 1995.

_____. *Statistical Brief: Poverty's Revolving Door*. Washington, D.C.: U.S. Government Printing Office, 1995.

_____. *Statistical Brief: Sixty-Five Plus in the United States*. Washington, D.C.: U.S. Government Printing Office, 1995.

_____. *Statistical Brief: Statistical Indicators on Women: An Asian Perspective*. Washington, D.C.: U.S. Government Printing Office, 1993.

_____. *Statistical Brief: Statistical Indicators on Women: An Asian Perspective*. Washington, D.C.: U.S. Government Printing Office, 1995.

_____. *Statistical Brief: The Earnings Ladder*. Washington, D.C.: U.S. Government Printing Office, 1994.

_____. *Statistical Brief: The Nation's Asian and Pacific Islander Population—1994*. Washington, D.C.: U.S. Government Printing Office, 1995.

_____. *Statistical Brief: The Nation's Hispanic Population—1994*. Washington, D.C.: U.S. Government Printing Office, 1995.

_____. *Statistical Brief: What We're Worth—Asset Ownership of Households: 1993*. Washington, D.C.: U.S. Government Printing Office, 1995.

_____. *Statistical Brief: Who Could Afford to Buy a House in 1991?* Washington, D.C.: U.S. Government Printing Office, 1993.

_____. *Statistical Brief: Who Owns the Nation's Rental Properties?* Washington, D.C.: U.S. Government Printing Office, 1996.

_____. *Statistical Brief: Who Receives Child Support?* Washington, D.C.: U.S. Government Printing Office, 1996.

_____. *Statistical Brief: Women in the United States: A Profile*. Washington, D.C.: U.S. Government Printing Office, 1995.

_____. *The Asian and Pacific Islander Population in the United States: March 1991 and 1990*. Current Population Reports P20-459. Washington, D.C.: U.S. Government Printing Office, 1992.

_____. *The Black Population in the United States: March 1991*. Current Population Reports P20-404. Washington, D.C.: U.S. Government Printing Office, 1992.

_____. *The Black Population in the United States: March 1994 and 1993*. Current Population Reports P-20-480. Washington, D.C.: U.S. Government Printing Office, 1995.

_____. *The Black Population in the United States: March 1995.* Washington, D.C.: U.S. Government Printing Office, 1996.

_____. *The Dynamics of Economic Well-Being: Health Insurance, 1991 to 1993.* P70-43. Washington, D.C.: U.S. Government Printing Office, 1993.

_____. *The Hispanic Population in the United States: March 1990.* Current Population Reports, Series P-20, No. 449. Washington, D.C.: U.S. Government Printing Office, 1991.

_____. *The Hispanic Population in the United States: March 1992.* Current Population Reports P20-465. Washington, D.C.: U.S. Government Printing Office, 1973.

_____. *The Nation's Asian and Pacific Islander Population—1994.* Washington, D.C.: U.S. Government Printing Office, 1995.

_____. *U.S. Population Estimates by Age, Sex, Race, and Hispanic Origin: 1990 to 1995.* PPL-41. Washington, D.C.: U.S. Government Printing Office, 1993.

_____. *We Asked, You Told Us: Ancestry.* Census Questionnaire Content, 1990 CQC-14. Washington, D.C.: U.S. Government Printing Office, 1993.

_____. *We Asked, You Told Us: Education.* Census Questionnaire Content, 1990 CQC-13. Washington, D.C.: U.S. Government Printing Office, 1994.

_____. *We Asked, You Told Us: Gender.* Census Questionnaire Content, 1990 CQC-3. Washington, D.C.: U.S. Government Printing Office, 1993.

_____. *We Asked, You Told Us: Language Spoken at Home.* Census Questionnaire Content, 1990 CQC-16. Washington, D.C.: U.S. Government Printing Office, 1993.

_____. *We Asked, You Told Us: Place of Birth, Citizenship and Year of Entry.* Census Questionnaire Content, 1990 CQC-12. Washington, D.C.: U.S. Government Printing Office, 1994.

_____. *We Asked, You Told Us: Race.* Census Questionnaire Content, 1990 CQC-4. Washington, D.C.: U.S. Government Printing Office, 1993.

_____. *We Asked, You Told Us: Residence in 1985.* Census Questionnaire Content, 1990 CQC-15. Washington, D.C.: U.S. Government Printing Office, 1993.

_____. *We Asked, You Told Us: Work Experience in 1989.* Census Questionnaire Content, 1990 CQC-23. Washington, D.C.: U.S. Government Printing Office, 1994.

_____. *We the Americans: Elderly.* WE-9. Washington, D.C.: U.S. Government Printing Office, 1993.

_____. *We the Americans: Foreign Born.* WE-7. Washington, D.C.: U.S. Government Printing Office, 1993.

_____. *We the Americans: Our Homes.* WE-6. Washington, D.C.: U.S. Government Printing Office, 1993.

_____. *We the Americans: Women.* WE-8. Washington, D.C.: U.S. Government Printing Office, 1993.

_____. *We the Americans: Asians.* WE-3. Washington, D.C.: U.S. Government Printing Office, 1993.

_____. *We the Americans: Blacks.* WE-1. Washington, D.C.: U.S. Government Printing Office, 1993.

_____. *We the Americans: Hispanics.* WE-2R. Washington, D.C.: U.S. Government Printing Office, 1993.

_____. *We the Americans: Our Education.* WE-11. Washington, D.C.: U.S. Government Printing Office, 1993.

_____. *We the Americans: Pacific Islanders.* WE-4. Washington, D.C.: U.S. Government Printing Office, 1993.

_____. *We the First Americans.* WE-5. Washington, D.C.: U.S. Government Printing Office, 1993.

Index

A

AFDC (Aid to Families with Dependent
  Children), 32
    African Americans, 32
    Asian Pacific Americans, 51
    Hispanic Americans, 83
    Native Americans, 101
    Non-Hispanic Whites/European Americans,
      114
Afghanistan, 42
African Americans
    Age Distribution, 26
    Agriculture, 34
    Definition/Origin, 19, 23
    Educational Attainment, 27
    Elderly, 26
    Family Composition, 31
    Housing, 33
    Income, 29
        Family Income, 29
        Individual Income, 30
    Introduction, 23
    Labor Force Participation, 28
    Major City Concentrations, 25
    Marital Status, 31
    Metropolitan Concentration, 25
    Occupations, 28
    Population Growth, 23
    Population Projections, 23
    Poverty, 32
    Regional Dispersion, 24
    State Populations, 24
    Southern Regional Concentration, 24
    Voter Turnout, 34
Age Distribution
    African Americans, 26
    Asian Americans, 45
    Hispanic Americans, 79
    Native Americans, 99
    Non-Hispanic Whites/European Americans,
      112
    Pacific Islander Americans, 47
Agriculture
    African Americans, 26
    Asian Americans, 54
    Hispanic Americans, 54
Alabama, 24
Alameda County, 46

Alaska Native Village Statistical Areas, 98
Albuquerque, 76
Anaheim, 76
Anglo-Americans, 18
Apache, 98
Arabia, 42
Arizona, 76
Arkansas, 24
Aryan Nation, 18
Asia, 42
Asian Indians, 41
Asian Pacific American Center for Census
      Information and Services, 51
Asian Pacific Americans
    Age Distribution, 45
    Agriculture, 54
    Definition/Origin, 19, 41, 54
    Educational Attainment, 48
    Family Composition, 52
    Geographical Breakdown, 41, 54
    Housing, 51
    Immigration, 43
    Income, 50
        Family Income, 50
        Individual Earnings, 50
        Per Capita Income, 50
    Introduction, 41
    Labor Force Participation, 48
    Laws Affecting Immigration, 41
    Market Power, 51
    Occupational Distribution of Recent
        Immigrants, 49
    Occupations, 48
    Population Growth, 45
    Poverty, 51
    Regional Dispersion, 45
    Voter Turnout, 54
Australia, 111

B

Baby boom, 137
Baltimore, 25
Bergen-Passaic, 52
Blackfeet Reservation, 99

Brownsville, 78
Bureau of the Census, 20
Bureau of Economic Analysis, 20
Bureau of Justice Statistics, 20
Bureau of Labor Statistics, 20

C

California, 24
    Civil Rights Initiative, 17
    Gold Rush, 41
    Registrar's Office, 20
Canada, 111
Census of Agriculture, 34
Center for Policy Studies, 18
Cherokee, 98
    Cherokee Americans, 19
Chicago, 25
China, 41
Chinese Americans, 19
Chinese Exclusion Act of 1882, impact on
        Chinese immigration and
        citizenship, 41–42
Chinese Student Protection Act of 1992, impact
        on immigration, 43
Chippewa, 98
Choctaw, 98
Civil Rights, 23
Civil War, 18
Cold War, 43
Colombia, 84
Columbus, Christopher, 97
Colorado, 76
Colville, 102
Compromise of 1877, 34
Congress, 34
Cook County, 46
Corpus Christi, 76
Creek, 98
Cuba, 75
    Cuban Missile Crisis, 79
    Cuban Revolution, 75
Current Population Survey, 20

D

Dallas, 76
Department of Agriculture, 20
Department of Commerce, 20
Department of Housing and Urban
        Development, 20

Department of Veterans Affairs, 20
Detroit, 25
Directive 15, 19
District of Columbia, 24

E

East St. Louis, 25
Ecuador, 84
Edinburg, 78
Educational Attainment
    African Americans, 26
    Asian Americans, 48
    Hispanic Americans, 80
    Native Americans, 100
    Non-Hispanic Whites/European Americans,
        112
    Pacific Islander Americans, 55
El Paso, 76
El Salvador, 84
Election Data Services, Inc., 20
Emancipation Proclamation, effects on African
        American citizenship, 41
Energy Information Administration, 20
English, 85
Environmental Protection Agency, 20
Equal Employment Opportunity Commission, 20
Eskimo Americans, 19
Ethnicity
    Definition, 19
    In relation to race, 19

F

Family Composition
    African Americans, 31
    Asian Americans, 52
    Hispanic Americans, 84
    Native Americans, 101
    Non-Hispanic Whites/European Americans,
        115
    Pacific Islander Americans, 56
Fifteenth Amendment, effects on voting and
        citizenship, 34
Filipinos, 41
Florida, 24
Foreign Miners' Tax, 41
Fort Apache, 99
Fort Lauderdale, 33
Fort Peck, 103

Fourteenth Amendment, effects on voting and
    citizenship, 34
France, 111
Fresno County, 46

G

Gadsden Purchase, 75
Geary Act of 1892, extension of Chinese
    Exclusion Act of 1882, 41
Gentleman's Agreement of 1907, 44
Georgia, 24
Germany, 111
Gila River, 99
Glass Ceiling Commission, 17
Golden State, 52
"Grandfather Clause"
    Definition, 34
    Effect on African American voting
        registration, 34
Great Migrations, 18
Greece, 111
Guam, 54
Guatemala, 84

H

Hacker, Andrew, 19
Harlingen, 78
Hawaiian Americans, 19
Hispanic Americans
    Age Distribution, 79
    Agriculture, 85
    Citizenship, 70
    Definition, 75, 19
    Educational Attainment, 80
        Variations in, 81
    Elderly, 79
    Ethnic and Cultural Background, 76
    Family Composition, 84
    Foreign-Born, 79
    General Demographics, 75
    Health, 85
    Housing, 84
    Immigration, 79
    Income, 82
        Family Income, 82
    Introduction, 75
    Language, 85

    Market Power, 83
    Nativity, 78
    Occupations, 81
    Population Growth, 76
    Poverty, 83
    Regional Dispersion, 76
    Residential Dispersion, 76
    Voter Turnout, 85
Hispaniola, 97
Hollywood, 33
Honduras, 84
Honolulu, 46
Hoopa Valley, 102
Hopi, 99
Housing
    African Americans, 31
    Asian Americans, 51
    Hispanic Americans, 84
    Native Americans, 102–103
    Non-Hispanic Whites/European Americans,
        115

I

Illinois, 25
Immigration Act of 1990, 43
Immigration and Nationality Act Amendments
    of 1965, 41
Immigration and Naturalization Service, 20
Immigration Reform and Control Act of 1986, 43
Income
    African Americans, 29
    Asian Americans, 50
    Hispanic Americans, 82
    Native Americans, 101
    Non-Hispanic Whites/European Americans,
        113
    Pacific Islander Americans, 56
India, 41
Indian Removal Act of 1830, 136
IndoChina Migration , 44
Internal Revenue Service, 20
Iran, 42
Ireland, 111
Irish Americans, 19
Iroquois Confederacy, 98
Isleta Pueblo, 102
Israel, 111
Italy, 111

J

Jackson, 25
Jamestown Colony, 23
Jim Crow laws, 23
Johnson-Reed Act of 1924, 42

K

Kennedy, Robert F., Senator, 43
King, Rodney, 17
Kings County, 46
Korea, 41

L

Labor Force Participation
    African Americans, 28
    Asian Americans, 48
    Native Americans, 100
    Non-Hispanic Whites/European Americans,
        113
Laredo, 78
Leibowitz, Patricia, 136
Long Beach, 46
Los Angeles, 25
Los Angeles County, 46
Louisiana, 25
Louisiana Purchase, 75
Lumbee, 98

M

Manhattan, 25
Maryland, 24
Mason-Dixon line, 18
Massey, 17
McAllen, 78
McCarran-Walter Immigration and Nationality
        Act of 1952, 42
Medicaid, 85
Medicare, 85
Memphis, 25
Mescalero Apache, 102
Mestizo, 75
Mexican American War, 75
Mexican Revolution, 75
Mexico, 75
Miami, 34
Michigan, 98

Minneapolis, 52
Minnesota, 52
Mission, 78
Mississippi, 25
Mississippi River, 98
Montana, 99
Monterey, 77
MSA (Metropolitan Statistical Area), 25

N

Nassau-Suffolk, 33
National Center for Education Statistics, 20
National Center for Health Statistics, 20
National Opinion Research Center, 49
National Technical Information Service, 20
Nationalization Act of 1790, 42
Native Americans
    Age Distribution, 99
        Children, 100
        Elderly, 100
    As opposed to "Indians", 97
    Definition, 19, 97
    Educational Attainment, 100
    Family Composition, 101
    Income, 101
    Introduction, 97
    Labor Force Participation, 100
    Metropolitan Concentration, 98
    Occupations, 100
    Population Growth, 97
    Poverty, 101
    Regional Dispersion, 97
    Reservation Housing Characteristics, 102
        Equipment Fuels, 103
        Plumbing Facilities, 102
        Structural Characteristics, 102
    State Populations, 98
    U.S. Populations, 98
Naturalization Act of 1790, 41
Navajo, 98
    Reservations, 99
Neo-Nazis (skinheads), 18
Netherlands, 111
New Jersey, 24
New Mexico, 75
New Orleans, 25
New World, 75
New York, 24
    Cattaraugus Reservation, 102
Newark, 77
Nicaragua, 84

Non-Hispanic Whites/European Americans
    Age Distribution, 112
        Children, 112
        Elderly, 112
    As opposed to "white", 19
    Definition, 19, 20, 111
    Educational Attainment, 112
    Family Composition, 115
    Health Care, 115
    Housing, 115
    Introduction, 111
    Labor Force Participation, 113
    Metropolitan Concentration, 111
    Moving, 115
    Net Worth and Income, 113
        Per Capita Income, 114
        Family Income, 114
    Population Growth, 111
    Poverty, 114
    U.S. Population, 111
    Voter Turnout, 116
    Whiteness, 19

O

Oakland, 52
Occupations
    African Americans, 28
    Asian Americans, 48
    Hispanic Americans, 81
    Native Americans, 100
Office of Management and Budget, 19
O'Hare, William, 48
Orange County, 46
Oregon, 55
Other Race, 27
Oxnard, 77

P

Pacific Islander Americans
    Age Distribution, 55
    Educational Attainment, 55
    Family Composition, 56
    Income, 56
    Introduction, 54
    Labor Force Participation, 55
    Language, 56
    Nativity, 55
    Population Growth, 54
    Poverty, 56
    Regional Dispersion, 55

Papago, 99
Pascua Yaqui Reservation, 102
Pennsylvania, 18
Peru, 84
Philadelphia, 25
Philippines, 41
Pilgrims, 75
Pine Ridge, 99
    Reservation, 99
Plessy vs. Ferguson, 135
Plymouth Rock, 75
Poland, 111
Pompano Beach, 33
Population Growth
    African Americans, 45
    Asian Americans, 23
    Hispanic Americans, 76
    Native Americans, 97
    Non-Hispanic Whites/European Americans, 111
    Pacific Islander Americans, 54
Portugal, 111
Poverty
    African Americans, 32
    Asian Americans, 51
    Hispanic Americans, 83
    Native Americans, 101
    Non-Hispanic Whites/European Americans, 114
    Pacific Islander Americans, 56
Proposition 187, 17
Public Use Microdata Sample, 20
Pueblo, 98
Puerto Rico, 75

Q

Queens County, 46

R

Race
    as a social construct, 18
    definition, 18
    governmental definition, 18
    significance of, 18–20
Reconstruction, 34
Refugee Act of 1980, 43
Refugee Assistance Act of 1975, 44
Regional Dispersion
    African Americans, 24
    Asian Americans, 45

Regional Dispersion, *continued*
    Hispanic Americans, 76
    Native Americans, 97
    Pacific Islander Americans, 55
Riverside, 78
Rosebud Reservation, 99
Russia, 42

S

Salinas, 77
Salt Lake County, 46
San Antonio, 76
San Carlos, 99
San Diego, 46
San Francisco, 46
San Jose, 46
Santa Ana, 52
Santa Clara County, 46
Santa Fe, 75
Seaside, 77
Seattle, 46
Simpson, O.J., 17
Sioux, 98
Social Security, 30
Social Security Administration, 20
South Carolina, 24
South Dakota, 99
Southern Regional Council, 18
Spanish, 85
Spanish surname, 75
Spanish-American War, 75
Spanish/Hispanic, 75
St. Paul, 52
St. Petersburg, 77
St. Regis Mohawk, 102
Summary Tape File 1C, 46
Supplemental Security Income, 141
Survey of Agriculture, 54
Survey of Income and Program Participation, 28

T

Tampa, 77
Tennessee, 25
Texas, 24
Thomas, W.I., 19
Trail of Tears, 135
Treaty of Guadalupe Hidalgo, 75
Trust Lands, 99
Tucson, 76

Tufte, Edward R., 17
Tydings-McDuffie Act, 42

U

U.S. Census, 19
U.S. Bureau of Census, 18
U.S. Commission on Civil Rights, 20
U.S. Constitution, 34
U.S. National Science Foundation, 48
U.S. Small Business Administration, 20
U.S. Supreme Court, 34
U.S.S.R., 111
Union, 75
United Kingdom, 111
United States, 18
Utah, 55

V

Ventura, 77
Vermont, 24
Vietnam War, 44
Virginia, 46
The Visual Display of Quantitative Information, 17
Voter Turnout
    African Americans, 34
    Asian Americans, 54
    Hispanic Americans, 85
    Non-Hispanic Whites/European Americans, 116
Voting Rights Act of 1915, 34

W

Warm Springs Reservation, 103
Washington, D.C., 25
West Indies, 138
West Virginia, 24
Whites, 18
Wisconsin, 52
Women, Infants, and Children (WIC), 33
World War I, 75
World War II, 19

Y, Z

Yugoslavia, 111
Zuni Pueblo, 99